'Stephen's book helped ̲ ̲ ̲ ̲ ̲ ̲ ̲ ̲ ̲ how profound my love for Willy was. The day he died, I lost my protector, and the world lost a treasure.'

Bob Kapell, brother of William, and a lawyer and retired business consultant

'This thoroughly engaging book tells a touchingly personal story of an immense musical personality whose life was cut so tragically short. It's a must for any pianist or musician's bookshelf.'

Richard Egarr – Music director, Academy of Ancient Music, professor of fortepiano and harpsichord, Amsterdam Conservatory, and jury member at the 2012 William Kapell International Piano Competition

'By exploring both Willy's youth and his posthumous existence in long-buried Australian recordings, Stephen Downes's splendid new biography of William Kapell adds a dimension to our understanding of the pianist's intense, brief life and gives us new perspective on the Kapell phenomenon.'

Jerome Lowenthal, American concert pianist, Kapell's first student, and a member of the piano faculty at the Juilliard School

A LASTING RECORD

STEPHEN DOWNES

HarperCollins*Publishers*

HarperCollins*Publishers*
First published in Australia in 2013
by HarperCollins*Publishers* Australia Pty Limited
ABN 36 009 913 517
harpercollins.com.au

HarperCollins*Publishers*
Level 13, 201 Elizabeth Street, Sydney NSW 2000, Australia
31 View Road, Glenfield, Auckland 0627, New Zealand
A 53, Sector 57, Noida, UP, India
77–85 Fulham Palace Road, London W6 8JB, United Kingdom
2 Bloor Street East, 20th floor, Toronto, Ontario M4W 1A8, Canada
10 East 53rd Street, New York NY 10022, USA

National Library of Australia Cataloguing-in-Publication data:

National Library of Australia Cataloguing-in-Publication entry
  Downes, Stephen.
  A lasting record / Stephen Downes.
  978 0 7322 9484 7 (pbk.)
  978 0 7304 9990 9 (ebook)
  Kapell, William, 1922-1953.
  Pianists – United States– Biography.
786.2092

Cover design by Jane Waterhouse, HarperCollins Design Studio
Cover image: William Kapell Playing Piano © Bettmann/CORBIS
Back cover image: Myer Emporium, Bourke Street, Melbourne, 1945 by National Archives of
Australia: A1200, L3984
Typeset in 11.5/16pt Bembo Std Regular by Kirby Jones
Printed and bound in Australia by Griffin Press
The papers used by HarperCollins in the manufacture of this book are a natural, recyclable
product made from wood grown in sustainable plantation forests. The fibre source and
manufacturing processes meet recognised international environmental standards, and carry
certification.

5 4 3 2 1   13 14 15 16

In memory of Anna Lou, and to Bob, Dave, Becky, Ann, and the younger Kapell-family members

CHAPTER ONE

A Wrong Turn

'I, for one, am sick and tired of going along in any way with the public "taste". Many artists do not realise that by doing so they are slowly dying creatively. And when artists die, so does art.'

William Kapell, three days before turning thirty-one, during his 1953 Australian concert tour

'Death cancels everything but truth; and strips a man of everything but genius and virtue.'

William Hazlitt

'This is the day I lost my protector and loving brother and the world lost a treasure.'

Bob Kapell, Willy's brother

RESOLUTION'S FOUR PRATT and Whitney engines droned a soothing contralto note. The flight had been routine, thought Captain Bruce Dickson. He peered at the blanket of clouds below him. There was that small problem with a prop climbing out of Honolulu. Easily fixed. And now – after nine hours – San Francisco was down there somewhere. When wasn't Frisco overcast? he asked himself. He'd flown in here so many times. Over a hundred? Must be. Many on instruments, too. But gee, it was a long haul from the islands. And you had to keep your wits about you coming into Frisco. Any airport, really. But at Frisco, there were mountains. Not very high mountains, but mountains nonetheless; bristling with redwoods, the world's tallest tree. The shortcut quickened your descent, of course. Just a break in the clouds. That's all he'd need. A bit of visual.

The air – piped and conditioned – smelled crisp and lush. He was flying the queen of the skies. There was no better passenger aircraft. You could have your Constellations. He was from Sydney, a DC-6 man, uncomplicated, just like the scrappers of Cronulla, the suburb in which he grew up. Just nicer planes, they were, the DC-6s. Less fancy. More Australian, in a way. Even though they were Yank. He remembered he'd once said that to Frank, beside him in the first officer's seat. He smiled at Frank Campbell. The co-pilot grinned, wondering what Bruce was thinking.

With the help of navigator George Murtagh, flight engineer Charlie Cattanach and radio officer Vern Walker, he and Frank had cruised VH-BPE well within its 270-knot top speed for hours on end. Without the slightest hitch. Just like the textbooks say. Around 300 miles an hour, hour after hour. She really was a piece of machinery. Dickson hoped the eleven passengers behind him had slept well. With a bit of luck, BCPA flight 304/44 would soon be nudging the chocks. Bit of luck … Long haul into San Fran. Always the shortcut.

★ ★ ★

William Kapell sat up in his bunk, thumbed the flint-wheel of his Zippo and lit up a Craven 'A' cork-tipped. He inhaled and grimaced. British cigarettes. He'd run out of Luckys and Camels. Proper American brands. Wished he could run out of all cigarettes of any sort, altogether, forever, one day. But not now. He was beat. He needed a smoke despite the coughing. Thirty-seven concerts in fourteen weeks. Less than fourteen, actually. Gruelling. That was the word for it. Brutal schedule, as he'd put it to the Australian Broadcasting Commission and its useless managers. He'd seen every corner of Australia but none of it. When he hadn't been on the road or playing concerts he'd been practising. The halls! The pianos! Honky tonks, some of them.

The cool air in the cabin and the nuttiness of the tobacco blended nicely, he thought. Great to have Anna Lou with him for a couple of months. At least *that* was great about the tour.

And he'd never played better. That was the best thing.

He listened to the engines. Murmuring, they were. A nice word for it. All sang the same note. Hey, in unison. An engine quartet. Close to middle C. Yeah, middle C. He'd *never played better.* Comforting to know that. He'd showed 'em.

He took a coffee from the hostess and told her he'd slept okay. Her name was Kay, she'd said last night. Thirty-two, and he'd just turned thirty-one and had two little kids, David and Rebecca, the cubs, back home in New York. They were waiting for their daddy to return from playing in the country of kangaroos. Where they jump about in the streets? Kay had said. I hope you didn't tell them that, she'd added with a cute smile. They'd laughed.

You're the famous pianist? she'd asked. He'd nodded and grinned.

Kay wasn't the only person Kapell had spoken to en route from Australia. He'd chatted with fellow passengers, at least one of them at length. They would have noticed his dark good looks, smart deep eyes and enormous blow-wave of Brilliantined chestnut hair that swept back from a book-thin forehead. He was shortish, and looked the brooding type. And you could tell he was a pianist from those perfect strong hands. Clean. Short fingernails. Manicured. And didn't he look like John Garfield, the Hollywood glamour-boy tough-guy? some would have said to themselves. Even that new bloke, Brando. Sexy.

Willy looked out the porthole alongside his bunk. Clouds of rolled lead stretched unbroken to the horizon. When were they due in? Around a quarter of nine, wasn't it? It'd be foggy in the city by the bay. Whenever wasn't Frisco foggy?

He lay back and let his mind pinball among the letdowns and triumphs of the tour. His Steinway, broken before it landed. The sum the ABC was going to demand from him for their expenses if he abandoned the tour. His *playing*! Gee, that was something. The rats of critics. Sydney critics! Never better, he'd played. *Never* better.

★ ★ ★

Douglas DC-6s were the aircraft every kid drew postwar. Powered by four piston engines, the DC-6 was easy – plain – on the eye and even easier for small hands to draft. Big silver cigar, sharply rising windshield, nicely rounded ends to the wings and stabilisers, and a lovely curving rudder rising at the tail. A big silver bird that was originally designed for military transportation, it first flew in 1946. Over the next dozen years, 704 of them were built. After World War II, DC-6s competed with Lockheed's Constellation, of the famous triple tail and dolphin-shaped fuselage, for what smart money saw as a potentially huge and growing market – long-distance air travel. While both aircraft were successful, the Constellation was sleeker and slightly faster than its rival. It pierced a corridor through rare air, sucking cheaper travel and more passengers into its slipstream.

British Commonwealth Pacific Airlines was half-owned by the Australian government. New Zealand and Britain owned thirty per cent and twenty per cent. Set up to provide a cross-Pacific service, the airline was incorporated in New South Wales the year DC-6s first flew. Its first passenger service – provided by a DC-4 – left Sydney on 15 September of the same year. With an eye on the lucrative American market, one of its early brochures featured a drawing of a jaunty koala hanging off a eucalyptus limb, its front right paw extended in greeting. Below the image, a slogan reads, 'Australia will welcome you … New Zealand thrill you'.

Two years later, the airline acquired the first of four modified DC-6s and was advertising 'slumber seat comfort'. 'Sleeper' DC-6s were easy to spot; a line of small portholes ran along the fuselage above the usual windows. The seats were lazy wide compared with even most modern business-class counterparts. Upholstered in tartan fabric, they amounted to armchairs in the sky. Above them were fold-down Pullman-type bunks with sheets, blankets and pillows. Enjoying BCPA's 'sleeper service' across the blue vastness was, in short, a luxury for elite travellers.

The airline's four DC-6s were named after ships either commanded by James Cook or that sailed with him on his three Pacific explorations.[1] Equipped with the latest in navigational aids, the propeller-driven version of *Resolution* could carry forty-eight to eighty-six passengers. It or its sister DC-6s would leave Sydney at 11 a.m. on Saturdays and Wednesdays and were in San Francisco in less than two days after stops in Auckland, Fiji, Kanton Island (one of the Phoenix group belonging these days to Kiribati) and Honolulu. But you needed to be a person of means to buy a ticket. The one-way fare was £285 15s and a return journey cost £514 6s. In 1953, the recently increased Australian basic wage was £11 16s a week and a new Holden motor car was priced at £1023.

Despite its romance, air travel was still comparatively dangerous half a century after the Wright brothers' first flight. You might be rich, but you ran a mortal risk among the clouds. Since records began, 1950 was the 30th deadliest year – 1834 deaths; 1951 came in 42nd (1616); 1952, 39th (1681) and 1953, 50th (1562). Bearing in mind the relatively few passenger miles flown in the 1950s, the numbers terrify. Elite athletes, artists and musicians were always well-represented among the dead. In 1958, film producer Mike Todd, eight members of the Manchester United football team and six members of Egypt's national fencing squad died. In 1953, the sublime French violinist Jacques Thibaud was killed. (His compatriot, the equally magnificent fiddler Ginette Neveu, had died in an air crash four years previously.) The following year two gospel singers in the Blackwood Brothers Quartet died, and two years later the young and brilliant Italian conductor Guido Cantelli was killed. And in February 1959, the music died altogether – according to Don McLean – when Ritchie Valens, Buddy Holly and the Big Bopper were killed in the best-known air crash in which musicians were victims.

★ ★ ★

If there was a single constant in Australia it'd been the quality of his playing, Willy thought. Especially the Chopin *Funeral March* sonata in Geelong, the last concert. He'd demonstrated the maturity the critics were always at him about. Just hadn't he! There must be recordings, too. Even if they couldn't give me one. An organisation like the grand little ABC would keep recordings of all its concerts. If only to have them. Drip-feed them out.

He lit another cigarette, engulfed the nicotine. All young artists are accused of immaturity. My God! They've been punting for years on the moment when I was going *to mature fully* as an artist. That's all they can talk about, the critics. The kid's got talent, but will he mature as an artist? Well, I have. Simply and plainly. I have. And this tour proved it. *Absolutely.* The Sydney rats! I meant it on the tarmac. I'd never come back. *Absolutely.*

He'd been fifteen minutes on the phone to Anna Lou when the plane was refuelling in Honolulu, he remembered. Golly, it was nice to hear her voice. He couldn't wait to see her and the kids. And she thought he was strung out. Wanted him to rest for a few days in Hawaii. Even had the hotel booked. He needed to relax, she said.

Ha! Can't wait to get home, I said. Couldn't wait in Hawaii. Can't wait now. I wasn't going to sit on any beaches. Sand up my ass. And Heifetz wanted me in LA for a day to record. Very exciting. The world's greatest violinist wants a second dose of me accompanying him. Heifetz and Kapell. What a doozie of a duet! Straight home after that, me. Gee, I can taste a Katz dog right now. On the tip of my tongue.

He looked out the window. A dirty-white quilt was about to envelop the plane. Can't be long.

★ ★ ★

San Francisco International Airport was then – and is now – on San Francisco Bay, not quite ten miles south of the city. Coming from Hawaii, aircraft cross the Californian coast over the town of Half Moon Bay and continue north-east, hurdling a hump of peaks that can be well over 2000 feet above sea level before lining up the runway. The highest redwoods can add another 300 feet to the obstacle. About ten miles after crossing the coast, pilots begin a clockwise loop at the outer fan marker south-west of Coyote Point, complete it over the bay and drop down in a north-westerly direction to land.

Bruce Dickson squeezed the control wheel of *Resolution* a little more firmly. For all the modernity in the cabin, the piped air and pressurisation, he was guiding the DC-6 with a thin black wheel. It looked like a Morris Minor's. He contacted San Francisco traffic control, which cleared him to descend according to 'visual flight rules'. He should stay at least '500 feet' above the clouds, the controller dictated. Dickson got Vern to acknowledge. He looked at his watch. It was 8.15. He eased *Resolution*'s nose into a shallow dive and headed for the clouds. The weather wasn't all that bad, he thought – broken ceiling, visibility nine. There might be a break.

George Murtagh turned the lucite rings of his Dalton wheel. He and Frank checked while George did the numbers, crunching ground speed, airspeed, altitude and air temperature to get *Resolution*'s where and when. They peered at the finely etched lines and digits and scribbled calculations. In a little while, they would listen for a continuous series of dashes in their headphones, watch for the blue light's flashing and see the needle reverse direction to say they'd passed over the outer marker – if they bothered to wait. He knew where they were. Confident he knew exactly where they were. *Exactly*. So many times he'd come in here. And the shortcut was tempting. The back way. Or front way, as it might be called. Straight in. Saved time. He ordered landing gear down and flaps to fifteen. All he needed was a break in the clouds.

At 8.39, Dickson asked Vern Walker to tell San Francisco they were over Half Moon Bay and 500 above the soup. Vern relayed the message. What'd you call us? the skipper asked. 'Air Pacific Echo', said Vern. San Francisco cleared *Resolution* for an instrument landing on runway 28, wind west 15, 'cross the outer marker initially at least 500 on top, report when inbound, ceiling 1200, visibility nine, altimeter 30.14'. Three minutes later, Vern called again. The air-traffic controller acknowledged: 'Air Pacific Easy, roger, south-east, turning inbound. Check passing the ILS outer marker inbound'. Easy?

About two minutes later, a call to flight BCPA 304/44 went unanswered. San Francisco tried several times to reach the plane without success. Search and rescue agencies were called. Flight 304/44 was overdue.

★ ★ ★

Resolution ripped through forest on a mountain ridge about seven-and-a-half miles south-east of Half Moon Bay, badly off course. Its left wing hit the first tree at over 2000 feet, losing about 13 feet. The fuselage hurtled on for several hundred yards, crossing a ravine and eventually crashing through branches and undergrowth. It came to rest at an elevation of 1950 feet. Below the crash site was Corte Madera, a canyon that might be translated as wild. The sheared wing and left stabiliser, which was also lost in the crash, were found more than 300 feet from the main wreckage. The DC-6's four engines were widely scattered. An inferno broke out, and VH-BPE was destroyed. Much of its aluminium melted into bright-grey misshapes. All nineteen passengers and crew were killed.

The official Civil Aeronautics Board accident report says that the landing gear was down and locked. Wing flaps had been extended properly to between 15 and 20 degrees. The plane's props had been set at the right pitch. The engines had been turning at the correct speed. As far as could be determined, 'there was no indication that a malfunction or failure had occurred prior to impact'. Ground instruments guiding VH-BPE had been working properly.

Many Californians heard *Resolution* just before it hit the mountain. Seven provided written statements. They generally agreed that the crash site and surrounding terrain had been shrouded in fog on the morning of the accident, 29 October 1953. *Resolution* could be heard but not seen. It appeared to have been flying 'very low with the engines sounding normal'. One witness who heard the impact thought VH-BPE was heading east rather than north-east. He or she thought that about one to two minutes elapsed between its passing overhead and the tragedy. Other witnesses near the crash site 'substantiated that the course of the aircraft immediately prior to impact was north-east', which might suggest a change of course or even the turn the radio messages implied.

In its analysis of the catastrophe, the board said it was 'obvious the flight did not maintain at least 500 on top and descended in weather conditions which precluded visual reference to the ground'. It continued: 'Thus it is likely that when the pilot reported "Southeast, turning inbound", his actual position was southwest of the airport'. It was probable, it continued, that after reporting over Half Moon Bay, Dickson or his crew either saw the terrain momentarily through an 'unreported break in the overcast' or, because of a radio navigational error, became convinced that their position was farther north-east. They 'started to let down over what [Dickson] believed was the proper area for … descent'.

The report ends with a 'probable' cause – 'the failure of the crew to follow prescribed procedures for an instrument approach'.

Just why *Resolution* was significantly off course remains open to debate. The report also throws up ambiguities. How was Dickson to descend through fog and make an instrument landing according to 'visual flight rules'? The report states that when VH-BPE radioed to say it was turning to land, it simply hadn't the time – with flaps and wheels slowing its speed – to cross the mountain range between it and the airport and be in the correct position to alter course by 90 degrees for descent. And if that was the case, why hadn't San Francisco air-traffic control queried the early turn? Moreover, what can be made of the confusion in call-signs 'Echo' and 'Easy'? (A new phonetic alphabet was being introduced, 'Easy' the old and 'Echo' the new for 'E'. It might have distracted some pilots.) And perhaps there was just a touch of easy-go-lucky Cronulla-boy bravado to Bruce Dickson. He knew where he was. And if you knew where you were, and you'd landed at Frisco over a hundred times, you could bend the rules and fly in quicker.

★ ★ ★

From a private plane, a *San Mateo Times* photographer Ray Zirkel was first to spot the wreckage. He reported 'absolute devastation'. Nothing moved, and great chunks of 'unrecognisable debris' were strewn across the mountainside. Check-Six is a website devoted to aviation history. It says a doctor and airmen were first on the scene. An air force helicopter had landed them in a clearing about a quarter-mile from the wreckage and they beat their way through undergrowth to discover no survivors. Small but extremely fierce fires had broken out, and it wasn't until the afternoon that a bulldozer forged a path to the disaster and firefighters and rescuers reached the scene.

Splashing news of the disaster on its front page, the *San Francisco Examiner* said that *Resolution* had needed only another 50 feet of altitude to clear the mountain range. Fires caused by the accident burned over a half-mile radius. More than two hundred people worked on a 60-degree slope to retrieve the bodies by cable and winch. Ten of the victims were found, burned beyond recognition, in the crushed fuselage. Dickson and Campbell were 'still at the melted controls, their headsets intact on their ears'. Bodies were taken to a temporary morgue in the National Guard Armory in Redwood City ten miles to the north-east. Donald Allen, a dentist from San Carlos, and three doctors identified them. For the first time, dental records were used to determine who was among the victims of an air crash.

Like the *Examiner*, the *San Francisco Chronicle* splashed its story on pages one and two. Both papers called *Resolution* a 'British' aircraft. The *Chronicle* reported that, nine hours after the accident, examiners had found one of the DC-6's wheels at the bottom of a ravine and another more than 200 yards up a 'precipitous slope'. *Chronicle* reporter Bruce Benedict hiked to the accident through a tangle of brush, 'sometimes on hands and knees'. He came to a clearing 'ripped through the trees and boulders for about 400 yards, straight up the mountainside'. He saw airmail fluttering free of the wreckage, shreds of clothing, body parts, and 'puddles' of molten aluminium.

Several victims had survived the wreckage only to die in the infernos. One report said that Willy Kapell was identified by his sports jacket. He was found lying face-down, the tweed beneath him burned incompletely. Most victims were cremated, and the ashes sent to relatives. One source says that Kapell's body was hurried from the site and returned to New York. Rabbi Edward Klein delivered the eulogy at a funeral service on 2 November at the Stephen Wise Free Synagogue on West 68th Street, Manhattan. Martha Lipton of the Metropolitan Opera sang Bach. Burial followed at Mount Ararat Cemetery near the village of Farmingdale, Long Island.

On 30 October, fewer than twelve hours after the accident, the *Herald* in Melbourne also splashed the disaster. Fourteen of the nineteen on board were Australians, including the Victorian Railways' superintendent of locomotive maintenance and its assistant chief electrical engineer. Beneath their names in the list of the dead is the mention, 'World famous concert pianist, William

Kapell'. The *Herald* said *Resolution* had 'failed to clear the top of a mountain by 300ft., bounced off a ridge full tilt into the side of a ravine, blasting out a bomb-like crater and disintegrating as its petrol tanks exploded.' (The *Herald*, it might be said, was farther from the action.) On page two, its music critic John Sinclair began a tribute with, 'It is very hard for me to write today about William Kapell'. Sinclair had spent the pianist's final hours in Melbourne with him the weekend before. The *Herald* called the crash the worst on a 'direct Australia air route outside Australia'.

★ ★ ★

Those interested can walk today to the site of the disaster. Beginning at El Corte de Madera Creek Open Space Preserve, you take a series of poorly indicated, winding tracks through redwoods and dense brush west of Skyline Boulevard for about a mile. Though the mountains here are relatively low, their sides are steep – more than escalator-steep in places. Fairly quickly, the route narrows and roughens from pavement suitable for firefighting vehicles to less than a pace wide. A valid preconception is that you're being funnelled into the essence of something sinister, the site of a tragedy that should never have happened. Mid-brown sandstone gibbers and rocks punctuate the track, which is a favourite of mountain-bike riders. In places it's very rough, and it ascends and descends felicitously. Its last few hundred feet were hewn by the rescuers of 1953. While you weave among some stands of awesomely large redwoods, tortuous madrone trees dominate, corduroy bark sloughing to reveal silken khaki boughs. And there is also scrubby manzanita, which burns hot and fast. This is regrowth – since the accident.

You turn a blind corner, and without warning, sign or cairn the hillside indents, as if a giant finger has pressed it in. It's where the nose and the cockpit of *Resolution* came to rest, perhaps three to four hundred feet below the clearing where rescuers based themselves. Up above, helicopters landed. Looking from the indent in the direction from which the dismembered *Resolution* approached, you appear to be at the bottom of a snare, as if the nineteen on board and their chattels – and the aircraft itself – were being acquired by fate. Compulsorily. No escape.

Beneath the track, sliding down the steepness, is wreckage – bits of fuselage, coils of wires, strands of plaited fabric, tubes and pipes and springs and big steel gear that might have once been struts that supported *Resolution*'s wheels. Dig about in the soft brown soil above the track and you'll find small pieces of thin glass, perhaps from cockpit instruments, ruptured rings of alloys in all sizes and shapes, press fasteners that might once have attached twill to a seat or a bunk. On several of the nearby boulders, fossickers have exhibited collections of wreckage, remnants of the disaster. Off a bough of madrone three metres above the track, a wreath of twigs woven many years ago has lost its flowers.

Looking again to the south-west, *Resolution*'s approach, redwood tops on a ridge appear to be about half a mile away. One of them – or perhaps several – took the airliner's left wing and rear stabiliser. Christopher O'Donnell, a retired photography teacher and a kind of warden of the crash site, says you can see where one of the trees has been truncated. Some sources claim, he says, that *Resolution* turned on its side after losing its wings and flew belly-up for seven seconds before the fatal collision. O'Donnell has established a website about the accident, and in 2009, largely because of his work, a sandstone memorial cairn closer to Skyline Boulevard was unveiled. On polished black marble, it lists the dead in alphabetical order. Just 'William Kapell'.

And then there is the silence. Standing at the crash site, it is so profound, so complete, that it sets you listening to the noise inside your head, the soft white noise of absence. Every now and then, passing jet engines sigh overhead.

CHAPTER TWO

Prodigious Prodigy

'He took to the piano. He was like Mozart.'
William Kapell's brother, Bob

'I made a mistake, and it's never going to happen again.'
William Kapell

I WAS ASTONISHED that no one had written a complete Kapell biography. During his short life – and long after it – several musicians and critics had called him America's greatest home-grown pianist. There was also the tragedy of his demise at thirty-one, and the eeriness of his scheduling Chopin's brilliant, profound and melancholic *Funeral March* sonata at what was to be his last concert. The story itched in several other ways, too, and once I'd read about it – in a brief newspaper article – the writer in me just had to scratch.

I discovered first that Willy Kapell was called Willy at a time when the word probably had no other connotation. Occasionally he went by Bill, even signing it on publicity photographs. A little cyber-searching revealed that he had only one sibling, a younger brother called Bernard, who was known as 'Bob'. I wondered if Bob were still alive.

A little more Googling produced a piece written in 2007 by New Jersey author and journalist, Warren Boroson. One Bob Kapell had emailed him to say he'd enjoyed his critique in a local newspaper of a regional opera performance. Warren and Bob had had breakfast soon after, and – possibly over hash browns – Warren had asked if Bob was related to William. 'He was my brother,' said Bob.

I contacted Warren, who contacted Bob, who emailed me to say he'd be pleased to tell me all about Willy and their young lives as 'children of Russian-Polish immigrants' in the poor Yorkville area of Manhattan. Bob and his wife, Ann, lived in New Jersey but they also had a small apartment in the Lincoln Center precinct of New York.

Bob soon revealed the odd news that, apart from a telephone interview he had once given about Willy, no one had ever bothered to sit down with him at length to discuss his brother. He was overjoyed that I was interested in him. My wife and I had scheduled a New York holiday, and I put Bob on the itinerary. As our meeting approached, Bob turned it into an invitation to lunch. We took a bottle of red wine and chocolates, as I recall, and Bob met us at the elevator door. A tall eighty-five-year-old, he was handsome, gaunt and grinning broadly. He wore a zip-up sky-blue track top, and his right hand was big and crushing.

He and Ann didn't drink, but the wine would go to the children, he said, showing us into a small, modest studio apartment containing a few chairs, a corner kitchen, bed, a small upright piano and stacks of CDs and music programs. Ann was elfin and pretty. She had fixed a simple lunch of cheese, crackers and fruit – blueberries, if I remember rightly – and we talked and ate for more than three hours.

To my first and most obvious question, Bob threw back his head and laughed. He had 'no idea' where Willy, older by four years, had acquired his genius. 'You tell me!' he hooted. Their parents loved great music, but neither played an instrument. Hyman ('Harry') Kapell and Edith Wolfson had emigrated from Poland – or Russia, as it was for 122 years after its partition in the late 18th century. Edith came from the village of Narewka, which is these days near the Belarus border. Predominantly Christian, Narewka had also been the home of many Jews since the late 17th century. (Almost all its Jewish population were to die in the Holocaust.) Edith spoke Russian, Polish and Yiddish. Her elder brother, Abraham, sponsored the immigration of his mother and two sisters – Edith the younger.

According to Bob his father was something of a 'mystery man'. Harry was born in a small Russian village that Bob is unable to name. Harry's father was Russian, and his mother, who was of Spanish-Portuguese Sephardi-Jew origin, died giving birth to him. He was taken to the United States as a baby, and joined the US Navy in his mid-teens. In World War I, he served on ships that escorted war vessels. In return for service he was granted citizenship and joined the Merchant Marine after hostilities finished. On shore leave he went to concerts, once hearing the great tenor Caruso, he liked to tell his sons.

Edith, the daughter of strict, orthodox Jews, dropped her religious beliefs and their trappings once she tasted freedom in New York. She had never learned music but, according to her musician son, loved profoundly the folk tunes of her native land.

Harry was a crew member on the ship on which Edith, her sister Olga, who had had voice training in Russia, and her mother came to America. He noticed this attractive young woman who was very seasick, and struck up a conversation. Six months later, he looked her up in Manhattan, where she was working at her elder brother Abe's dental practice. She could speak fluent English! In six months! Harry had to marry her. He popped the question, and Edith said yes on one proviso: that he gave up being a sailor and get a job. Harry agreed.

Harry and Edith were so devoted to the great composers that when America's first classical music radio station, W2XR (later WQXR), began broadcasting in 1936 the only radio they possessed was rarely tuned elsewhere. Bob wanted to listen to Dick Tracy serials and had a 'hard time' doing it. An old upright piano got shuttled with their chattels among several apartments they rented on Manhattan's Upper East Side, which was not so gentrified then as it is today. Indeed, the Kapells lived in the 'Yorkville' section which, ironically, was the home of many ethnic Germans. Even the lower-middle classes had pianos – it was 'important to that generation', as Bob Kapell puts it. No one played the Kapells' until soon after Willy came along on 20 September 1922. At the age of perhaps two or three he began to reach up for the keys. On occasions, Edith thought he could pick out melodies. Bob says that Willy developed his love of music because Edith sang Polish songs to him. She was keen for her son to have piano lessons, and they began when Willy was about eight. (Bob later learned violin and piano.) Willy once told a Californian newspaper that Edith first sent him to a French piano teacher, who taught him to play pieces by ear – without reading notes. A second teacher slapped his hand and he 'quit on the spot'. Yet another gave him children's pieces to learn when all he wanted to play were the 'big chords' of Chopin. He didn't get the teachers he wanted, in short, and the lessons lapsed. He also wouldn't practise enough, and the family was struggling financially.

Abe had at first set Harry and Edith up in a small stationery shop. By the time the Depression bit with most force, though, they had a bookstore in Lexington Avenue. Debts piled up, and they were forced to file for bankruptcy. (Over several years they paid off what was owed, 'a hundred cents in the dollar', says Bob.) Their financial despair coincided with Willy's wanting to take up playing again. He was ten, and his Damascene conversion occurred during a weekend upstate outing. A girl about his own age played a short bracket. Suddenly, he wanted to be a pianist, and there was no cash for lessons. Edith scoured the city for a teacher who might take on Willy *gratis*. She found Mr Sheridan, who would consider teaching Willy, he said, but he'd first have to see what the boy could do. Willy plinked out one of the earliest little pieces he'd learned. Mr Sheridan told him he didn't like the way he played it. Taking over the stool, he showed Willy how the music should be executed. Willy said, 'I don't like the way *you* play it.' Yet another teacher had to be found.

Edith 'scouted around', says Bob, finding the Third Street Music School on the Lower East Side, quite a hike from the Kapells. She had stumbled across something of a utopia of musical education. Set up in 1894, the first American community school of its type originally employed live-in social workers. It bathed the children of poorly off immigrants as well as teaching them music. Its founder, Emilie Wagner, believed high-quality music education could provide 'hope and inspiration to the impoverished immigrants of New York's Lower East Side', according to the school's website. Teaching at Third Street was Dorothea LaFollette, who could see that Willy had something. She took him on.

It's uncertain whether Mrs LaFollette taught Willy for nothing or if the lessons cost as much as two quarters each. What isn't in dispute is that they went for three to four hours sometimes three times a week over several years in Mrs LaFollette's studio in West 84th Street. Only weeks after taking up with his new teacher, he was among several students from community schools invited to share a Thanksgiving turkey with musician José Iturbi at his apartment. Working at the bookshop, Edith couldn't make it for Willy's contribution to the soirée, but mothers of other children welcomed her with rave reports when she went to pick him up. Her son was by far the best of the bunch and, in Bob's words, they 'practically wept at her feet'. When Willy visited Uncle Abe during school vacations, he would play constantly. 'I would have to beg him to stop [and] take some refreshment,' Abe wrote in a tribute read at a memorial concert at Miami Beach soon after Willy's death.

From a child who hated to practise, Willy became obsessive about it. Ann recalled his spending two hours repeating a single phrase of a couple of bars because he'd bungled it at a concert. He'd said, 'I made a mistake, and it's never going to happen again.' Apart from genial and infrequent mixing with important others, such as Bob and his parents, very little else mattered to Willy. (Bob learned violin from Mrs LaFollette's husband and was good enough to be appointed concert master of the All City Symphony Orchestra, which was composed of New York's public-school children.)

Mrs LaFollette did much to lay the foundation of Kapell's fiery and brilliant technique. In particular, she helped him develop supple wrists. For the rest of his life, he would return to her if he felt they were a little stiff. He is quoted as saying that Mrs LaFollette was 'an angel with me'. She took 'infinite pains', and he wondered how she'd 'managed never to lose her temper'. In the summer of 1935, she took him – Edith accompanying – by bus to La Jolla in California, where she visited her mother. He studied and practised for six weeks and played a recital for the first time – not yet thirteen – at a beachfront hotel (the Casa de Mañana), these days a retirement village. Willy played Bach – a 'Preambule', and the E major 'French' suite for keyboard. He played Bach, he told a local reporter, 'because it is strengthening'. The journalist found his performance 'energetic and clean-cut', and Willy's talent had already been recognised by several fine New York musicians. Another reviewer found his playing 'amazing' for someone 'whose small fingers could not yet stretch an octave comfortably'. He was a 'slight little lad with intense brown eyes and hair', and for encores he played two of his own works, 'Russian Medley' and 'A la Chopin'. He also played works by Mendelssohn and Goldmark. A hat was passed around and Willy made $60 for his effort. (A new car cost on average $625.) Not just a prodigy at twelve, he was also a pro.

Bob said – smiling – that Willy was 'not a normal boy'. In a host of family photographs he certainly appears normal. He and Bob are usually in short pants or swimsuits at the beach, once with a neighbour's cat, at other times relaxed in long grass or leaning against a wall. Every family member is handsome, faces symmetrical, dark eyes reflecting perhaps a little scepticism about the American dream. Willy smiles lightly in several.

He played no sports, had no close friends and no pets. He enjoyed reading, especially Thomas Wolfe's immense and hugely popular *Of Time and the River*, an American try at Proust, and biographies. From an early age he painted, a hobby he dropped in the late 1940s. He contracted rheumatic fever, several allergies, asthma and quite severe acne. He was allergic to cotton and had to wear expensive silk shirts. As if in compensation, though, he had magnificent large and rectangular piano hands. Photographs show that his palms were broad, fingers long and strong. His little fingers were near ring-finger length. Bob says Willy's hands were similar to his but bigger. Once you've shaken Bob's mitt you understand how suited Willy's must have been for his life's work. (At least one source claims that Willy felt his thumbs were short, forcing him to work hard to get fast scales and passages even. At one point, he also consulted a surgeon and family friend about cutting what he believed were longer than normal webs between his fourth and fifth fingers. The surgeon refused.)

Bob remembers Willy's asking him to bang down on the keyboard – anywhere. Willy turned his back. Bob struck five notes with each hand. Willy named all of them. Willy taught Bob two other keyboard tricks: the chords he needed for a basic boogie-woogie, and how to get what Willy called an 'Oriental' sound out of a piano by playing the black notes.

Willy and Bob were exceptionally close – essentially deckhands on a family vessel skippered by a mother and crewed by a hardworking, if introverted, father who had sailed rough seas before. Bob's love for his big brother was – and remains – as profound as a Pacific Ocean trench. While they were young, Willy was his 'protector'. He taught him how to ride a bike, for instance. To get out of New York's summer heat, Edith arranged for the boys to go to summer camps. Willy ensured that Bob – a five-year-old with a good appetite – had enough to eat. He remembers Willy writing home to their mother phrases such as 'Bobby is eating well'. On his own admission, Bob was a poor swimmer, and his brother made sure he didn't get rough-housed in the water. Much later, Willy was Bob's best man.

Over several years, the boys' favourite hobby was stamp-collecting. Willy ran the show, deciding what they would buy and how much they could afford to spend on first-day covers. They haunted Manhattan's Maiden Lane, the stamp district, looking for affordable buys. Bob, these days a retired lawyer and business consultant, wanted to invest fairly heavily in Hindenburg stamps issued in the early 1930s that celebrated the airship's voyages before the 1937 disaster. Willy curtailed the spree, insisting that they purchase only a few of the cheapest issue.

He was an exceptional student. The New York Board of Education rated children monthly in those days. Out of sixty-three marks on two cards, Willy scored a dozen B+s and five Bs. All the rest were As. Soon, his musical development had progressed to such an extent that he was allowed to do his schoolwork from home so that he could practise. And he rehearsed with gusto, so much so that about every two years the Kapells changed apartments. Leases were hard to keep. 'He played so loudly,' says Bob. Two months after his thirteenth birthday, Emily Nosworthy, the principal at Public School No. 6 on 85th Street, wrote to Columbia Grammar School on behalf of Edith, pleading with 'whom it may concern' to enrol Willy on a scholarship. He is 'unusually musically gifted', and it would be difficult for a public high school to offer him the program he needed. His school record was 'exceptionally good', she wrote. He was a boy of 'high intelligence, splendid character and good instincts'. His work had always been 'superior', and his pianistic ability was of such a 'high order that in the future it will be a credit to any institution to have had a part in furthering his ambitions'. He got the scholarship.

Dorothea LaFollette was well connected, introducing Willy to the cream of New York's pianists, Josef and Rosina Lhévinne, and Arthur Rubinstein. The Lhévinnes had arrived in New York from Russia via Berlin in 1919. Both had been gold medallists at the Moscow Conservatory. Moreover, they had taught Mrs LaFollette. Rubinstein, another pianistic gypsy who fled wars and anti-semitism, had spent most of his life outside his native Poland. His reputation in the United States developed relatively slowly, and he became an American citizen only in 1946. By the 1930s, he had toured widely and his magisterial renditions of the Romantic piano literature had gained significant respect. In a memoir, Rubinstein wrote that Willy had tried to be chummy by criticising his 'best friend' Josef Lhévinne. He alleged that Kapell asked to be taken on as a student. Rubinstein refused because he was away a lot. Kapell thought Rubinstein was hugely gifted but lazy. Relations between the two men remained cool over several years. But they stayed in touch and, in 1942, Rubinstein dedicated a photograph of himself to 'my dear Willy Kapell, with admiration for his wonderful talent'.

And Willy met Olga Samaroff, who became his second important teacher. There is some difference of opinion as to whether LaFollette was pleased with the move because she felt she had taught Willy everything she knew, or whether she was upset by his jumping ship to a better connected coach. Olga Samaroff said LaFollette asked her to hear Willy, with a view to his switching teachers. Samaroff asked why. LaFollette reportedly said, 'Madame, he is very difficult, and I am hoping you can manage him.' And so began, says Samaroff, a ten-year association with 'the most gifted, loveable, unpredictable, often inspiring, sometimes exasperating and altogether unique member of my large musical family'. There was no doubting the musical connections and didactic skills of 'Madame' – as her students called her. Born Lucy Hickenlooper in San Antonio, Texas, she became Olga Samaroff at the suggestion of her agent. (The name reportedly was borrowed from a distant relative.) Her family's business in Galveston was wiped out by the infamous hurricane of 1900, which might have killed 12,000, and she went to Europe to study, the first American woman admitted to the Paris Conservatoire.[1] Willy's indebtedness to Samaroff is best demonstrated in a four-stanza poem he wrote entitled 'To Madam'. It begins:

See the star!
That twinkles through its joy
O happy thing that nothing can destroy –
And though when there were fleeting clouds
Its smile was robbed from sight,
See now the radiant star
Its face is filled with light!

In *The Great Pianists*, Harold Schonberg describes Samaroff's playing as 'fiery and temperamental', two epithets that may be attached to Willy's early and middle performances. The impeccable young man from the Upper East Side first studied with her at the Philadelphia Conservatory. In 1940, he entered Juilliard to continue with 'Madame', and promptly won the Philadelphia Orchestra's Youth Contest, making his debut with the orchestra under Eugene Ormandy in February the following year. For the rest of his life, Ormandy could not contain his praise. A little after, Willy took out the Walter W. Naumberg Award, its prize a debut recital to fifteen hundred concert-goers at the Town Hall on West 43rd Street. His thank you letter begins, 'I am afraid that words are futile as a means of expressing the deep gratitude I feel, but I hope that they convey a little of it to you.' He goes on to say that Naumberg's kindness allows young musicians to give 'their first big concert'. He's very lucky to have the chance, and he will 'try to live up to it'. The letter finishes, 'I wish I could tell you what my heart feels, but the more I write, the more impossible it becomes.'

Willy had been playing less formal concerts around Manhattan for several years, but he was well aware that the Town Hall recital on 28 October 1941 would launch his career. He chose a courageous program, beginning with Bach – the C sharp minor Book I prelude and fugue, and an A minor suite. Until Glenn Gould made Bach popular late in the 1950s, the world's greatest composer was infrequently listed in recitals. (Gould made his debut at the Town Hall fourteen years after Kapell.) But Bach was only one of seven composers on his program. Three of them – Medtner, Rachmaninoff and Shostakovich – were still writing.

The audience and critics loved Willy. Howard Taubman in the *New York Times* said he was 'generously gifted, one of the most talented' Naumberg winners. He had 'imagination and sensitivity'. At times, he played too fast, Taubman felt, but he also didn't come to grief. He 'should be spending a good deal of his time on the performing side of the footlights in seasons to come', he finished. In the *Herald Tribune*, Jerome D. Bohm was left 'with a feeling of exhilaration not often carried away from the concert hall'. Imagination and sensitivity were again cited, and Mr Bohm thought Willy had captured the 'true flair of the Polish Master's idiom' in Chopin's F major ballade. 'I shall consider myself fortunate if I hear another performance of [the work] this season as satisfying as this one,' he concluded. His 'technical equipment is that of a true virtuoso'.

Four months later, Arthur Judson, the biggest and best agent to America's most important classical musicians, signed up Willy for three years. He would tour the States and the world, he told the young man. He would be a superstar.

★ ★ ★

Great pianists fascinate me, mostly because I wanted to be one. My teacher urged my parents to send me to Europe for advanced training, but they refused. My hands are fairly small, too, and the idea of playing the piano as a career mutated from desire to yearning, leaving something like a lifelong obsession with keyboard artists and what they do.

The challenges they face can't be exaggerated. The last two pages of Prokofiev's seventh sonata – a mere thirty-six bars of music – require the pianist who can play them to strike 1103 notes. Depending on the player, the notes are hit in forty to forty-five seconds, or at a rate of about twenty-five a second. Restrained in his directions as to whether music should be played loud or soft, Prokofiev marked the manuscript here either *f* for *forte* (loud) or *ff* meaning *fortissimo* (very loud). No relief. Many of the notes are grouped in four-note and five-note chords in the right hand and two-note, three-note and four-note chords in the left. The chords differ constantly, and within each, the pianist should attempt to sound the highest notes loudest. He should not play wrong ones, it goes without saying, and each chord needs to be given a weight relative to other chords sounded before and after it.

This third and final movement – section – of the piece tumbles to its conclusion like the controlled implosion of a derelict skyscraper. A critic once described the piece as a steel factory at full blast. It takes a little over three minutes to play: seven similar pages have preceded the last two. Above the first bar of the last movement Prokofiev wrote '*Precipitato*', which music sources agree means that the music should be hurled at listeners. And if you can add your own curve to the ball, all the better. There is no doubt that anyone who takes on Prokofiev's seventh is playing *precipitously* – in danger of tumbling over the edge of art.

In twenty-two pages before the *Precipitato*, the elite pianist has negotiated a long opening movement that should be speedy and 'unsettling' – Prokofiev's instruction was '*inquieto*' – and a lovely singing movement of walking pace marked '*caloroso*'; to be performed with warmth. The whole work is between seventeen and eighteen minutes long, and it will be only one of several items a pianist will play in a recital usually lasting more than an hour in playing time

On 25 July 1953, for instance, Prokofiev's seventh was the second item on William Kapell's program at the Melbourne Town Hall. It followed 'God Save the Queen', which opened every Australian classical music concert in those days, and Mozart's B flat sonata (Köchel 570), a quarter-hour of relatively straightforward playing that dares pianists to coax more mystery and imagination from the score than appears to inhere in the notes. *Appears.* After interval, Kapell gave his interpretation of the four-movement Schubert A major sonata, a monumental thirty-two-minute work composed in 1828 in the last months of the composer's life.[2] Leaving aside 'God Save the Queen' and encores, Kapell's recitals in 1953 had playing times of sixty-four, sixty-five and seventy-two minutes. Thousands of notes at each performance, all repeated from memory, all struck dead-centre, all unspoiled by sharps and flats on either side of them. Each note given its due weight, too; a crucial criterion. Each its artistic relevance. Each hit with unerring hand–eye coordination. In a typical week during the 1953 tour, Kapell played three concerts. In some, he would be on stage for only the half-hour or so it would take to perform a concerto with an orchestra. But twenty out of the thirty-seven concerts he performed were recitals – alone on the platform with only a keyboard and his nerves to work with. From 21 July, for instance, he executed five in Melbourne and Adelaide in fifteen days. Between 3 and 12 September, he played five in Sydney, Newcastle and Maitland. No wonder he called the schedule 'brutal'.

The elite pianist is a rare athlete, a highly trained digital gymnast who has acquired stupendous hand strength and dexterity. In tiny fractions of a second, he or she can vary the direction of attack and the force with which his or her fingertips strike the keys. But he or she must also be a marathon runner. Considerable physical – and mental – stamina is mandatory.

Unsurprisingly, there is an optimal 'piano' hand, a best tool to use in becoming an elite pianist. In *The Technique of Piano Playing*, a classic text published in 1965, József Gát mandates a long thumb, saying that the 'relative length of the thumb is one of the most important factors of good – or bad – hand structure'. His comprehensive treatise devotes a dozen pages to detailed analysis of hand morphology. He discusses the optimal proportions of phalangeal to metacarpal bones, of one finger's length to another, of one finger bone's length to others, of the ratio of finger thickness to length and the nature of finger joints. But perhaps the most striking feature of the *Technique* is its collection of photographs of pianists' hands. Those of Sviatoslav Richter, Emil Gilels, Anton Rubinstein, Lev Oborin, Vladimir Horowitz, Arthur Rubinstein, Annie Fischer and Wilhelm Backhaus, to name a few, are on display. There are photos of plaster casts of Chopin's left hand, Mendelssohn's right, and both of Liszt's.

Most striking are the lengths of these great pianists' little fingers. In practically all cases they seem longer than normal. (Gát recommends long little fingers. The right-hand one, in particular, is given the responsibility of carrying a lot of the melodies in piano literature.) Pictures of pianists' hands with the fingers outstretched show that their tips form a shallow arch. Most people usually have quite a step down from ring to little fingers. As remarkable is the thickness of great pianists' fingers and the meatiness of their hands. Palms thick through. They are the tools of gravediggers, lumberjacks, fishermen and those who hold horses on a tight rein. They are the hands of peasants and tradesmen, in short; Annie Fischer's perhaps the ideal. You can scarcely imagine their being appropriate for long delicate passages of *pianissimo* (very soft) that abound in piano music. Only Chopin's left hand shows any delicacy: the ring and little finger are fine and seem somewhat fragile. But it could be a fault of the cast.

Richter was defensive about the size of his hands. They hung ape-like from his sides – like spades, a critic once remarked – when he strode to the keyboard. But if anyone told him his hands were shovel-blades from which salamis dangled, he took offence. He felt they were not especially big. One side German – his father was a German piano teacher in a Russian conservatory – he had no tradesmen or farmers among his recent forebears. (His mother was a landowner's daughter.) In Gát's book, though, the nails of Richter's right thumb and middle finger are dirty in more than one picture – as if he has just come in from heavy labour. He hasn't, and his wrists are stranglers'.

For someone aspiring to elite levels, possessing 'piano' hands, strength, flexibility, stamina, hand–eye coordination and memory are more or less necessary. But as important as all these are, the door to success will remain locked to any aspiring pianist without the key called 'musicality'. Hard to define, a pianist who has it easily convinces an audience that her playing sounds both authentic and moving. She – or he – can make hairs stand up on listeners' necks. She can make them weep. Her interpretations of the great works are exciting and sound right, as if she is playing them as their composers intended them to be performed. Even though they might be fresh interpretations – and sometimes radical – they sound legitimate.

Being 'musical' almost always means being highly intelligent. Great pianists are never stupid. The works they play are of such intellectual complexity and emotional depth that, without considerable nous, convincing performances of them are impossible. Many great pianists have been great readers and beguiling writers – take Glenn Gould, Alfred Brendel and William Kapell. Most have been unusually good at school. Learning the technical skills to play the piano at elite levels is usually said to take ten to twelve years from about the age of eight, practising for four hours and more a day. But parallel to this athletic training, the prospective elite pianist is reading and writing, studying mathematics and geography, among other subjects, and glancing sideways at how other arts, such as painting and film, go about creating.[3]

For all that, we often think that gifted musicians are born ready to play or compose. Lending credence to that idea, several studies have shown that the vast majority of us could never be Mozart, even if we sat at a keyboard and wrote music from infancy as much as he had. A reasonable conclusion is that many variables create a keyboard superhuman. But the way in which they combine is complex and possibly unknowable. We are left shaking our heads, falling back on speculation.[4]

As we must with Willy. Bob tells a story that helps us understand the degree of Willy's obsession, how dedicated he was to his art.

When Bob was about ten, Willy got into the habit of taking him to Carnegie Hall concerts. They got in for nothing.

As if they hadn't a care in the world, they'd stroll along 57th Street to an inconspicuous door. It led direct to an elevator, which whisked New York's top music-lovers to the best seats.

Willy and Bob would wait their chance and take the elevator. Its doors opened at dress-circle level, and they'd take cover until they were sure no one was around, especially an usher. Outside the lift, steps to the right led to seating. To the left, a corridor about fifteen yards long went past doors to private boxes. At its end was a fire exit that opened onto a spiral steel staircase that descended into the stalls. They'd run along the corridor, clatter down the stairs and mingle with crowds until the show was about to begin. Then find spare seats.

One day, an usher caught them. Where were their tickets? They didn't have any, Willy admitted. Then they'd have to leave, said the usher.

For a second or two, Willy was speechless. He knotted his fingers and rubbed the side of his nose. Then he knew what to say. Just like that it came to him. He pointed in the direction of the auditorium.

'One day, sir,' he told the usher, 'I'm going to be up on that stage.'

In a cruelly truncated career, William Kapell played Carnegie Hall many times.

CHAPTER THREE

Thousand-dollar Man

'WILLIAM KAPPEL [sic] VERY INTERESTED COMING
AUSTRALIAWARD. HE ASKS REPEAT ASKS ONE
THOUSAND DOLLARS PER CONCERT BUT FEEL ABC
CAN GET BETTER DEAL. HE WOULD LIKE TO …
COME VIA BOAT.'

Extract from ABC cables negotiating Kapell's 1945 Australian tour

'[Kapell] is young and, according to Ormandy, in the
Horowitz class. In the case of a young artist like this, who
will eventually become world-famous, we might have an
opportunity of getting him at reasonable rates.'

From W.G. James memo to ABC management

Two weeks before the German surrender in 1945, Eugene Ormandy, the renowned conductor of the Philadelphia Orchestra, wrote an astonishing letter to Charles Moses, head of the Australian Broadcasting Commission. Beginning 'Dear Charlie', Ormandy penned an adulatory page-and-a-half to introduce William Kapell, the 'greatest pianistic talent since Horowitz'. Under the auspices of the national broadcaster, Willy's first major concert tour outside North America would begin in three months.

Ormandy, who had toured Australia for the ABC the year before, hit his stride in the second paragraph. 'In private life [Kapell] is a very modest, natural, friendly, thoroughly likeable young man. At the piano, he is a whirlwind. I feel that he will create a sensation in Australia.'

'In spite of his extreme youth,' begins the next paragraph, 'he already ranks, in my opinion, among the giants of the piano – such as Rachmaninoff, Horowitz, Serkin.' Ormandy wrote that he was particularly proud of his friendship with Willy because the pianist had made his orchestral debut with the Philadelphia 'when still a mere boy of fifteen'. (He was, in fact, eighteen.) 'His appearance was an immediate success.' After a rehearsal with the orchestra, the letter continued, the conductor had taken the 'unprecedented step' of writing to Arthur Judson, Willy's agent and president of Columbia Artists' Management Inc., the biggest music promoter in America. He told Judson that Willy had made a 'great sensation' with him and orchestra members. 'He is doubtless one of the four or five great pianists today.'

The Ormandy letter would be conscripted by the ABC's publicity department, of course. Such an endorsement was priceless. But it was also an affirmation of the value of Charles Moses's plans to persuade the world's best musicians to play for Australian ears. A cynic might even speculate that Moses asked Ormandy to write it.

Lieutenant-Colonel Charles Moses – he was later knighted – had a unique musical vision: he wanted every Australian state to have a proper symphony orchestra.[1] The distinguished British conductor Dr Malcolm Sargent had urged him and his musical director Bernard Heinze to try for a single fine Australian ensemble. They resisted. Moses wanted a 'musical core' in every state, as he put it. Each would be accomplished enough to accompany the world's best instrumentalists and singers.

Willy scarcely needed Ormandy's recommendation. He had caused a sensation at his formal debut in 1942. Not long before it, conductor Efrem Kurtz and Willy heard together the premiere of Soviet-Armenian Aram Khachaturian's piano concerto, a new, percussive and pyrotechnical pastiche that American audiences fell in love with – most things Russian gained easy popularity as the allies slugged it out on different fronts in Europe. Kurtz conducted the New York Philharmonic's summer concerts, and asked Willy to learn the piece. (Judson negotiated a fee of $75.) It took him a week, according to Edith Kapell. Willy strode to the Steinway in Lewisohn Stadium and Kurtz raised his baton. By the time the thirty-five minute concerto was over, Willy owned it. Following that performance, he played it often, once in front of Andrei Gromyko, the Soviet ambassador to the United States and – later –

Cold War foreign minister. (Willy described it as 'Oriental and colourful', its slow movement 'very beautiful, suggesting a … bazaar'. But in other parts of the score you might hear jazz, ragtime and even a hint of Gershwin.) Composer and friend Aaron Copland dubbed Willy 'Khachaturian Kapell'. The euphonious alliteration no doubt helped in his thrust for fame, but that he became known as the supreme exponent of a collage of sound that sometimes scintillated and at others could be mistaken for the accompaniment to a B-grade western, he realised, wouldn't help his reputation as a Bach or Mozart interpreter. He was being seen as a leading interpreter of Russian music, and performances of Rachmaninoff and Khachaturian only reinforced this view.

In January 1944, Kapell was due to make the first American recording of the Khachaturian with Serge Koussevitzky and the Boston Symphony. They'd played it together seven times and, somehow or other, the recording schedule coincided with Willy's playing concerts in Cuba and taking a short holiday there. He interrupted his vacation to fly back for the session, curtailing rehearsal time. Dr Koussevitzky was beside himself, his brow under an ice-pack, as the story goes.

According to Willy, who loved to relate his version, Koussevitzky opened with, 'Where you was?' and 'When we rehearse?' Willy pointed out that he was on holidays, he'd come back for the recording session, and they'd played the piece many times and didn't need to rehearse. He knew the speeds the maestro liked to take the movements at. 'This is the Boston Symphony,' moaned the conductor. The recording began, Koussevitzky striking new tempi and stopping the Boston band from time to time to chide the soloist for getting ahead or falling behind. The recording was scrapped and the war was to end before the pair collaborated again on a benchmark performance. Kapell and Koussevitzky had been close before the first attempt to tape the Khachaturian. They had lunched and dined together to discuss the work. But Bob Kapell says his brother never got over Koussevitzky's embarrassing him in front of the Boston players.

Willy – and presumably Judson – worked hard to ensure that the tyro acquired a repertoire beyond the Russians. He played Beethoven's second and third concertos and Saint-Saëns's G minor. But – with his background – he could scarcely neglect music that sung of the steppes, and his Rachmaninoff broadened. In 1943, he played the composer's second concerto with the St Louis Symphony and was invited to return, which he did several times. After the first concert, the *Globe-Democrat*'s reviewer called Willy its 'pianist of the year'. Three seasons later he was its 'pianist for the Ages!'

He also composed – piano pieces, pop ballads and reportedly a concerto, which was so similar to inferior Rachmaninoff that he trashed it. 'Song of the Forest' in six-eight time is a slow violin solo accompanied by sweeping left-hand arpeggios on the piano. 'Never Again' – 'music and lyrics by William Kapell' – is a four-four ballad. Its lyrics begin, 'Right into my heart, you came walking along. Yet I felt somehow this could last, it seems that I was wrong.' The chorus pines, 'Never again, never again, shall I permit myself to fall again. If I had known that you didn't care, this last farewell would be easy to bear.'

In non-musical time, Willy read widely, moving on from Wolfe to the novels of John Dos Passos and the work of philosophers. Nietzsche, of God-is-dead notoriety, was a favourite. And he continued to paint, mainly in oils now, without really knowing how. His politics were 'liberal democrat', says Bob Kapell, and he admired the eloquent intellectual and Democrat Adlai Stevenson. He was pro-Jewish, proud of his forebears, and excited by the creation of Israel. Bob says that although family members were not practising Jews there was a lot of '*Yiddishkeit*' about them – they revered their antecedents' religion and deferred to its moral positions and customs. Music came first, however, and Willy was rarely distant from a keyboard, arranging practice time of four to five hours a day even when he travelled. If pianos could not easily be found where he was about to perform, he would arrange time in piano stores. A Judson flyer for the 1944–45 season begins, 'The eyes and ears of the musical world are on' – in huge block capitals – 'KAPELL'. He was the most 'talked-about artist of the past 2 years'.

In the coming season he would play with eighteen orchestras, it says. The bookings are astounding. Four concerts with the Philadelphia Orchestra in October and one in November before five more to finish the year with such ensembles as the Buffalo Philharmonic, the New Orleans Symphony and the St Louis Symphony. January is busier – nine concerts, including two in Indianapolis, two in Kansas City and one in Denver. February sees only one engagement, March one, two in April and a single concert in May. Judson garnished the flyer with rave reviews. C. B. M. – in those days it was common for reviewers to be simply initialled not bylined – in the *Oklahoma City Times* had thrilled to Willy's playing, adding that his 'dazzling technical command' includes a 'pianissimo which tosses off like spray, a fortissimo which rolls up to a tremendous climax but never hurts the ears, and a staccato as delicate and brittle as the rustle of dry leaves'. Willy was a fine artist and 'potentially he is a great one'. In the *Philadelphia Inquirer* following his 27 October performance, Linton Martin called Willy 'electrifying and exciting'. Rachmaninoff's *Rhapsody on a Theme of Paganini* 'provided an ideal medium for the display of Mr Kapell's fine musical sensibility, and his excellent physical and emotional equipment'. An important 'even though' followed. It would have reverberated in Willy's ears – he read all the crits and got upset at those that suggested, even in passing, that he was artistically deficient: 'even though,' continued Martin's paragraph, 'he has not yet attained full interpretive maturity'. Willy had just turned twenty-two, but the question of his maturity as an artist gnawed his psyche like a dog with a bone.

★ ★ ★

Judson blew a fanfare for his client every time his name was mentioned. Leith Stevens, the ABC's head of radio, had presumably gone to the US to scout for soloists. Stevens cabled from Hollywood, 'WILLIAM KAPPEL [sic] VERY INTERESTED COMING AUSTRALIAWARD. HE ASKS REPEAT ASKS ONE THOUSAND DOLLARS PER CONCERT BUT [I] FEEL ABC CAN GET BETTER DEAL … HE REQUESTED RETURN VIA PLANE BUT HAVE ADVISED HIS MANAGER JUDSON THIS IMPOSSIBLE. PLEASE HAVE ABC CABLE SOONEST THEIR TERMS IN DETAIL TO ME …'

Bill James, the ABC's federal controller of music, hadn't banked on paying Willy big fees. In a memo to Moses the month before, he had written, 'Ormandy mentioned to me the name of William Kappell [sic], who has come right to the front in America.' (Early in his career, few people spelled Willy's name correctly.) James continued, 'In the case of a young artist like this, who will eventually become world-famous, we might have an opportunity of getting him at reasonable rates.' The ABC subsequently cabled back to Stevens, 'ABC CANNOT CONTEMPLATE HIGHER FEE THAN 100 POUNDS AUSTRALIAN PER KAPPEL [sic] CONCERT HE UNKNOWN IN AUSTRALIA RELATIVELY UNKNOWN AMERICA. IF KAPPEL INTERESTED ABC SUGGESTS 20 SOLO CONCERTS THROUGHOUT AUSTRALIA PLUS 5 APPEARANCES ORCHESTRAL CONCERTS FOR WHICH FEE 50 POUNDS EACH'. Willy was asking more than £A400 a recital.

And recitals were what the ABC wanted, a policy that could advance a performer's artistic gravitas – and the ABC's credentials as a serious promoter – more than any number of performances with orchestras. Willy accepted a guaranteed £150 a recital and agreed to perform twenty. He took £100 for each of six appearances with an orchestra. The broadcaster agreed to pay his return travel costs from San Francisco and his travel expenses within Australia.

He was not the ABC's first choice for the 1945 season. Stevens wrote to Moses two months after his first cable to say that Judson's office had advised that Paul Robeson, the black bass with a voice as rich as cocoa butter, was 'out', Yehudi Menuhin, the violinist, was 'tied up' with another agency, but 'Kappel [sic] accepts with pleasure'. Willy would arrive by ship. Stevens needed only to cable to secure him.

A problem with dates quickly arose. For the first six weeks of Willy's schedule, the ABC was also touring Noel Mewton-Wood, a talented Australian pianist who had lived and studied in London since his teens. (In 1945, the ABC slated 105 orchestral concerts and 42 recitals.) To the day two months younger than Willy but taller, his rearing, wavy brown hair was almost as luxurious as the American's. Noel and Willy would make great photo fodder for the ABC's publicity department if they posed together. Kept apart, they could cross-market, though, increasing ticket sales for each other. If their performances clashed, box office could get hurt. It was a ticklish but delectable predicament. The broadcaster opted to separate their dates as much as possible. Willy would start later, which brought about its own problems because he had to honour commitments back in America in early October.

In mid-January, the parties finally decided that Willy would play twenty recitals and make eight orchestral appearances. Judson's office advised on 20 January that the terms were fine but the dates were 'unsuitable'. Kapell would be ready to leave on 15 June and make himself available for twelve weeks. He would need to leave Australia at the end of September. Robert McCall, the ABC's federal superintendent, wrote to the acting secretary of the Department of External Affairs. It was 'essential' that Kapell arrived in Sydney on 1 or 2 July. After the ABC had juggled auditoriums, orchestral players and other itineraries, there was room only for the New Yorker to begin his tour in Adelaide on 4 July. McCall's letter continues, 'We therefore are seeking your assistance in securing a passage for Kapell on a R.A.F. plane which would deliver him here at the end of June'. The US Office of War Information had helped in negotiations with Kapell, and McCall thought flying Willy out might encourage 'the closest co-operation between the United States and Australia, and enlarging [sic] the field of mutual cultural interest'. The Australian Legation in Washington finally cabled the ABC on 1 March to say that 'IT IS IMPOSSIBLE TO GRANT KAPELL A PASSAGE BY RAF TRANSPORT'.

A cable on 9 March insisted that Willy provide 'at least six recital programmes each approximately eighty minutes'. Judson's office replied at the end of March that 'since he only twentytwo [sic] he doesn't have six complete concert programs'. He did have four, though, that – the implication is clear – the ABC could lump or leave. The broadcaster was asked to okay 'these facts'. If it agreed, publicity material would be sent. 'If not will have to cancel Kapell's trip'. The ABC agreed, and its attention then turned to getting Willy back to America in early October. Launceston could be deleted from the itinerary – as could Perth.[2] There was no denying that the tour would have to be shortened. It might have to end in August if he couldn't fly home. Seven recitals and four orchestral concerts would need to be cancelled, one memo advises.

Perhaps if Willy had taken to heart the headaches his first major international tour was causing at the tail-end of a world conflict, he might have abandoned it himself. Ruth Walter, who worked for the American Office of War Information, pleaded with her employer to smooth Willy's path. She had had a recent lunch with him, she wrote to Bob Burlingame, the acting chief of the office's Sydney bureau. 'He is an awfully nice person but has not had very much experience on an out-of-the-country tour. He would like to be taken under your wing as much as possible, and this also means handling financial matters for him.' She also wondered if Burlingame could arrange for a collection of Willy's Australian press clippings to be sent to him.

And if windy preparations and Willy's inexperience weren't enough, the New Yorker would not be able to benefit from a tax loophole Ormandy had exploited. Several of Ormandy's concerts in 1944 had entertained troops. As a consequence, he paid no

Australian income tax. As Willy would not be performing for the services, the Taxation Department ruled, he would not be exempt.

Then there was the Steinway. The world's best piano-maker had a policy of lending instruments to the best pianists. All musicians had to do was pick up tabs for transport. Willy wanted to bring a favourite Steinway. A cable arrived in May advising that Steinway in New York would 'send and pay salary of Messerschmidt best piano mechanic and tuner to put all ABC pianos in top condition if ABC pay transportation'. Perhaps many people in New York still thought kangaroos bounced about the streets of Sydney and Adelaide. Although there is no evidence, Willy and Judson probably – and rightly – suspected that some Australian pianos would be inferior to a Steinway-supplied instrument, especially one that Willy liked. Concert grands have heavy – and sometimes quirky – touches; they're built for professionals and vary under the fingers. Pianists can be sensitive to their ways. And Messerschmidt's name was unfortunate. It was similar to that of a successful World War II German fighter plane, which perhaps triggered aversion in Bill James's unconscious. He thanked Steinway, but said that the ABC could not undertake to bring out Herr Messerschmidt. Australia's concert pianos 'would be OK', he wrote.

By June, keeping Kapell and Mewton-Wood 'as far apart as possible' was becoming an 'almost desperate' situation, ABC internal documents showed. Schedules were rewritten several times. Even so, on 'one occasion he [Kapell] will have to fly from Melbourne and appear in Sydney on the same night', said a memo. Not only was Mewton-Wood touring, but eighteen-year-old New Zealander Richard Farrell was waiting in the wings if Willy couldn't fulfil an engagement. Another ABC guest was Pnina Salzman, a Tel Aviv-born 'Palestinian' Jew of Willy's age and similar reputation. Several of the ABC's many bureaucrats were conscripted just to handle the arrangements of its plethora of tyro pianists, it may be fair to surmise.

Willy's final itinerary had him performing thirteen solo recitals and eight concerts with orchestras. The tour began on 12 July and ended on 3 September. Most recitals were kept at least two days apart. But his first solo performance in Melbourne was on a Monday, an orchestral concert followed on the Tuesday, a recital on the Thursday and another on Saturday. His gruelling lap of the nation ended in Sydney, where he played six concerts in a fortnight. Recital programs can demand a little or a lot from experienced keyboard artists. Willy's were weighty both technically and artistically. Number I began with Brahms's F minor sonata and a bracket of three Chopin pieces before interval. After it, he played ten preludes by Shostakovich, Rachmaninoff and Gershwin, and Liszt's bristling Mephisto Waltz, a challenge for anyone to get his fingers around. Program II included works by Mozart, Chopin, Debussy, Brahms and Liszt. (Brahms and Chopin were his favourite composers.) Program III included a Prokofiev sonata, and IV a six-dance Bach partita, Bach choral preludes arranged by Busoni, a Schumann sonata and Chopin pieces.

★ ★ ★

With Willy a passenger, the SS *Kookaburra*, according to cables, left San Francisco on 15 June and was due to arrive in Brisbane on 5 July. Unfortunately, as Burlingame told the American Consul in the Queensland capital, 'there is no piano aboard ... and therefore

Kapell will have had no chance to practice during his voyage'. Plans were made to get Salzman to replace him if he couldn't make two performances scheduled for the second week in July.

The *Kookaburra* not only tied up on schedule but Willy had reportedly been practising at sea on a 'dummy' keyboard. The ABC's publicity department was quick to get Willy and Mewton-Wood together. They met on 9 July and played for each other. A press photograph shows a vaguely amused Mewton-Wood at a keyboard, Willy stolid and senior to the side, hand on the back of the pianist's chair. The Brisbane *Telegraph* reported Willy as saying that Noel was a 'brilliant pianist'. Australia had a 'wealth of natural talent', Willy went on, 'but I always think it's a shame for musicians to study in foreign countries'. It was a way to 'lose their nationality and become imbued with the ideas of those people under whom they have studied'. (In an interview published in the Western Australian Communist newspaper *Workers' Star*, Willy was reported to have said that Mewton-Wood was 'now an English pianist'. Music was 'like a seed', he continued. You needed to give it the chance to grow in a player of genius. Then it would become 'truly Australian genius'.)

When he hadn't been hitting dummy keys on board the *Kookaburra*, he'd read, slept, chain-smoked and painted – five seascapes on surplus ship's canvas and board. He gave one to the captain and another to the *Kookaburra*'s first mate. Two owned by Bob Kapell are dark and stormy pieces. Waves bludgeon an unidentified rocky coastline. Foam surges. Though nowhere near so luminous, they are similar to the Australian Impressionist John Peter Russell's seascapes of Belle-île off the Brittany coast.

William Dobell, one of Australia's finest painters, had presented Ormandy with one of his paintings the year before. Willy had seen it in the conductor's apartment, and Dobell was one of the first natives Willy wanted to meet. It was arranged, and a press photograph shows a credentialled artist scrutinising one of Willy's fresh sea pictures. The caption says the painters had made a pact to swap works. Willy looks over Dobell's shoulder. In the many hundreds of images of him he rarely smiles. (In many he looks a little sulky. Perhaps women might have called this a smoulder.) In the Dobell photograph he seems a trifle anxious. The accompanying report says that, as children, Dobell had wanted to be a pianist and Kapell had wanted to be a painter.[3] After examining Willy's canvases, Dobell was reported to have told Willy he had talent. 'He shows a sense of drawing in his patterning and shape, great feeling and flexibility.'

Willy was even more enthusiastic about the older man. In his diary, he noted that they dined at Le Coq d'Or and that 'that guy Dobell is a fantastic artist. Serious such as one rarely sees. I am taken with him completely.' Bill had taken Willy to a party at the home of Sydney society photographer Jo Fallon, the diary reports. It continues, 'Got very drunk and played a lot of jazz. Relaxed completely. Bill Dobell slept most of the night in my room, and we had fun telling stories.'

In other interviews, Willy revealed that his favourite piece of music was the Brahms piano quintet, and what he liked most about being a student at the famed Juilliard School in New York was playing chamber music with other students. Since the outbreak of war, he said, the 'musical centre of the world has moved to New York'. There were so many musicians in the city that 'it isn't unusual to have twenty piano recitals a week ... during the winter concert season'. He loved British contemporary music, especially the works of Britten, Bax, Walton and Vaughan Williams. The latter's *London Symphony* was among the most beautiful compositions of the 20th century. Musical composition in the United States was at its 'zenith', Willy reported. 'Samuel Barber, Aaron Copland, William Schumann and Leonard Bernstein are among the most conspicuous of the many gifted composers in America whose works are being played all the time by the big American orchestras. There is a stipulation among most orchestras that at least one work by a local composer should be included in every programme.'

Halfway through the tour, 'Athena' wrote one of the most perceptive brief profiles of Willy. Filing from Melbourne for readers of the *West Australian*, who were about to hear him, she began with the words, 'Remarkable scenes ...' They referred not to celebrations following victory in the Pacific, which was still officially more than a week away, but to the behaviour of Melbourne Town Hall patrons at one of Willy's concerts. 'Large numbers,' 'Athena' wrote, mobbed the stage after his final encore. They sought the pianist's autograph. She estimated that almost five hundred waited outside the stage door for Willy to leave, and as he walked to 'a motor car he was cheered to the echo'.

She spent an hour with this 'tempestuous-looking young man, thin-faced, with deep-set eyes and a shock of dark hair' in the 'sitting room of his Melbourne hotel'. He'd insisted he was a 'dull subject'. Far from being boring, he was 'direct and friendly', she wrote. He had admitted that he was always nervous before concerts. 'I doubt any artist who is not,' he said. 'He is a machine not a poet.' Bringing enjoyment to so many didn't mean *he* enjoyed it; the responsibility was too great. Practising – when he played for himself – was a different matter. 'But once you walk on to a stage you no longer belong to yourself. You belong to the audience.'

Soon after arriving, a *Listener In* correspondent told readers that Willy thought jazz in America bore the same relationship to serious music as 'folk music does to art music in other countries'. Jazz and its progeny – 'swing, boogie-woogie and the like', as Willy was reported to have put it – were being 'increasingly absorbed into serious American compositions'. Judicious and precise words. For reasons unknown, Melbourne's *Argus*, however, appeared to corrupt Willy's views. The young pianist saw no musical merit in jazz, regarding it as 'decadent'. There was merit in 'negro spirituals', the *Argus* quoted Willy, which would 'have their effect in American composition'. A highly regarded newspaper, the *Argus* was not the sort of journal to misreport. A week or so later, 'Fidelio' tried to untangle the mess, opening his interview with an attempt to confirm Willy's opinion on jazz being the folk music of America.

'I hope not,' said Willy. According to 'Fidelio', the New Yorker's words were terse and emphatic. He'd been misquoted. He'd meant that some American composers were using the rhythms of jazz in serious compositions. Jazz was 'just an entertainment to me', he said. He liked to dance to it, but never turned on the radio to listen to it. 'Fidelio' got Willy to opine on musical appreciation on a broader scale. He said Australians enjoyed music 'in a deeper way' than Americans. 'I think they get far more joy out of Brahms than most Americans do.'

Inevitably, there were reports on what Willy liked to eat. He told Vesta Junior in the *Argus* that his mother was a 'superb cook'. He liked everything she produced. He had his favourites, though. A potato soufflé contained three eggs, and potato 'beignets' one.

Pea soup was made with fresh peas, but also contained carrot, onion, 'chicken broth' or stock, butter and milk. The soup could be eaten hot or cold, Willy told Miss or Mrs Junior. Willy – 'Bill' in the article – liked mackerel. He preferred them filleted and fried in butter or margarine with a sauce made from 'a little fish stock with the bones and heads of the fish', red wine, butter and milk.

His direct and opinionated answers to routine questions told reporters and their readers that William Kapell was no one's twenty-two-year-old fool. He had ideas – as well as recipes – and he expressed them undiluted. Among many shy and wary Australians he would have seemed over-confident. Several vernacular – and pejorative – expressions were used then to describe this peculiarly Australian interpretation of self-confidence. He would have been 'blowing his own trumpet' or 'blowing his bags out'. He might have 'had tickets on himself' or was 'getting ahead of himself'. Or he might have been just a 'skite'.

For Bonnie McCallum, Willy was no skite. For twenty-eight years from 1936, her job was minding visiting musicians for the ABC's Victorian office. She also managed their publicity. She looked after Schnabel, Neveu, Lotte Lehmann, Claudio Arrau and Otto Klemperer, among many. Perhaps a decade older than Willy, she wrote much later in her memoir *Tales Untold* that he 'did not treat his hard-won success lightly'. She had observed the usual traits. Beneath his 'affected' brashness he had a 'deeply sensitive make-up'. Willy's mother 'meant everything to him'. (Bob Kapell confirms this. With his first earnings as a pianist Willy bought Edith a fur stole. Bob adds, though, that for all the floods of affection within the Kapell family, Willy sometimes yelled at Edith over career decisions she had made on his behalf.) McCallum wrote that Willy had told her he had grown up in a 'tall tenement apartment block ... to which the natural light and sun seldom penetrated between the canyon walls of the buildings'. It represented a challenge for him to get to the top. 'He strove both to reach the light, and push upwards to achieve his ambition.'

By the time he reached Melbourne, he had won the epithet 'difficult' because he wanted a piano and a studio as soon as he touched down anywhere. He also wanted to practise at any time of the night or day. McCallum was to treat Willy with 'velvet gloves'. It was superfluous advice. 'Willie [sic] came across from his plane at Essendon [Melbourne] airport, getting along with his characteristic insouciant walk, appearing to tilt forward on his toes. Scarf escaping from his baggy overcoat, he had even a gamin air that did little to suggest the serious artist.' Willy and Bonnie quickly became friends. When she fell behind his forward-slash walk in the street, he would tease her, 'wheeling back like an eager puppy' and threatening to carry her. His 'coal-black eyes, like those of a sad monkey until he smiled' gave him even more of an 'urchin air'. He rubbed the right side of his nose with a closed fist when he was uncertain. He told her she reminded him of his 'Mom'.

He was sometimes off-hand with the Press – before the interview with 'Athena', he had said, 'I'll see that babe of yours.'[4] McCallum organised the photographs with Mewton-Wood. At first, the pianists looked at one another 'askance'. But they became close, meeting several times and playing four-handed works by Schubert and others 'for hours on end, even late into the night!' Frank Drew, a veteran Oriental Hotel porter, told McCallum that guests often gathered on the landing outside suite 71–72 at midnight – even later – to listen to Willy.

Bonnie organised several photo shoots. In one, Willy holds a lamb and looks worried. In another, a kangaroo eats out of his hand. In a third, a possum is climbing up his chest, its claws hooked into Willy's coarse-woven jacket. The pianist appears to be trying to pull its tail to stop it reaching his collar and tie. Willy's bouffant hair is as big as the animal.

Willy left Bonnie a studio photo in return. He inscribed on it, 'To Bonnie – of whom I shall always think with sincere affection and deep gratitude'. He dated it, and signed it 'Bill'.

He made several friends in Melbourne. He visited pianist and teacher Jascha Spivakovsky and his wife Leonore at their home in Toorak, a posh suburb. He went to the home of psychiatrist and writer Dr Reg Ellery to listen to his vast record collection and play the family's grand piano 'sometimes literally through the night'. (The Ellerys also had Victoria's only harpsichord, which Mrs Mancell Ellery took to the Town Hall and played when symphonic repertoire required it.) The New Yorker also met Willi Serkin, a Melburnian and the engineer brother of the great Rudolf, and contacted Richard Farrell, who was studying in the city. He urged Farrell 'to go back with him' to New York, where he could get Olga Samaroff to teach him.

Judging by reviews, he played better as the tour progressed. He had, it appeared, plenty to skite about. Critics used the word 'brilliant' until it was numb. Melbourne's *Radio Times* said Willy 'proved himself possibly the finest pianist ever heard here … He certainly made the piano "talk" in a manner not approached since Percy Grainger's pre-war visit.' This 'serious young man has music in his soul'. Y. M. C. in the Brisbane *Telegraph* said the outstanding characteristic of his playing was its 'vigour'. But 'sweetness and clarity of the softer passages did not at any time suffer as a result'. The review continued, 'At times, the sheer brilliance of his technique was breath-taking and this was combined with rare depth and understanding'. 'Fidelio' wrote that the 'flinging forth' of an opening theme of an early Brahms sonata was 'electrifying'. It had 'leonine power in attack and grip … Only a bar or two were needed to tell us that here was a commanding musical capacity'. The sonata's scherzo featured 'massive, resilient, clean-cut masterfulness'.

'Fidelio' reported in a chatty arts column on the same day that a local pianist had damaged his hands applauding Kapell. Thorold Waters in the Melbourne *Sun* had followed all three young touring pianists. They had spread 'the loveliness of music before us'. All had 'uncanny wisdom and authority on the secrets of the composers' and not just technique. Kapell possessed more than the others. W. M. in Brisbane thought Willy's playing might persuade a listener that he was hearing an orchestra and not a piano. And in Adelaide, 'Orpheus' wrote that Willy's work had an 'infinite variety of shading'. Trying to explain his reactions, the *Listener In*'s reviewer said there was something 'intensely alive' in Kapell's interpretations that gripped him (or her) in a way that 'none of the others has'. Pianists with 'greater reputations have been almost too mechanically perfect, whereas there is always a provocative air about Kapell's playing. It certainly gets me.'

Only in Sydney did Willy fare less well. Kenneth Wilkinson in the *Telegraph* began his first review by describing Willy as a 'virtuoso of the first order'. Even when Wilkinson 'disagreed profoundly' with a Brahms interpretation, he found himself 'whipped along by the sheer force of his rhythm, the adroitness and brilliance of his detail'. The pianist approached the keyboard 'arrogantly' – he was 'out to show how magnificent he could make the Brahms F minor sonata sound'. He succeeded. But the work required a 'certain inwardness of feeling', which the young composer had underlined by writing above the slow movement a melodramatic quote from the poet Sternau about the uniting of two loving hearts in the gloaming. The next one-sentence paragraph was printed in bold type: 'There was no love in it last night.' Instead, wrote Wilkinson, wielding metaphor like a cudgel, the lovers were 'both of them showing off, and trumpeting at each other in a great flourish of egoism'. Willy's Chopin was 'sometimes incredibly lovely' and 'keenly intelligent' but a 'Chopin as yet without a heart'. He went on, 'Some day, it is almost certain, the young pianist will weary of the vanities of technical display for its own sake. The sharply etched lines of his style will become suffused with the colors of meditation and emotion. If that happens, he will be a great pianist.'

Two days later in his second review, Wilkinson accused Willy of his customary brilliance but also a 'certain shallowness'. The pianist was sincere, obviously, but 'he is still immature enough to prize resounding flourishes more than the slow, even development of the composer's thought'. Playing Rachmaninoff's third concerto late in the tour, Willy suffered again from an unwavering Wilkinson. The pianist's 'dash and flourish' and 'extraordinary bravura' were unabated. He 'galloped' through technical complexities. 'But the attraction lay almost entirely on the surface.'

In 1945, Neville Cardus was the *Sydney Morning Herald*'s music critic. A doyen of the fourth estate who was later knighted for his writings on music and cricket, Cardus was born in England, his father unknown to him. His mother and sisters worked as 'genteel prostitutes', as the *Australian Dictionary of Biography* puts it. He joined the *Manchester Guardian* at twenty-nine, and in a very short while became known for an 'intuitive' and personal approach to writing about his two loves. He made radio broadcasts and wrote books – eventually eleven on cricket and nine on music.[5]

At Willy's first Sydney recital fairly early in the tour, Cardus attacked the audience for liking the New Yorker's playing: they were 'indiscriminating'. He was only limbering up; his account of the second recital begins with a fine example of journalistic solipsism, a blend of lilac – if not purple – prose, breast-beating and analysis peculiar to British critics. It's the type of writing that often says more about its authors than what they are supposed to be reviewing. And, no doubt, it's the sort of scribbling that yearns for readers' applause. Willy, at any rate, showed 'something of the mastery of a rider clinging commandingly to a runaway horse', began Cardus. For the next several hundred words, he rampaged, finishing with a morsel of faint praise, an admission that Willy was 'undoubtedly promising'. His shortcomings were obvious. He strained his 'exceptional technique a little too far'. He made 'lavish use' of the pedal, obscuring errors. Often, he 'actually scatters wrong notes'. His 'musical penetration is not yet deep or poetic enough to ignore insecurities of execution which a keen ear can detect in an impressive show of velocity'. Willy's playing lacked nuance; he was either 'loud or soft'. A 'lovely soaring melody' in Brahms's scherzo was 'curiously cold, and hesitant and inhibited'. Mr Kapell did not seem to have studied 'tone relative to a composer's style'. In a quieter age, wrote Cardus, his undoubted skills would be given more time to mature.

Cardus and Wilkinson were stags with locked horns, and to hell with the pianist if he became collateral damage. Straining an exceptional technique didn't make sense. If a technique was exceptional, nothing in the piano literature would normally challenge it. Did Cardus mean Willy employed more technique than he needed, an impossibility? Using a sustaining pedal to mask errors suggested that Willy was dishonest; most critics and music-lovers agreed that playing the music the way he sincerely believed the composer intended it to sound was his performing trump. 'Actually' scattering wrong notes also implied fraudulence, the antithesis of Willy's approach and character. And remarks about his playing without nuance and warmth opposed other reviewers' opinions.

To his credit, late in the tour Cardus recanted. Perhaps the joust with Wilkinson was over. Perhaps he'd realised his earlier disingenuousness. At any rate, the rigors of performing and practising day after day had tamed Willy's 'youthful excess of energy', Cardus began one piece. '[His] grip on the keyboard was firm, but not aggressive; there was no virtuosity merely to excite us; the music was penetrated below the surface'. But it got better. 'This was the most revealing Brahms playing heard in Sydney in my time; also it was a lovable Brahms, saying so much of satisfying musical content in so wide and economical a language.' It was an 'extremely mature interpretation', neither 'adolescent' nor 'provincial'. Cardus found it a 'pleasure at last to make a favourable estimate of this young pianist's gifts; the sources of comprehensive interpretation are in him undoubtedly; the true artist's aloofness and hint of enigma should come to him with experience'. On the same day, Wilkinson still insisted Willy's playing 'did not come from the heart'.

The critic was a man alone. The New Yorker's visit ended a huge critical success, and for his twenty-one appearances, Willy took away cheque number 45430 drawn against the Gothic lettering of the Commonwealth Bank of Australia to the value of US$5706.18. An American skilled worker earned US$2842 annually in 1944 – about half what Willy had made in less than two months.

Few writers bothered to compare Willy's playing with Noel Mewton-Wood's. M. H. M. in Melbourne's *Radio Times* said the American was the better pianist, but partly because of the Australian's poor programs. 'Anyone who plays three numbers by Debussy on the same night has a lot to answer for,' he wrote. Willy's performances of Rachmaninoff's third concerto, on the other hand, 'confirmed the impression … that he was possibly the finest pianist heard here'.

Whatever his talent, the American offended Miss or Mrs D. Whiting of Roseville, a Sydney suburb. With a thick black nib, she told the ABC's new chairman, Richard Boyer, she was 'disgusted' to hear Willy play the 'American National Anthem … and then afterwards our National Anthem – God Save our King'. She considered it an 'insult to Australia and our King'. The pianist's 'lack of good manners' could be excused, but the ABC and Heinze, who was conducting on the night, could not. Miss or Mrs Whiting's reproof ignited a bureaucratic grassfire. Assistant program controller Ewart Chapple memoed the general manager to say that the director of music 'thought it would be a gesture not only to America, but also to the visiting artist' as it was the first concert after victory in the Pacific. After three weeks in the ABC's in-tray, the missive got a response. Boyer wrote back to Whiting that her complaint would receive 'the fullest attention'. Charles Moses finally sent a note to the controller of programs, saying that 'God Save the King' should always come first. (According to one critic, Willy had pounded the anthem in a show of petulance at an earlier concert.)

As Willy's tour ended, top ABC executives decided that they wanted him back; they tried to contract him for thirteen weeks in 1948. At first, he 'had more or less thought' that 1947 had been agreed upon, said a head-office memo. He would consider 1948, he said, but advised the broadcaster that it had to negotiate through Judson.

Despite efforts over several months, the ABC was unable to secure Willy a flight back to the United States and he left on 13 September from Melbourne's South Wharf on the *Empire Haigh*. The ship carried sand for ballast rather than cargo, presumably because of disruptions caused by the war. Family members seeing off passengers were kept hundreds of yards from the gangway behind what the *Herald* called a 'wire fence'. Willy told reporters that 'some of my dearest friends who came to see me off were shut out by aggressive officials'. He had remonstrated with them. He had heard that the ship had no piano and had bought one for £25 the day before sailing. Accompanying him was Farrell, who had, the month before, won a scholarship to study with 'Madame' following Willy's recommendation.

Once home, Willy wrote to Bonnie McCallum. In part, the letter says:

> Well … I must admit it feels pretty good to be back in my own bed and eating my mother's food! I feel wonderful – the sea trip was just the thing and I emerged from the ocean a rejuvenated fellow.
>
> In all the time I've been home I've had time for only one activity – work. I am learning several new notes (gross understatement!!) so I've not had time for much gallivanting. Good thing, too.

The ocean voyage was ... uneventful except for the fact that
the good captain bought the piano for his personal use!!! So I was
relieved of all worry concerning the bl---y instrument.

I painted only two or three pictures on the way but these are
pretty good! The best was still the yellow tree that wasn't quite dry
when we got on the ship. Did that watchman ever make a court case
of my swearing? I was really mad as hops, you know.

Willy went on to say that he had just come in from playing with
the New York Philharmonic. Richard Farrell had enrolled 'safely'
in the Juilliard Graduate School. He had 'impressed my teacher
considerably – he's a likeable chap'.

The letter ended with Willy sending his love to Melbourne
friends. He begins the paragraph, 'Well, cutie, give my love to the
Ellerys', and ends by calling a teenage Melbourne musician 'quite a
loyal fellow it seemed!'

★ ★ ★

Unique joy and contentment. A young man fulfilled. And one can
imagine his looking around, taking in the view the best soloists saw
from their pedestals and feeling that almost nothing could go wrong.

CHAPTER FOUR

Perfect Pianist

'He was God's least fool, was Willy. He wanted to learn, learn, learn. What he wanted to learn is how I approached major classical and Romantic repertoire.'
Eugene Istomin on his friend Willy Kapell

'Twenty-seven years old and a figure of gauche dynamism, over whose face the sweetest of smiles and the angriest of frowns played in unpredictable alternation, Kapell seemed like the very flame of art.'
Jerome Lowenthal, Willy's first student

'The conflict between wanting to be an obedient daughter and wanting to marry the man I love is overwhelming.'
Rebecca Anna Lou Melson, in a letter to her parents

IN SIXTY-NINE INTERVIEWS with the pianist Eugene Istomin taped over several years, biographer James Gollin acquired a trove of material for his book *Pianist*. Istomin describes the great musicians of the 20th century with fondness, and he himself – a formidable player who joined Leonard Rose and Isaac Stern to form one of the best piano trios the world has known – is drawn in detail. The pianist was one of Willy's closest friends, and his succinct and detailed portrait of the maturing Kapell is touching and closely observed. It also strives to be objective.

What emerges is a man who is ruled by either a fairly simple psychology or a very complex one, depending on how you look at it. Complex, because he appears to have told no one *how* he thought, why he was so motivated. (He certainly told others *what* he thought.) Simple, because he could be reduced to two personalities: there was genial, restrained, well-mannered, generous and compassionate Willy, charming at drinks parties with a hot dog in his hand; and there was the second and more important Willy, who lived within the strait chamber of his mind, a place he preferred to be, a place of contemplation and penitence, where errors committed by himself or others were chewed over and regretted, where obsession and dedication and hard labour were everything. He wanted to become a perfect artist, and we know that at least once – in a provincial Australian city – he believed he had achieved it. (One can't imagine his joy.) James Gollin summarises Kapell like this: '[He had] a passionate drive for perfection, for growth towards some absolute and unreachable summit of attainment, in piano playing, in friendship, in love itself.'

Three years after Willy's Town Hall recital, Istomin, who was three years younger than Willy, followed the same path. Willy sought out the newcomer backstage after he had performed. 'Your Chopin,' began Willy. 'I've never heard anyone play Chopin like that. I'm not exaggerating. We have to get together.' Istomin was suspicious, wondering why Willy had flattered him. What had he in mind? But when Willy called a few weeks later he realised he was genuine. There was nothing more to it, and the men became great friends, talking, guiding and helping each other whenever they could.

Willy had street smarts, said Istomin. He just knew that certain ways of behaving were an aid to his career, the most important thing in his life. Istomin believed Willy made friends with powerful artists such as Rubinstein and played at soirées attended by other eminent New Yorkers to help him mount the career ladder. Rubinstein introduced Willy to Frederic Mann, for instance, a Philadelphia businessman who made a fortune from cardboard boxes while still in his twenties. His first love was music, though, and he played the piano. Mann became Willy's patron, backing him financially and even, according to a *New York Times* obituary, helping him to negotiate contracts. He also provided moral support and guidance, and once advanced him $1500 to buy a Picasso. (When Willy died, Mann played a big part in funeral arrangements and 'made it as easy as it could be', as Bob puts it, for his parents. Mann also supported the Philadelphia Orchestra and led out of penury the Robin Hood Dell concerts, where Willy played.)

Unlike Istomin, Willy obliged when it came to Arthur Judson's plans to promote him. He'd pose for photographs in swimming trunks, on diving boards, or wearing an apron and whisking what appear to be eggs, even if he never cooked and beneath his bib was a natty necktie. And there are endless images of him playing or leaning against a grand piano. He almost never looks at ease, and in many – even keyboard photos – a cigarette dangles from his lower lip. (A reporter for *Musical America* counted the number of cigarettes Willy smoked during an interview at the pianist's apartment late in 1952: seven.) Judson wanted the concert-going public to fall in love with a sensitive new classical headliner. Far and wide, newspapers reported about a giant of a pianist who looked like Sinatra, painted like a Renaissance master, liked his 'beef rare' and his 'music straight'. He was a revelation for bobby-soxers, according to the publicity, and, once, when the hype spilled over the top, Willy had to deny an addiction to boogie-woogie. One stunt had him accepting that deaf and blind Helen Keller enjoyed his performance of Rachmaninoff's second concerto on a 'snowy evening', as the Judson machine put it. Sitting in one of the forward boxes, Keller delighted in the 'vibrations which are her only contact with the outside world'. She was taken backstage after the concert to meet the star of the show.

He worked and performed incessantly, bleeding as well as sweating for his art. In *Music and Maestros*, a history of the Minneapolis Symphony Orchestra, John K. Sherman writes of 'a sight rarely seen in a concert hall: a gory keyboard'. Willy split a fingertip playing the Khatchaturian concerto in January 1945 but 'carried on with savage intensity despite pain and slippery keys'. Other observers noticed that he sometimes taped his fingertips to prevent splitting them.

He charmed powerful critics such as the New York *Herald Tribune*'s Virgil Thomson, who was also a composer, and Claudia Cassidy of the *Chicago Tribune*. The latter's frequently abrasive reviews of other artists earned her the nickname 'Acidy' Cassidy. But for Willy, her tartness was neutralised by a base of praise to produce a salt of the musical earth. 'Mr Kapell, who is every day of 27, is already one of the great pianists. [He] plays magical Mozart and monumental Bach, and [he has] the grand manner of Rubinstein and the fingers of Horowitz.' She thought that, after a Brahms sonata, Willy not only had 'brilliance, but the deep roots of lyricism and poetry and that quality you simply can't define, for it is an inner blazing fire'. Kapell had the 'makings of magnificence'. Thomson was more subdued. He wrote in 1947 that a 'certain maturity' had appeared in Willy's work and was to its advantage. His rendering of a 'difficult and exacting work' [Prokofiev's third concerto] was that of 'a master pianist and master musician'. Olin Downes in the *New York Times* agreed. Kapell had 'magnificent artistry and an admirable range of dynamics'. He showed 'how consistently and rapidly he is maturing in his art'.

Despite overwhelmingly favourable notices, however, Willy was almost never happy with his performances. He was sceptical about good reviews and deeply hurt by anything casting even the slightest doubt on his musicianship. (His technique was a given.) In short, if he performed even slightly below his best he was winded. In a letter, he threatened to punch the nose of critic Irving Kolodin, who didn't like a recording he had made. And at a post-concert party the bell rang and seconds cleared the ring for Willy and Jay Harrison of the *Herald Tribune*. (Cocktailers separated them before damage could be done.) Bob Kapell tells the story of going backstage after a concert and seeing Willy being gladhanded, backslapped and congratulated on a sublime performance. But he practically hissed to Bob, 'Didn't they hear those wrong notes?'

He was equally adamantine about fellow pianists. He once told Gary Graffman that he played like a 'pig'. Graffman supposedly smiled and accepted Willy's critique because he believed his friend knew what he was talking about. Bob Kapell says Willy's frankness was what made him a stupendous artist. 'What people saw in Willy's great playing,' says Bob, 'was his complete honesty in saying [sic] what he thought and let the chips fall where they may.' Audiences knew how he was, and when he walked on to the stage he electrified them, says Bob. Charisma? His forthright personality? His artistic honesty? Perhaps a combination of all these things, aided and abetted by a businesslike stride.

And as he performed three tours in South America and annually cut wide artistic swathes across North America, his standing in Columbia Artists' Management rose. In Istomin's view, Willy and he were eventually not too far behind Judson's big two – Rudolf Serkin and Robert Casadesus.

Willy kept diaries and notes and wrote long letters. On 1 January 1948 he noted the standard of some of the instruments he had played. Under the heading 'POOR PIANOS', he scribbled that Pittsburgh's was too stiff and dull, Kansas City's 'awful', Denver's 'terrible', Portland's 'appalling', Seattle's 'bad', and Victoria's 'too dull'. A New Orleans piano was 'simply ghastly. No tone, no resonance, no brilliance. Like a rubber tire – flat. Was very low and discouraged'. Only Longview in Washington State emerged unscathed; its piano was 'excellent'.

His diaries reveal recurring themes that arose from his single-mindedness: depression, obsessive work, fatigue, anxiety, illness (usually respiratory-tract infections and inflammations), and constant finger, wrist and hand injuries. (He believed pianists could never overcome injuries. They had to manage them.) In February 1949 he ran a temperature of 101.5 degrees Fahrenheit and had 'no desire to work. Depressed. Learned a nocturne. Went to Rubinstein recital. Fair.' A week in October of the same year is typical. On the Monday he practised for six hours. On Tuesday he managed a further six. On Wednesday five hours were 'pretty tough all the way'. (He pounced on repeated octaves for two of them, rewarding himself with Jimmy Cagney's *White Heat* that evening. The movie was 'so-so'.) On Thursday after a further five hours he was 'tired and depressed. Stopped early.' And on Friday he did seven hours because he had to 'make up one hour. Pretty good work.' His six hours on Saturday were 'boring' because he couldn't concentrate properly, and he applied the same epithet to a following six hours on Sunday. He would frequently practise so intensely – sometimes into the early hours of the morning – that he needed to sleep for half a day or more to recover. If his playing was good enough, it was 'clean'. If he – or anyone else, for that matter – failed to reach even the least of one of his benchmarks, he or she had played like a 'pig'.

A more complete picture of how his music constancy affected his life is provided in the last three years of his life. In 1950 his diary logs a series of visits to Professor Gustav Bychowski, a leading New York psychiatrist and academic. Willy was increasingly troubled by anxiety before playing and wanted ways to tackle it. The diary shows that he had an appointment with Bychowski at the end of May – perhaps a first – that was followed by eight in June and one in July. They appeared not to have helped to any great degree, because he reported sickening nervousness before concerts for the rest of his life.

The effects of his fierce practice routine were compounding, too, and by 1952 his fingers and wrists were often injured. He cancelled a concert in January because of a 'terribly inflated index finger [left hand]' that mandated a night in hospital. On 4 February he wrote that 'both wrists hurt. Worked too hard. Stiff, painful'. He had practised for eight hours. After massage – 'Praise the lord' – they were much better. Three days later the fourth finger of his right hand was 'very painful'. He had worked five hours before a concert with the San Francisco Symphony and that night he judged his performance 'wonderful. Clean, powerful beautiful'.

Despite the compulsory torture of an elite pianist's life, he was heading towards imparting his knowledge of musicianship as far and as wide as it would reach. A long article in *ETUDE* magazine in 1950 is, like its author, earnest. 'There is beauty in the sheer skill of playing an even scale. One can derive pleasure from a rippling arpeggio, a warm pearly touch, an absolute equality of fingers.' To make the mechanics of piano-playing interesting, musicians had to 'clarify their aim'. It was to create beauty, even with the dullest of five-finger exercises. Willy said he still practised the Hanon exercise canon, which rehearses the basic digital gymnastics required by top pianists. He insisted that the musician had to perform them 'as music'. The article continues with a discussion of the 'shaping' of tonal meaning and the constant and necessary attribute of its making – to create beauty. By the late 1940s, he had taken on a few of his own students. (When he died, he was about to begin teaching at Juilliard.) The first was Jerome Lowenthal, who wrote an affectionate tribute to a 'figure of gauche dynamism … [who]

seemed like the very flame of art. His playing was quite simply electrifying ...' Even before the pair had met, Lowenthal wrote, Willy was 'my god'.

In an article in the February 1984 edition of *Clavier* magazine, Lowenthal comments on Willy's uncompromising approach to both teaching and pianism. At first, they worked on finger-strengthening, using scales, arpeggios, exercises written by Czerny, and the right hand of the Chopin B minor Scherzo. Willy talked about the importance of 'having steel in the fingers'. One element was a ground bass to the lessons, says Lowenthal: the 'intensity of Kapell's commitment and the generosity of his spirit'. When Lowenthal played well, Willy called in 'the beautiful Anna Lou [his wife]', and when he didn't 'my hands swam in sweat'. He used metaphor to encourage art. Bach's counterpoint could be bawdy, intervals (the sound made when two notes are played one after another) had colours, and each phrase or passage of music had a 'biology'. Along with Willy's second-hand cigarette smoke, says Lowenthal, he inhaled a 'sense of art and of the artist's vocation which, from my lungs, entered my bloodstream and spread throughout my being'.

Not to be confused with Lowenthal, Raymond Lewenthal was another fine American pianist who owed Willy a tremendous artistic debt.[1] He played for him only twice – while he was preparing for his Carnegie Hall debut in 1951. 'But I learned more from him ... in those two afternoons than I ever learned from anyone before or since,' he wrote two decades later. He had the qualities of a 'very great teacher', being able to explain what he knew. Moreover, he was 'willing, *wanted*, and *had* to explain'.

Willy himself learned constantly. For a while he was coached by Schnabel, who had many students; some, like Clifford Curzon, became famous, and others advanced no farther than giving suburban piano lessons. Schnabel stressed many things, but among the most important were 'playing' the pauses (rests) in a score, being aware of their length and capacity to convey drama. He also taught that in executing runs the student should keep in mind a string of pearls whose gradations were even. Willy elevated the latter skill to transcendent levels – even in passages played at rocket speed. And in his mid-twenties, he remained so willing to learn that he sought 'Madame's' – Olga Samaroff's – advice. In a very long letter that was written at the end of ten days of musical discussions with Willy, she outlines twelve attributes that 'make a pianist an artist'. The tenth is particularly perceptive: a musician should guard against a 'method of work' that wastes a 'major part of his life … playing music the way he does not intend to perform it'.

Despite his sober approach to the art of pianism, Willy also loved fun. Like the most serious artists, he would leaven the intensity of his profession with humour. He loved telling amusing anecdotes and would imitate the great conductors – in their accents. He and the great Horowitz lived on opposite sides of East 94th Street between Madison and Fifth avenues. Like most east–west thoroughfares in Manhattan, 94th is narrow, and no more than forty yards separated the pianists' open windows. Being neighbours, they socialised and discussed music a lot. But one day they went to their respective keyboards and decided to volley between them 'The Star-Spangled Banner', the American national anthem. And so it ricocheted across 94th like a ball across a net, the pianists adding variations with each 'shot'.

Bob and Ann were students at the University of Michigan when Willy and Eugene Ormandy played Prokofiev's third concerto for its spring festival. The four went for supper of sandwiches and coffee in a student cafeteria. The muzak was loud. Willy conspired with Ormandy to get the volume lowered. Ormandy called over a waitress, and in what Bob describes as Ormandy's 'beautiful patrician voice', he said, 'Would you please turn down the muzak.' Pointing to a deadpan Willy, he added, 'My friend here doesn't like music.'

Infrequently, he over-indulged in alcohol. He had a night out at the home of Isaac Stern. Also invited was the unconventional Austrian pianist Friedrich Gulda, who was eight years younger than Willy. 'Gulda here,' he wrote later in his diary. 'Interesting evening. He played boringly. No imagination. Got very pickled.' The following morning Willy was hung over and feeling 'rotten'. His back hurt, he wrote, and he was tired.

In *Pianist*, James Gollin relates what, at the limit, might be called a simple slight. Istomin was involved in it, and he later called it 'shameful'. Six years younger than Willy and of similar Russian-Polish-Jewish stock, Byron Janis was a twenty-year-old keyboard sensation. He was also specialising in the Romantic Russian repertoire, and Willy wanted to know if his turf needed fencing. He persuaded Eugene to go with him to hear a Janis recital in Chicago. Janis played well, but for Willy he was just a 'very talented boy, but misguided badly'. Instead of the two older and more experienced pianists going backstage after the performance to congratulate Janis, Willy insisted that they return to the airport and catch the first flight home.

Willy's ego was large but delicate, it may be averred, and you criticised his work at your peril. But Rebecca Anna Lou Melson, a piano student who was learning from Sergei Tarnowsky in

Chicago, poked a stick into the lion's flanks through the bars. A very pretty young woman, she had grown up in Portland, Oregon, in the exquisite fir-clad north-west of the United States. In the last week of January 1947, Willy joined the Chicago Symphony for Rachmaninoff's second, and twenty-year-old Anna Lou was invited by George and Mildred Kuyper, the symphony's manager and his wife, to the performance.

Mildred asked Anna Lou if she would like to meet the pianist after the show. Anna Lou's letters – mostly to her parents – log a courtship that began in light warm winds but turned cyclonic. On 5 February 1947, she told her parents that she had hesitated to meet William Kapell – already famous – because she thought he had played too fast. She was also a pianist, and he was bound to ask her what she thought of his playing. She gave in to Mildred, though, and when Willy asked the imperative question, she responded by enquiring where the 'fire' was in his performance. 'He had played so fast that I could not hear all the notes,' she wrote. No response from Willy. But no left hook, either. And when George Kuyper invited Willy to join them for dinner the following night Willy said, 'Yes, if you bring her,' indicating Anna Lou.

The four dined at the Cliff Dwellers Club, an exclusive hangout for artists and their supporters where the food was 'nothing to rave about', as Anna Lou put it. At a concert afterwards, Willy was escorting the elegant and mink-enwrapped wife of a steel magnate and told the girl from Oregon that, naturally, he was obliged to sit with her. He had been uncomfortable during the show, Anna Lou had noticed, and it amused her and Mildred. But after the concert, he deposed Mrs Jeanne Butler in her limousine and took Anna Lou down to the basement of Orchestra Hall, the Chicago Symphony's home. Steinways were stored there between concerts, and Willy and Anna Lou played for each other until one in the morning. He played the swoon-filled eighteenth variation from Rachmaninoff's *Paganini Variations*, a giveaway for romantic feelings. She played Bach.

Two nights later, they went on their first true date to a Budapest String Quartet concert followed by dinner and dancing at the swanky Pump Room of the Ambassador Hotel. Anna Lou enjoyed herself because she hadn't danced since leaving home. And while the Pump Room was posh, it wasn't worth 'the money you pay to be there'. She practised all day Saturday, but on Sunday spent the day with Willy – 'breakfast, lunch and dinner with much talking and walking in the snow'. He had to leave in the evening to play in Toronto.

Anna Lou found him an 'interesting boy, very romantic'. Despite his success, fame and money, he was 'very much like all the rest of us'. He was 'rather shy and quite lonely as he never stays in one place long enough to make attachments'. She wrote that he seemed to like her, and she, in return, admired him and wanted to 'help' him. He needed to develop more confidence with people. 'He is very handsome, dark and glamorous. He looks a bit like John Garfield, the film actor, and like Garfield he has something of the Dead End kid about him.' She looked forward to seeing him again.

Romance has its own perfume, and Anna Lou's considered lines – even to her parents – are steeped in it. She writes of her non-musical studies, buying flat heels because she goes out with short boys, supplementing her income with modelling at $5 an hour rather than fifty cents an hour over summer doing less glamorous jobs. But Willy was responding to her correspondence, and her letters reveal a sharpening focus. Even if they hadn't liked the Prokofiev concerto he played, she was 'glad' that her parents had gone to the trouble of listening to his art, she wrote. (It is unclear whether they went to a concert or merely heard a recording.)

He was supposed to visit Chicago in April but didn't. The following month, he was back in town, though, and calling her from the Kuypers. They met, and he apologised and explained why he hadn't been able to come earlier. She decided she should be firm but not 'too rigid' as Willy had many problems. They ate out, and Willy bought her a new recording he had made with William Primrose, the viola player. A photo studio had rung to ask her to pose at a Baldwin grand piano for $10, she told Willy. He said he was 'jealous because no one asks him to sit at the piano for a picture in which he is an adornment'. (He was being playfully disingenuous, of course. In many, many photographs he did just that.)

Despite Willy being a 'very difficult person', she had a grand time with him on succeeding dates. He generally did not care to meet people because they chased after him and made nuisances of themselves. Because his mother had spoiled him 'unmercifully', he was 'not always as considerate of others as he should be'. On the other hand, he was generous, idealistic and a 'fine boy'. She felt their friendship was growing, and she went 'early' to the airport with him just to watch aircraft take off.

By March the following year, however, if their passion hadn't exactly cooled, she was at sixes and sevens about her friend 'Mr Willy', she told her parents. He had arrived in Chicago to play Chopin's first piano concerto and 'everything was upset for a few days'. He didn't like the idea of her 'going steady' with fellow pianist

Leon Fleisher, who was six years younger than Willy. Indeed, he was 'furious' with her, and when they played four-handed pieces at a party 'he quite intentionally tried to beat me to death'. She hadn't taken his attentions to be anything more than 'friendly interest'. But since leaving Chicago he had phoned her 'long distance' every night. He seemed to be 'quite serious' and was making 'meaningful remarks' about a future together. There were moments, though, when she couldn't take him seriously. At others, his calls kept her 'sitting on the stairway outside our door near the public phone where rats the size of cats run up and down the steps'. She wouldn't dream of marrying someone she didn't see for months on end.

Willy was due to play in Portland and wanted to take Anna Lou's Presbyterian folks out to dinner. Anna Lou dictated how they should behave – and they shouldn't fret about it. Unless he thought he had played badly he would be 'natural and friendly …' He had a 'terrific sense of humour' despite being a serious artist. They would discover a 'simple, sweet person'. She asked her father, who sold 'pots and pans', as she put it, and her mother, who taught school, to be patient with her about the 'Kapell affair'. They shouldn't refer to their relationship, and if Willy talked about it they should act as if they knew she and Willy were 'good friends'.

Although Anna Lou's parents were far from pleased that Willy was Jewish, Ray Melson wrote a 'wonderful' letter to his daughter about the blossoming relationship. It was an unusual concession, because several members of the Melson clan were plainly and simply anti-semitic. She read parts of her father's letter to Willy, she told her parents, and although she wasn't quite certain that Willy was right for her, he was keen to get married. Financial security was 'of little or no consequence'.

She clearly wrestled with a life-changing decision, canvassing the problems of partnership with a musician and its requirement of 'so many hours of solitude'. She should not make a 'precipitate decision'. She had been well brought up, and the last thing she wanted to do was 'betray' her parents, she told them.

But by the end of April, the thought of having a pianist husband and children was becoming increasingly appealing, she wrote, 'even though it seems that Willy might be the last man you would choose for me'. In fact, she repeated, he was a 'sweet, sincere boy', and they should be patient with him, even if the lives they might lead 'must seem an awful trial to you'. The following sentence thumps like a goodnight punch: 'Maybe I will suffer one day for my sins with my own children as mother has always said I would.' Her teacher Tarnowsky advised her to do what her heart decided; marriage to Willy would be an 'ideal compromise' if she had to relinquish her concert aspirations.

A week later, she had made her decision and was in agony. How she wished she could cry on her parents' shoulders, she wrote them. It was so hard to be in love with a boy a thousand miles away and have family even farther distant. 'The conflict between wanting to be an obedient daughter and wanting to marry the man I love is overwhelming.' She asked them not to think she was being selfish. A bride wanted happiness for 'all those around her'. She wished they could see her engagement ring. No girl had had a lovelier one. The band was platinum, the principal stone a deep-blue sapphire. On either side of it were smaller diamonds. 'I hope that some day when we can all agree as to time and place it will be joined by another plain platinum band.' Willy's parents were wonderful, and Harry had asked her to tell her father that they should have a contest to see who could sell more books or pots and pans. Edith asked her to tell them that they were simple people 'who would like to have me for a daughter who smiles in their home'. It wasn't true, she told her father, that she was marrying Willy to get a trip to South America, as he had at some point suggested.

Anna Lou and Willy spent early May in a 'tizzy'. They wanted only their families at the wedding, and an announcement made after it. If marrying two months after getting engaged was disgraceful, she wrote her parents, then she was 'disgraceful'. She wouldn't regret giving up her own concert aspirations as her interests were too broad, her personality too extraverted. She had a strong intellectual as well as artistic bent. She would hate to think that her folks would be 'disappointed' with her for the rest of their lives. She loved them, even if she was a 'problem child'.

She was twenty-one, she wrote in the following letter, and they would have to accept that she was an adult. And as to religious belief, no amount of research or learning could prove that God did or did not exist. The next paragraph demonstrates the uncommon humanity and generous intellect of an astonishingly mature young woman.

For the individual, the most important thing is to respect the humanity of each other person whether or not he is a ditch digger, a housewife, a porter on a train, a salesman or a concert pianist. To a greater or lesser degree most human beings have the same capacities. How these capacities develop is determined by what they can do with the opportunities offered by their environments. Do you realise, daddy, that you could have been in Willy's position? If instead of being Christian pioneers in Canada, Grandma and Grandpa

*Melson had been Jewish refugees starting a small newspaper store
in New York City, you might have become a concert pianist and
experienced the same struggles as Willy has. Mother, if you had
been born to parents like mine, you might have found yourself in the
position I am now in.*

Anna Lou – her intellect already honed – was steady in response to
her father calling her 'selfish', even if it upset her 'profoundly'. She
finished her letter by saying that Willy wanted to love her parents,
and it would take time and effort on both sides. His life made huge
demands on him, and they would do best by trying to understand
that. They also needed to accept him. 'This may be difficult for you
because he is Jewish and he knows how you feel about that.'

On 18 May, they married privately in Chicago, a justice of
the peace officiating. Anna Lou wore an aqua wool suit, the first
garment she had bought for herself. They phoned their families to
break the news. Edith had something sad to tell them in return:
Olga Samaroff had died. Willy had lost his artistic beacon, and Anna
Lou had shattered her parent–child relationship. Both families held
receptions for the newlyweds, but in Oregon the celebrations were
soured by anti-semitism. Anna Lou loved her paternal grandmother
but, with tears welling, Grandma Jeffcott told her that the Jews
had killed Christ and her children wouldn't have blue eyes. On the
plane back east, Willy told Anna Lou that her family had made him
feel like a 'plumber'.

His rocky entry into marriage had no effect on his artistry,
however, and less than three years later Willy was recognised by
an important new voice in music criticism. Harold Schonberg had
only just arrived at the *New York Times*. Nine years later he was to

become its chief music critic, a post he held for twenty years. After a March 1951 recital, Schonberg wrote a review of Willy's playing that hinted at the pianist's potential for genius. Schonberg began by saying no one doubted Willy's 'innate talent'. (Of course, most of it wasn't innate at all but a harvest after endless ploughing.) But was he going to remain a 'permanent member of the "promising" group of younger pianists?' The concert he had just heard resolved the issue. Schonberg wrote:

> *It showed that Mr Kapell is on his way to becoming one of the great pianists. It showed a clarification of the emotional problems that must have beset him, and it showed a maturity far in advance of anything he has displayed in this city.*

Willy had been guilty in the past, said Schonberg, of performing music with which he had 'no emotional affinity'. But at this concert he played pieces he understood – a Bach partita, Copland sonata, Debussy and Liszt – and they were 'polished' and 'possessed of musical understanding'. As well, they 'sang out – and a singing tone in the past has been a rare experience at a Kapell recital'.

It seemed that nothing could stop Willy's charge towards the artistic perfection he yearned for. Two years later, as he headed to Australia, music-lovers, musicians and critics alike buckled in for the musical ride of their lives. What excited them was his boundless potential. It seemed inevitable that he would become a keyboard god. Glenn Gould was yet to arrive, and Richter was not yet known in the West. A few great pianists – such as Wilhelm Backhaus and Wanda Landowska – were much older than Willy and at the ends of their careers. Dinu Lipatti, the sublime Romanian, had died three years earlier at the age of thirty-three. Schnabel had died in 1951, and Clifford Curzon, thirteen years older than Willy, and Claudio Arrau, nineteen years older, were yet to develop the esteem in which they were held later in their lives. Even pianists of around Willy's own age such as Paul Badura-Skoda, Alicia de Larrocha and Arturo Benedetti Michelangeli were yet to advance in their professions as far as he had.

Lovers of art music in the early 1950s therefore held the highest expectations for the New Yorker. He was already ranked among the greatest masters. If he can captivate us now, how sublime will his interpretations be in ten, twenty, thirty or forty years? Even half a century? How profound will his musicality be? What wonders are in store? Look at it. Pianists perform into old age. Horowitz returned to the concert platform at eighty-two and played majestically. The great French master Vlado Perlemuter had a long hiatus in a career that blossomed again in old age, playing his last concerts when he was eighty-nine. Imagine Willy in his eighties! How great will that be? What sublime music he'll make. What wonders are in store!

The premise being, of course, that Willy would live to old age. Over that proposition, his 1952 diary cast several doubts. At 11 a.m. on 10 April he had a chest x-ray. A week later, when a diagnosis might be expected, he recorded that his playing at a Vancouver recital had been 'excellent, inspired, despite constant coughing on the stage'. A doctor had advised him not to play, diagnosing bronchitis. The *VANCOUVER PROVINCE* ran a front-page picture of the pianist in bed on a 'liquid diet'. Willy said the illness made him feel as if he had been 'pulled through a keyhole'. Four days later – after having practised for five hours – he described a performance as 'way under par, close to mediocre, tired, arms heavy, head cloudy, clinkers here and there, audience enchanted ...'

A month after the x-ray there is still no mention of a diagnosis, but he wrote that he was 'very low and depressed over Lord knows what'. On 17 May he had dinner with a Sacramento pianist called Anthony Harris then went to the movie *Dracula*. Five days later he had a gum abscess and was 'feeling lousy'. He had also 'strained a muscle in [his] stomach from coughing'.

Summer was not without fun. Willy and Anna Lou had Oscar and June Levant for dinner. Levant was a pianist and composer better known as a comedian and Hollywood actor. The quartet had a 'very enjoyable evening' talking music and sex. With other friends he discussed ways of making 'easy money'. The way he made it was 'too hard, much too hard'. It was 'blood money'. In July, he noted that he was beginning to think – at last – that his daily grind of eight hours at the keyboard was a 'ridiculous amount of time to try to concentrate'.

By the end of August he was willing himself to try to enjoy life more and work a little less. And, on 10 August, he listed three 'things to attend to'. The first was 'Lung condition – immediately'. The second was a 'memory problem', followed by a note to see an analyst. And the third was 'teeth and gums', which he told himself he should look after 'very well'. Not a single word indicates the nature of his pulmonary disease. Nor are there references to doctors' demands that he should quit smoking.

At a Carnegie Hall concert on 27 November – a year before his death – he played a Mozart concerto. He reported that he had been 'nervous all day'. He saw Dr Bychowski at 1 p.m., and at 8.40 p.m. arrived at the hall 'very jittery over memory. House sold out'. In the next paragraph, he penned a rare entry that dredged the depths of his psyche. 'At the first sound of [the] orchestra … cold terror gripped my hands. I thought I would have to run away, or stop. Nothing so terrible as this feeling. Played very well in spite of it.' He made three 'clinkers' in the first movement's cadenza – cadenzas are showy interludes near the end of a movement in which the orchestra stops and soloists play alone – and came in late once in the second. But his tone had been 'lovely'. Less than a fortnight later, he wrote, 'All bones and ribs sore from coughing for 48 hours.'

★ ★ ★

Days after the crash that took Willy's life, the Associated Press news agency despatched three devastating paragraphs. Its source was Anthony Harris, Willy's dinner companion the year before. Describing Kapell as a friend, Harris said he had asked him about his punishing schedule – why he was driving himself so hard. Willy allegedly replied that he had to do everything he could 'while there's time to do it'. He was living on 'borrowed time', he told Harris. He reportedly added, 'I've got cancer. The doctors have given me two years to live.'

CHAPTER FIVE

Tour Triumphs

'Maybe that is the true humility. To feel you can't fulfil the songs and dances of the great, and to be happy as a child when a stroke of lightning hits you, and you find yourself floating on the wing of a butterfly, and find yourself deep in the current of a Schubertian or a Mozartean or a Chopinesque stream of beauty. To be happy as a child! Because when that hits, that is the reason we ever studied music.'

William Kapell in a letter to composer Virgil Thomson

'Not last week.'

Willy, responding months before his death to a broadcaster enquiring whether he had found himself

PERHAPS WILLY WAS right to be wary of Byron Janis's growing reputation. A draft of an ABC letter in mid-1949 discusses the artists it wants to invite for the following year. Edwin Fischer is top of the list, followed by Robert Casadesus. If they are unavailable, it says, 'we shall probably negotiate with Byron Janis and William Kapell in that order through New York office'. Two years later, an extract from the minutes of the commission's Overseas Artists' Tours Committee states that it 'would be most useful for us to have an idea of Kapell's fees'. On a New York mission, the broadcaster's music director William James cabled back, 'KAPELL STOP WOULD BE INTERESTED THIS PIANIST STOP CONSIDERED HERE AND AGREE TOP RANK HE MADE AMAZING PROGRESS STOP HE JUDSON WILLING CONSIDER TOUR 1952 FEEL CAN NEGOTIATE REASONABLE TERMS ADVISE URGENTLY'.

A week later, James had reported that he had had a 'further talk with Kapell, who is very keen to make another tour of Australia'. James thought Kapell's recital terms would not have altered from 1945. He would want a higher fee for orchestral concerts. He ended his report: 'Kapell is coming right to the fore and is one of the small group of pianists who can draw a large audience in this country. He has greatly developed.' Five days later, James had secured Willy to tour Australia either in 1952 or 1953. The fee for recitals (£150) would be the same as in 1945, but Willy would charge £125 for playing with an orchestra, a £25 increase on the 1945 sum.

Supposedly canny, the ABC and William James failed to appreciate the quality of the goods they had ordered. Already a star in the galaxy of classical music, Willy could command an average fee in his home country of $1500 a concert. Judson was keen for Willy to tour in 1953 but, by October 1951, the commission was trying to postpone his visit by a year. 'Confidentially', as an ABC memo described it, the broadcaster was attempting to book Gulda. Kapell, a note showed, would be an 'unwise' booking because it would amount to bringing 'two fairly young pianists with much the same appeal in the same year'. The bureaucrats probably hadn't forgotten the difficulty of scheduling the young pianistic talent they had booked in 1945.

The Gulda strategy fell through, and by February of 1952, the ABC's tours committee was showing increased interest in Kapell. It had developed a vision for music beyond Australia's big cities, and it felt that Kapell would suit it. Each year, 'one or two of the more expensive artists' were asked to perform to provincial audiences in small towns. It directed that 'our country audiences are entitled to have at least one to attract audiences'. Perhaps the New Yorker would be happy doing that. Yet he was 'fairly expensive ... for country and youth concerts', the committee noted. By country audiences, the ABC meant music-lovers in regional cities such as Maitland in New South Wales or the tiny wheat-plains town of Horsham, say, in the west of the state of Victoria.

Wrangling continued between Judson and ABC management throughout most of 1952. Willy wanted – and got – a slightly greater share of profits if they exceeded his slated fees. A grumpy tours committee commented in April 1952 that Willy's 1945 concerts had resulted in a net profit for the ABC of only £4. There was also a problem concerning when Willy could begin – he had Israeli dates in the northern summer to contend with. Judson's associate, Ruth O'Neill, told the ABC's New York representative, Nell Fleming, that nothing should hurt his chances of playing in Australia because he was 'very eager indeed'. A shock arrived, though, when Fleming told the commission Willy was married and would be bringing his wife – 'we had been thinking in terms of one return fare', wrote music director James.

A draft schedule was put together in June, and it was agreed that Willy should start the tour in July the following year. He had 'stipulated' that his season begin in Sydney, which the ABC thought would set a 'dangerous precedent' if it agreed. He wanted to tour for no longer than ten weeks – the ABC wanted fourteen. O'Neill wrote to Fleming in her Fifth Avenue office. She had just heard from Willy, she said. He had written, 'I shall agree to stay in Australia for 14 weeks, a long time indeed, but only if they can promise that the first concert in Sydney whenever it is, will be with orchestra. The debut in Melbourne is of secondary importance, but an orchestra appearance to start there is good too.' A little later, he had a further requirement – that his opening concerts in Melbourne and Sydney, Australia's biggest cities, should be two-concerto programs. He informed Fleming that he and Anna Lou had two small children, David and Rebecca, and he hoped that the ABC could find a house in Sydney for the family, preferably by the harbour, and a 'nursemaid'. (The ABC replied that it could not 'guarantee' a nanny.)

Bill James sent off a long and genial letter to Ruth O'Neill in August. The ABC had drafted an itinerary, omitting the smallest (island) state, Tasmania. He went on to explain something of the broadcaster's philosophy, defining its 'Red' and 'Blue' series of concerts, and its 'Youth' performances for subscribers between sixteen and twenty-five. Another feature of recent Australian development, the letter continued, was the ABC's activities in 'provincial centres – where interest in music had been stimulated by broadcast programmes to the point where there was a demand to see and hear the artists in person'. There were sixteen ABC provincial Subscription Series, and it was expected that visiting artists 'give a few recitals in these smaller centres'. James continued, 'Hotel accommodation, halls and pianos, naturally are not of the same high standard as in the capital cities and, frankly, there is little prospect that the artists' percentage will exceed the guaranteed minimum fee'. The ABC made no profit in these cultural outposts – indeed, they had to pay the musicians and the costs of staging the shows. But for visiting performers they were ways of filling in 'blank' periods between more important engagements, wrote James.

When it was finally sent, the draft contract for Willy's engagement filled two pages of small type. Mailed in early August 1952, by mid-September it was still unsigned. Then came a surprise. Fleming cabled senior ABC executives on 18 September to say that O'Neill had returned the contract with 'suggestions for amendments'.

O'Neill told Fleming that the pianist had used 'extreme and harsh language' when he'd read it. The women had decided to tell Australia about it in 'more modified' words than the ones Willy had used. O'Neill was not too alarmed about Willy's 'violent objections to certain parts' of the document, wrote Fleming. She had a 'great understanding of the Kapell temperament'.

Under the letterhead of Columbia Artists' Management Inc. and signed by O'Neill, a letter next day landed on the desk of acting general manager Arthur Finlay. Kapell was in California, it said, but he had certain suggestions about the proposed itinerary. The Geelong recital should be placed 'somewhere else or cancelled'. He objected to the date of the first Melbourne appearance, saying he would need three days to prepare for it. In parts of the suggested itinerary, Willy had written that 'the spacing is brutal'. Then came the crunch. While most of the contract was 'entirely satisfactory', a clause like paragraph ten had 'never before been submitted to him'. The rest of the letter is worth quoting in full.

> *[In] view of his standing as an artist and his known integrity, he is somewhat disturbed that such a condition was included in the contract. I can assure you that in our ten years of managing Mr Kapell we have had no experience which would lead us to believe that he would ask for payment without performing a service ... and I think you can take our word for it that there will be no trouble whatsoever in this regard. I sincerely trust, therefore, that you will not insist on the inclusion of these terms, since they seem to have affronted Mr Kapell's sense of honor. He states that he is "a professional and not an amateur" and that ... he could not consent to putting his signature on an agreement which contains these provisions.*

The offending paragraph said that Willy would not be paid if he did not perform or if he 'may not complete [a] performance by reason of illness or any other cause'. Its second sentence, though, was what riled him most. It stipulated that if he were too ill to play, the ABC could – 'at its option' – cancel or postpone a concert. On the last day of the month,

Finlay wrote to O'Neill saying it was understandable that Willy took exception to paragraph ten, 'since on his previous visit he did not sign a written contract'. The stipulation had been in contracts with the ABC's visiting artists for many years, and Kapell's was 'the first complaint we have had'. The ABC resubmitted it with the term 'by mutual consent' replacing 'at its option', and Willy signed on 23 October.

Fleming's covering letter to Finlay said that, despite rejigging certain dates, Willy still found the draft itinerary of thirty-nine appearances over fourteen weeks 'brutal'. He asked for changes. Almost incidentally, Fleming wrote that she had had to go to Bristol, Virginia, to get his signature. 'Bristol is a small town ... and I was amazed at the rapt attention this large country audience gave to [his] cosmopolitan program. It speaks well of Kapell's playing, and I should like to add that it was one of the finest piano recitals I have ever heard.' The letter continued:

> *Both you and Mr James are aware that Kapell has a reputation for*
> *being extremely temperamental and often times difficult to handle.*
> *I say this because I would like you to know that I found him to*
> *be most affable and enthusiastic over his return visit to Australia.*
> *His explanation of his reticence in signing the contract was sincere*
> *and logical. He suffers with bouts of asthma and hay fever and the*
> *tight schedule ... frightened him. However he is now trusting to*
> *providence that he will be able to carry through with no interferences*
> *due to these conditions.*

Back in Australia, the ABC's wisest heads concluded that if Miss Fleming had not chased Willy to Bristol, he might never have returned to Australia.

By November, the tour was locked in, and Willy and Anna Lou had decided not to bring the children. David and Rebecca would stay in Oregon with Anna Lou's parents, and she would join him (at his expense; he signed a statement to this effect) for only some of the fourteen weeks.

And even if the ABC had succeeded – some might say despite itself – to sign up Willy, there were still minor preoccupations. Four months before the pianist was due to strike his first key, Bill James had reservations about the recital programs. Four concerts without orchestra were scheduled for both Melbourne and Sydney, and in a letter to Willy, James wondered if it were 'wise from both public interest and the critical point of view' to play Mozart sonatas and 'not to include, say, a Beethoven'. Willy is said to have regretted that he learned little Beethoven; 'Madame' had shepherded him towards the florid Russian repertoire. And while it was developing more limpidity as he aged, his Mozart playing was the weakest part of his game. Bill James also thought it was unwise that a Bach partita took up the whole of the first half of one of the recital programs. 'Our concert halls are large,' wrote James, 'and in order to attract "full" houses, our experience is that one has to appeal to the less discriminating as well as the connoisseurs and critics.' Nell Fleming wrote back three weeks later to say that Willy 'seems to have a keen desire to cooperate most fully with all your suggestions, and in my dealings with him these past few months, he seems to have acquired a gentleness and a sense of "give and take" that has not been so much in evidence in past years'. He wanted to keep the Bach, agreed that his programs were over-Mozarted, and suggested several changes. (By the time he played them, his recitals were models of musical balance.) She ended correspondence on the matter by hoping that

'Willie's [sic] ... season will be sufficiently successful to compensate for all the trouble he has given us with his program material.'

In the same letter, Fleming said she had received word from the general manager that Australia's two biggest music agents – in Sydney and Melbourne – had 'proposed sending a specially selected Steinway piano for Kapell's concerts'. She went on, 'I should like to say that this is the first I have heard of [it]. I have been in constant contact with Kapell for the last few months and if the proposal was instigated by him I can now understand why he did not mention it to me.' She realised how silly the 1945 Steinway redux was, and recommended that 'Head Office' send him a missive. (Willy had left New York for concerts in Israel and at Pablo Casals's festival at Prades in southern France.)

Four months before the tour was due to begin, Steinway & Sons in New York, who made the world's best and costliest pianos, wrote to its agent in Melbourne, Allan's (Allan & Co.), who were also the city's biggest retailer of sheet music and instruments. Mr A. W. Greiner, manager of Steinway's concert and artist department, told Allan's that Kapell wanted the piano-maker to ship to Allan's a concert grand he 'specially likes and uses frequently ... (CD384)'. He asked Allan's to inform him about Australian government regulations that might affect the project. Geoff Allan, Allan's general manager, wrote back in April to say that the idea 'is full of difficulties, and frankly seems impractical'. The instrument could not be packed and unpacked to suit Kapell's itinerary, which criss-crossed the island continent. Ships were out of the question, and Melbourne to Adelaide, for example, was two days by road. So the Steinway would have to be transported by air within Australia, and 'places like Bendigo, Horsham, Geelong and Shepparton do not have air facilities'. Nicholson's in Sydney (Allan's counterpart) thought similarly. If the project proceeded, a 'special' import licence would be required, a 'special arrangement' with customs would need to be negotiated, and refundable duty would need to be paid, among other things. Geoff Allan concluded that 'we frankly suggest Mr Kapell will find the Grands here equally as good as his own, and save him a lot of headaches'. He copied his letter to the ABC, saying a tuner might have to travel with the New York Steinway. The instrument would need constant attention – packing and carting needed specialists. Three days later, Bill James wrote to Nell Fleming, asking her to tell Willy that the ABC would be making 'satisfactory arrangements ... covering piano requirements' wherever he would appear. Fleming wrote back immediately, saying it was all a surprise to her and she did not understand 'why he failed to mention such an enormous undertaking'.

Steinway – and probably Willy – were undeterred. After all, some of the greatest artists toured with a favourite piano in the hold. Willy's neighbour Horowitz was one. Greiner wrote to Colonel Moses in May to inform him that the piano was on its way – sent to 'our dealers in Australia', Allan's. Steinway understood that for practical reasons Willy would use the instrument in only Sydney and Melbourne. But could the ABC arrange to pay the refundable government bond, insurance and shipping costs totalling £800? Mr Kapell was on tour, and could not make the payments. Mr Greiner ended his letter by reminding Moses that sending a selected instrument was 'no reflection at all on the Steinway pianos which you have'.

Nell Fleming was flabbergasted. She rang the piano firm. A Mr Fitzgerald had agreed that sending the piano was 'needless', but a 'special Steinway' had been despatched to Israel and one was being sent from Paris to Prades for Willy's use. He worried, though, about the 'fate of the piano when it reaches Australia'. Ruth O'Neill at Columbia Artists' Management was 'surprised and embarrassed' by the whole fiasco, according to Fleming. In a letter, she had said, 'Between you and me, I know Willy has gone to this expense, but after all he is the doctor and it is up to him to say how he wants to spend his money.' Willy was 'someplace in Europe' and would return to New York on 10 July, staying for only two days before flying to Australia. Fleming wrote to Moses, who was against the ABC's getting involved. But, in the end, the commission agreed to cover the bond, and Willy would pay shipping costs. As soon as he touched down in Australia, he was asked first to initial then sign a thirteen-line legal undertaking to pay £650 should the piano be 'totally damaged', that he would be responsible for removing it from Australia after the tour, and that £150 could be deducted from his fees to pay for shipment within Australia and back to New York.

In the end, Willy used the 'special' Steinway only once – at his opening concert in Melbourne. Details are light on, but according to an ABC inter-office memo, he had made a 'final inspection' of the instrument at an Allan's warehouse and decided that it was 'obviously damaged in transit from America and would be of no use to him'. After the first concert, it was returned to New York on the SS *King David*. The escapade cost Willy a little over £118.

★ ★ ★

Just before Willy left New York for Israel, Nell Fleming organised the only long recorded interview he gave. She had put a lot of thought into finding 'just the right person' to interview him, she told ABC publicity bureaucrats. Several radio presenters and journalists were contacted. All were unsuitable. 'I eventually met a Mr René Erville (some sources write the name 'Herville'), who occupies the French desk at the "Voice of America" and who … showed a keen interest in taking on the assignment'. He was prepared to turn ABC interviewing into a long-term arrangement – he could do four or five of the ABC's touring artists a year. He wanted payment to be made into an account in Belgium, and 'had considerable experience [talking with] celebrities in Europe'. He also had a 'great knowledge of music'.

The interview was duly recorded, and Fleming noted that Kapell 'may sound somewhat ponderous and slow'. But he was discussing 'musical matters which are most important to him'.

Erville, who has a French accent, begins the tête-à-tête with a long prologue, calling Willy, among other things, 'young and distinguished'. In the background, Willy is sniffing. It's spring in New York and Central Park's blossoms are out. Erville tells Willy a couple of recent magazine writers have thought he has achieved 'maturity'. What does Willy think of that?

'Well,' he says, beginning the answer as he begins several throughout his twenty-two minutes on tape, it's a difficult 'point to discuss'. He defines maturity as 'inner growth', something that is 'very gradual and rather sustained and rather difficult to measure in a test-tube'. Willy's voice is clear and clipped, his words enunciated, lightly inflected with a Manhattan accent.

After a brief to-and-fro about maturity that resolves nothing, Willy and René talk about the works he plays, Willy suggesting that the Copland piano sonata is the 'greatest solo piano work' written in America in the past twenty-five or thirty years.

Erville moves on to a debate about Chopin's B minor sonata. There has been a tendency in the past to 'overplay the so-called romantic aspects of the music', Willy suggests. But lately, the younger generation of pianists has become convinced from recent research that Chopin is 'primarily a purist'. So sentimentality, while important, has to be balanced against the music's 'objective' power. Perhaps to lend the discussion more clear gravitas – and thereby hinting at *immaturity* – Willy cites such attributes as 'cadential strength', 'excessive *rubati*' and a 'Byronic or Shelleyian approach' to interpretation. He pronounces *rubati* (playing music faster or slower than written) as an Italian would, and 'Erville' in the French manner. The middle section of the 'Largo' is 'rambly and dreamy and full of dark little harmonic shadows', he decides.

Erville returns to 'growth', and Willy suggests that the younger generation, a term he uses often, is growing in reaction to an ugly world. Young musicians share basic philosophies and communicate with one another. From 'true inner freedom comes outer freedom', he says. Refraining from adding yes, yes, how wise, Erville asks if Willy has found himself. 'Not last week,' says Willy. Finding yourself continues 'throughout your life'.

Willy declares his profound respect for the 'very unpretentious' Schnabel, who made 'angelic' recordings and was 'adored' by music-lovers throughout the world. The Austrian 'was a medium ... he reacted against ugliness'.

They exchange views on the difficulties of getting music into a microphone in a recording studio. But a moment comes, says Willy, when the microphone is an audience. Then you can play music. Willy, who has ended several of his responses with a chuckle, completes the interview with 'Good day'.

★ ★ ★

Reports suggest that Willy loved the Israeli concert-goers, revelling in their worldliness and energy. He sent 'love and greetings' on a postcard to his parents from Haifa, where he had played the week before. At his last recital in Tel Aviv, he remarked, he played nine encores. In Prades, he accompanied soprano Maria Stader, who sang Schubert songs, played a Beethoven violin sonata with Arthur Grumiaux and the Köchel 414 Mozart piano concerto, Pablo Casals directing his own festival orchestra. As a personality, Casals failed to impress, Willy wrote to a friend. 'But his way with Bach is something to adore,' he said. 'It has heart and soul. It is human and overflowing, and grand. It warms and soothes and makes happy. Isn't that what we all want?' He transited in New York before flying to Australia, landing in Sydney on 11 July.

His welcome to Australia included an apology from William James for not being able to greet him and a smallpox vaccination because his 'health papers' were irregular. Soon after, he began inevitable and endless press conferences and interviews. He told Melbourne *Herald* journalist E. W. (Bill) Tipping, whose column 'In Black and White' was elegant and informed, that his favourite hobby was 'day-dreaming'. He charmed 'Alice', another about-town writer, with his 'small boy's enthusiasm for cocktail sausages and tomato sauce'. She had met him at a party in his honour and asked him to smile for her photographer. 'I never smile in photographs,' she alleged he said. Another reporter sought Willy's views on piano hands. That musicians should have long sinuous fingers was all 'hooey', he said. The ideal piano hand was short, squat and broad-palmed, with a long stretch between fingers. Psychologically cornered, the reporter pronounced that Willy's hands were 'short and squat, with broad palms'. He or she clearly hadn't shaken them, measured the finger lengths or, especially, the small differences in Willy's fourth and fifth fingers.

A week after arriving, he played Prokofiev's third concerto and Manuel de Falla's *Nights in the Gardens of Spain* at his opening concert with the Victorian Symphony Orchestra, Joseph Post conducting. The *Herald*'s 'guest' music critic Arthur Jacobs began his review with the observation that Willy had 'spring-loaded steel hammers where most people have fingers'. The same age as Willy, Jacobs was born in Manchester and had already contributed reviews to many of Britain's best-known newspapers and periodicals. Five years after Willy's tour, he edited the first edition of the *Penguin New Dictionary of Music* and went on to revise its several editions, write books on music and teach. His review of Willy's 1953 debut was largely favourable, saying that the pianist was 'positively pulling' at an orchestra that had seemed a little 'dispirited'. Prokofiev's third had 'vigor and conviction' and 'such a brilliant and masterful style of piano playing is a rarity'. The pianist's 'aggressive, percussive' style suited the work, but just occasionally Jacobs wished for 'warmer and more ingratiating' playing. He couldn't resist firing a salvo at the Town Hall's empty seats and a woman and three men who talked and rustled a newspaper throughout the show. They were 'musical barbarians' at whom he threw a glance that would 'freeze a whole block of stalls in London'. It didn't work with the colonials.

In the *Sun*, Linda Phillips wrote that in eight years Kapell had become a 'more mature and thoughtful pianist'. He had always been a dazzling technician, coming at times in the past 'perilously near tricks in a kind of spectacular, exciting way'. But his version of the Prokofiev was a 'terse, brilliantly rhythmic reading, astringent and pointed and clear as glass'. The de Falla performance was similar, 'where one expected a more sultry atmosphere and a richer musical palette in tonal contrasts'. Even though she didn't like the word, she said Willy was 'slick' in a 'masterly' sense, robbing the performance 'of soul, though not of interest'.

If these were cautious, thoughtful and well-weighted critiques, three nights later Jacobs called Willy's first recital 'superlative'. Kapell's Bach was 'splendid', he wrote – 'restrained but alive, sounding spontaneous throughout'. Willy's spontaneity, indeed, 'distinguished the recital'. There were a few small mistakes in Mussorgsky's *Pictures at an Exhibition*, 'but they counted nothing against the power, characterisation, and sense of climax that went into [the performance]'. But Mr Kapell had an Achilles heel; a single encore would have been a pleasure, two 'permissible', but four had begun with Schubert and ended with 'I know not what finger-twaddle. What a pity!'

At the second recital, the *Herald*'s staff critic John Sinclair found Willy an 'uncommonly serious musician'. While his Mozart was too 'high-powered', it was also 'finely cultivated'. Prokofiev's seventh sonata was played with 'astonishing power and brilliance, and with a shrewd and incisive sense of character'. The *Age*'s music critic – a writer neither bylined nor initialled – remarked on Kapell's versatility; three sonatas (by Mozart, Schubert and Prokofiev) without 'falsifying a mood or a note'. He had taken his audience with him, the seventh's *Precipitato* a 'burst of instrumental dynamics'. Here was 'one of the greatest and most discerning pianists of his day'.[1]

After his third and final recital in Melbourne (he performed three in a week), Kapell wrote on 29 July to friend and fellow pianist Shirley Rhoads, in America:

> For the past 2 weeks I have literally worked my head off, so that at last night's concert I thought I would have to stop in the middle of the Suite Bergamasque, put my head in my hands, and just sit on the stage like an idiot. Actually, it went off all right, but that was the sign to take a breath, and lay off for a couple of days. The doctor said "exhaustion", and I was snickered. I only have 3 months of back-breaking tour ahead of me.

The same letter hinted that critics had already got under his skin. He told Rhoads that the public knew the difference between a 'shoe-cobbler and the poet'. The press usually 'does not, or will not, because it can't or won't'. He continued, 'So it leads the public astray, because the public has little confidence in itself, and needs a leader, a guide. Except that these guides are up the wrong tree most of the time'. The following night's recital was cancelled, the only concert in the tour that he failed to perform.

A 'special correspondent' for the Adelaide *Advertiser* interviewed Willy in Melbourne before he left for the South Australian capital. She or he found him 'extremely articulate', but he paused when he'd been asked if he felt he was a changed musician compared with the pianist who had visited eight years before. It was hard to say, he said, but he had 'certainly developed as a person, and that must mean I have changed as a musician'.

Adelaide critic Nadra Penalurick in the *News* agreed. What she hadn't been prepared for in his second and final recital in the city was the 'added authority, maturity, and, at times, electric brilliance which this pianist now so commandingly brings to [his] work'. She added that his performances were 'unforgettable'. Dr Enid Robertson in the *Advertiser* said Kapell was 'conspicuously master of his every fine shade of technique'. He almost imperceptibly 'lingers over, and caresses with dulcet inflections, details which he plainly loves'. For James Govenlock in the *Mail*, William Kapell practised the art of piano playing with 'incredible subtlety and skill'. He showed 'absolute mastery of every period of keyboard music'. Govenlock began another review with the sentence, 'American pianist William Kapell is now a mature artist.'

'Fidelio', Arthur Jacobs and Biddy Allen were among the most impressed. Allen made the observation that Willy was a 'master of silence'. He understood the 'language of the pause better than any great pianist to visit Melbourne in the last decade'. A 'rest' in a piece was never used as 'time off the job'. Time and again he 'transformed [silences] into functional pressure points on a two-way circuit − recharging and indicating the intensity of rhythmical circulation'. Whatever she had meant by the last two words, she was clearly convinced of it. Starting from scratch 'with a handful of notes he erects tonal skyscrapers of extraordinary dimensions, strength and flexibility'. 'Fidelio' began a review, 'the poet who resides behind Mr Kapell's waistcoat ... took full control at last night's solo recital'.

Willy played Brahms's first concerto with the Sydney Symphony and 'transformed', Jacobs wrote, a concert that had lacked lustre before he had walked on to the platform. It was 'one of the finest solo performances imaginable'. In the next paragraph, the critic declares that Kapell is 'one of the great pianists of our time'. He used his technique to make the whole concerto 'seem one', bringing out the 'continuous musical structure'. Pianist and conductor [Post] 'played a near-perfect duet'. Jacobs admitted that he found the Brahms first 'tedious and turgid' if it was mishandled. But this performance was 'memorable; it was one I shall remember Sydney by'.

Early in the tour, Willy had arranged an informal première of Aaron Copland's sonata for Melbourne critics in his suite at Menzies Hotel. His thinking was that they needed an understanding of the contemporary American composer, who was also his friend. Phillips, Dorian le Gallienne, who wrote for the *Age*, and Sinclair attended. All three were composers of varying significance. Willy was about to start playing when in swept Anna Lou from America. Rather than rush to her husband, she took a seat like the others. Embraces waited until Copland was still.

Anna Lou frosted Willy's cake. He was an excellent father, she told reporters, and they tried to travel as a family when he toured. The Australian itinerary was too strenuous for little children. She knitted and ran up her own dresses, even taking a portable sewing machine on some circuits. Her day frocks, she told the *West Australian*, were of wool jersey and orlon, a 'synthetic material that strengthens the wool'. Fully-pleated skirts needed only to be hung as soon as they were unpacked and they were 'ready to wear'. Taffeta was best for evening because 'the creases fell out quickly'. For this trip she'd bought her first long frock since getting married five years ago. She also had 'several street-length evening gowns'. Journalists had no option but to find her uncommonly pretty, her hair 'long golden-red', her eyes deep and blue. On tour, she became her husband's secretary and book-keeper. One day, she yearned to have a home in Connecticut about an hour's drive from the nearest big town. Willy was easy to feed, she confessed. He liked steaks, chops and vegetables – 'he's very conservative that way'.

They'd given up their New York apartment, she told Melbourne's *Argus*, and stored their furniture because Willy was touring so much. Except for short visits, they wouldn't be back in America for two years. South American and European concerts were to follow Australia.

Woman magazine got its man with this vignette:

> *Anna Lou is as calm and unruffled as Kapell is a tense bundle of artistic nerves.*
>
> *'I guess Bill has grown up now,' Anna Lou commented, giving her husband a speculative look out of her pretty blue eyes. 'Having two babies in the house tames any man down.'*
>
> *'Some kids,' said 'Willie' Kapell.*

Woman insisted that Willy joked, clowned 'in a poker-faced way', gestured 'with his finger and thumb together' and spoke quickly and 'jerkily'. His chain-smoking was noted.

Countless photos were taken and published. In two of the last, Anna Lou, her nails lacquered, holds a lighter for Willy. A cigarette in his mouth, he regards the flame and bends to meet it. In the second, he looks his thirty years but rested and at peace. His wife nestles into his chest and seems no more than a teenager. His left hand caresses the side of her neck. She smiles up at him. Willy is grinning, but only slightly, and his view is beyond the frame, distant.

By mid-tour, there had been only a single bump – cancellation of the fifth of his Melbourne concerts on doctor's advice. The medico had diagnosed 'nervous exhaustion' with muscular trouble in his back, shoulders, torso and upper arms. An urgent cable from the ABC's acting Victorian manager David Felsman to Colonel Moses asserts, 'WHEN KAPELL RETURNS MELBOURNE [26 September] WILL GO THROUGH COURSE OF INJECTIONS WITH DOCTOR TO HELP HIM THROUGH REMAINDER OF SEASON'.

What he was to be injected with and why he was exhausted and on his nerves went unexplained. Moreover, there is no record of further treatment. Bill James urged Willy in a telegram to 'look after' himself. Two days later in Adelaide, he showed, as Govenlock wrote, 'absolute mastery of every period of keyboard music'.

CHAPTER SIX

Depression, and Rats of Critics

'I do not remember Willie making any remark of his doubts about whether he had "long to live", but he was in a rather depressed frame of mind on the last occasion when I saw him, and muttered once or twice that he would never come back to Australia again.'

From a letter written by Joseph Post, conductor, and the ABC's acting director of music, to journalist Alan Gemmell

' … I knew that his playing at that point was exquisite.'

Anna Lou Dehavenon

'One must have a chaos inside oneself to give birth to a dancing star.'

Friedrich Nietzsche

'I shall never return.'

William Kapell to Eunice Gardiner

EVEN BEFORE HE had struck a key in Sydney, Willy was welcomed to Australia's biggest city with a backhander headed 'No Fancy-Dress Mozart, Please'. The *Sydney Morning Herald*'s music critic Lindsey Browne was on song. In a long preview to the New Yorker's first concert, Browne criticised the way Kapell *might* play his debut. He began by patronising Willy – he was 'now a grown man'. And being a grown man, Browne implied, Kapell must provide not just fireworks but musicality. His second sentence announced that the pianist would play Rachmaninoff's third concerto 'perhaps for fear that Sydney might be losing its familiarity with the work's drenched decadence'. Browne followed the insult to one of Willy's favourite composers by opining that the pianist might play the second item, Mozart's G major concerto (Köchel 453), 'as a kind of fancy-dress ball in 18th century costumes, a matter of perukes and patches and snuff with everybody waggishly pretending to be Marie Antoinette or Louis XIV in between cigarettes, corn-massage, cocktails (or Bourbons), and arguments about the baseball games'. Kapell would not be the first to make Mozart sound like 'so many toy peacocks metrically pecking at tin grain'. Advance reports 'speak highly of him', wrote Browne. But advance reports were often 'misleading'. Only by the third column of his stool-warmer did he concede that Willy *might* play well.

In fact, he had already played ten concerts *superbly*. On 14 August, he wrote again to friend and fellow pianist in America,

Shirley Rhoads. Much of the letter's first page discussed the art of pianism, the differences between technical brilliance and playing with your 'insides'. He recommended that Shirley persist, that she see technique only as a means to arrive at the end of art. The craftsman could never be an artist, but the artist should have something of the craftsman about her. He believed that his own fingers and hands were still inadequate facing up to the scherzo from Chopin's third (B minor) sonata. He wrote, 'Sometimes my fingers work, sometimes not – the hell with them! I want to <u>sing</u> anyway. And my heart seldom doesn't work.'

Unlike the overall sunniness of the 1945 tour, a month into this one Willy reported that he didn't like Australians: 'They seem rough and rude.' Audiences were dull, managers were invisible, and you were expected to do your job, no questions asked. After he had cancelled the Melbourne recital, a 'delegation' of four checked his story with the doctor. He was appalled, but too tired to argue. Already exhausted, he had been 'trying to keep up a standard of playing that would not leave me with a poor conscience'. He hoped only that he could 'hold out', because he and Anna Lou had done the sums and his income after expenses was 'depressing'. He wrote, 'It comes to almost nothing in the face of nearly forty concerts. Certainly, under these conditions I'll never return.' He was 'killing himself' with work and wondering how he could keep the repertoire under his fingers. He listed for Shirley's interest the big pieces, including Brahms's first piano concerto, the Rachmaninoff third and a Mozart concerto he was scheduled to play in less than three weeks. Audiences seemed to like him but didn't show it half the time. Reviewers were generally favourable, but their critiques were far from 'sensational' and he played to half-full houses.

Tendons in his arms and fingers were acting up, and he wished he was in 'beautiful California under a cypress!'

At least initially, Browne, who also composed crosswords for the paper, was blindsided by his Sydney peers. An unnamed *Daily Mirror* critic called Willy's opening show a 'remarkable tour de force' not just because of the playing: the pieces were so 'widely-contrasted'. He performed Rachmaninoff 'brilliantly', and his Mozart was 'suave and elegant'. The opinion continued, 'Both emotionally and technically, this young pianist has matured immensely since his 1945 visit.' His playing had 'enviable clarity and certainty of tone'. Some Mozart moments were 'exquisite'. But the *Mirror* woman or man disliked something others had missed. Willy, who had perfect control over his instrument, had an 'unfortunate lack of control' over his own movements. That his head and body beat time with the music during rests was 'disconcerting'.

He or she was also less generous about Willy's first concert without orchestra, a 'mixed bag'. The 'illumination of the spirit' demonstrated so convincingly on opening night with the Sydney Symphony was 'frequently missing' as a soloist. He played Chopin best, but the 'famous *Funeral March* movement' was executed with 'almost indecent haste'. And some of the pictures in Mussorgsky's exhibition were 'capriciously interpreted'. The gnome sounded more like a giant than an imp, and the ballet of the unhatched chicks was as shrill 'as if they had been out of the shell for weeks'. His Bach suite, like many opening numbers, was a 'mere statement of the music'.

M. L. in the *Sunday Herald* interviewed Willy. He was 'more like Hollywood's conception of a trouble-shooting "private eye" than Hollywood's conception of a concert musician'. He looked 'shrewd and practical, and his speech is crisp and idiomatic'. His manner was 'slightly aggressive', and he chain-smoked throughout their chat. Modern composers lacked a sense of beauty, said Willy, because they expressed the world today – 'and that ain't pretty'. People said Bartok's violin concerto was wonderful 'but it sounded like a lot of hens in the farmyard to me'. And while Australian radio had fostered interest in serious music, its American counterpart – and television over there – gave little opportunity for conscientious artists. 'Music over the radio is rather cheap', said Willy. Australia wasn't entirely blameless, because a minute had been 'chopped' off the end of a broadcast of one of his Melbourne programs 'to make way for a sports announcement or something'. He understood that there had been a row about it.

Max Keogh in a long piece in *Tempo* was vicious. He warmed up with a few light strokes. To say Kapell was a technical master was a 'limping understatement', and the experience of watching him was 'colossal'. He was more a pianist 'to be seen than an artist to be heard'. The opening recital showed that he could play 'louder and softer and faster and more accurately than any pianist in my experience'. Then this: 'If he were a typist, how the copying and duplicating business would fight for his services! As a mechanic of the keyboard, he gives a thrill a second and should cause endless swooning among those citizens who attend recitals primarily to "see the pianist's hands"'. Consequently, the music 'is forced into secondary importance in Mr Kapell's mind, despite his published statements'. He had 'something of a singing tone, but a true legato from [him] is rare'. Then, 'His wish to re-create the composer's feelings ... is unfortunately distorted by the fictitious beliefs of Hollywood and commercialised culture'. Keogh continued by deriding American pianism in general, and concluded that Willy's technique dominated his playing to the extent that it 'suffers exaggeration and distortion'.

Most critiques of the first Sydney recital appeared the day after, on Friday 4 September, and Willy played for the second time the following night. One writer called the second 'not very moving'. He or she continued, 'The noisy and spectacular seem more to Mr Kapell's taste than the melodic and contemplative'. Willy 'began badly' with Mozart's Köchel 570. His was 'hard, arid playing, very efficient but austere and chilly'. But there was enough in his performance of Schubert's A major sonata to suggest that he was a 'virtuoso pianist who may one day be a very great artist'.

At some stage over the weekend, at any rate, Willy must have had a gutful. He explored the idea of quitting. The commission's archives have no record of telephone or telegram correspondence between him and ABC executives, but on Monday 7 September, when offices re-opened, he was sent a letter at the Hotel Australia. R. G. Gifford, assistant controller of administration (finance) wrote, 'I have been asked by Mr Moses to let you have the attached statement showing the details which you requested as to the amount to be refunded in the event of you cancelling your contract.' The letter continued that because of 'many implications', especially concerning broadcasts, 'we would naturally like to have your decision on this matter immediately'. Gifford asked him to give scheduled recitals through the week in the regional towns Maitland and Newcastle even if he decided to cancel the tour. Enclosed was a single foolscap sheet headed: 'COMPENSATION PAYABLE FOR CANCELLATION OF CONTRACT FOR EXPENSES ALREADY INCURRED'.

They were considerable. Hall rental bookings amounted to £185, a quarter of his return fare £158. 'General' publicity and advertising, which included the cost of spruiking recitals in Newcastle and Maitland that he might not have played, came to £275. Ticket printing was £63, programs £95, postmaster-general's charges for broadcasting lines £27, forfeited hotel deposits £15, and refunds to program advertisers £72. The ABC decided that he would need to find £222 10s for their administrative overheads. Most of his 'wife's overseas fare' and Steinway's shipping costs would also need to be covered. Willy's bill came to over £1513, but the sheet's last line was generous: 'Say: £1,500'. The penalty amounted to a dozen orchestral concert fees before income tax. Willy played on.

At his third – and last – Sydney recital the following Saturday, he played 'The Star-Spangled Banner' before 'God Save the Queen', the Australian anthem. Elizabeth had officially ascended the throne only two months before, and Willy appeared to be at it again. In the local vernacular, he understood what would get up Australian noses, how many Mrs Whitings of Roseville were out there, scattered among Sydney's top folk. The *Sunday Telegraph* was aghast. 'ANTHEM SHOCK AT CITY CONCERT', shouted its heading. Kapell had 'astonished' his audience. He had played the American anthem at earlier concerts, but always after its Australian counterpart. Then, after 'striding brusquely' on to the stage, 'last night Kapell shocked the audience by reversing the anthems'. Several concert-goers sat down when they realised what was going on. Others complained to ABC officials at interval, said the *Telegraph*. And a strange thing happened. A broadcast of the concert went 'off the air' after a fuse allegedly blew in a control booth.

Charles Moses, the chief himself, explained in newspapers the next day that a 'genuine error' had caused the anthem reversal. He said Kapell had wished to play both – as he had at earlier recitals – and the ABC duty presentation officer for the third recital had advised him to reverse their order. Moses continued, '[Kapell] believed he was acting correctly to avoid the situation that occurred the previous Saturday night when [he] played the British anthem and the audience had to rise again for the American [one]'. The explanation sounded marginally credible but almost certainly wasn't.

An easy suspicion is that the ABC and Willy Kapell were playing tit-for-tat. In the same newspaper, T. F. M. found Willy's playing not so impressive as at earlier concerts. 'Much of it was surly and lacked crispness and character'. He had lost a great opportunity, T. F. M. pointed out, because the audience was among the biggest Sydney had seen at a recital. (Taking £407 12s, it topped the box office for the whole tour, its earnings exceeding the second-most lucrative Kapell concert by more than £100.) There was also program choice. Willy played the Copland sonata, which for one critic was a 'mass of jangling discords, formless and probably meaningless to any but the composer'. Whether Kapell played it well or badly 'wouldn't have mattered in the slightest'.

At Willy's fourth and last recital in the New South Wales capital, Browne blended broadsides with praise. The pianist's performance of Debussy's *Suite Bergamasque* was 'stylish'. Bearing in mind what Willy eventually said of Browne, it is worth quoting most of the five-paragraph review: '[Kapell] made out for Copland's 1941 Sonata just about as good a case as could ever be made for this dry, austere work.' It was performed 'incisively, with the air of stubborn defiance that suits its percussive chords, and he was careful not to let the work go soft during the bellringers' harmonies of the first movement.

'In a work that could easily seem scrappy and improvisatory, the pianist did well to find and preserve a firmly unified design.'

Browne had actually been tougher earlier. 'Mr Kapell's aggressive approach to four Scarlatti sonatas ... with tones as hard as New York asphalt and moods twitching like Times Square neon, must have left his audience quite unprepared for the antic [sic] elegance, the exquisite transparencies of texture, and the subtle tasting of vintage sensations in his Debussy playing.'

Pulled apart, the critique balanced favour and disfavour. It was smug, though, and gratuitously insulting. Only a perfectionist – such as Willy – might have perceived it as, in sum, damning. But it hurt. Ten years later, Joseph Post, who had conducted orchestras many times while Willy played, replied to a letter of inquiry from Alan Gemmell, a Melbourne journalist and photographer who worked for Australian United Press but also filed for overseas magazines and newspapers. Gemmell was a friend of the Ellerys' son John, and in his mid-twenties was bowled over by a virtuoso only a few years older than he was. The Sydney critics, Post told Gemmell, 'enraged him – and he told me all the way to Adelaide in the plane what scoundrels they were. I can still hear him spitting out with great venom, the epithet "the rats!!!"'

Olga Samaroff had once warned Willy in a letter not to let critics get him down. If there were people who failed to recognise the genius of Mozart, Beethoven and Brahms, she wrote, 'can Willy Kapell or any other artist expect to find only praise?!!' She went on, 'Dear Willy, the prime requisite is to master one's own soul!' If he wanted to do that, she advised, he needed to 'curb [his] tongue'. He had the 'usual crop' of enemies through jealousy. 'But your worst enemy is your own tongue, thoughtlessly used!'

Willy first revealed his feelings about Browne to Shirley Rhoads three days after the last Sydney recital. The 'fellow who had sat on the fence got off it and tore the whole concert to pieces, and 2 papers copied him, as he is ringleader'. The Sydney critics were 'laymen' – they were 'terrorizing' Australia. They were 'all young, all queer' and had 'gotten after me'. They had paid him some of the 'prize insults of my career'. Yet he had played well, one recital in particular a 'beauty'. ABC management had not said a single word about the 'unjust press' and didn't seem to care. 'It is all very disheartening, because I have given these stupid, cloddish people playing they probably won't hear again.' Kapell continued, 'So, we will never come back, for love <u>or</u> money.' He had already played eighteen concerts like an 'angel' and received only 'coldness' and 'insults' in return 'and no money to speak of, and a sickening fatigue. And <u>blockheads</u>! I am completely fed up with them, and their so-called "musical life". This is <u>the</u> most unmusical place on earth, probably more than Iraq.' Australians were 'basically unfriendly' and should be 'left alone with their sullen thoughts of inferiority to the rest of the world'. On the way home he'd spend a day in Los Angeles, he told Rhoads. But apart from that, he couldn't wait to leave Australia. 'How I wait for that plane home you have no idea.'

* * *

In Adelaide in mid-September, Willy paid two guineas (£2 2s) to consult a Dr Goode. Whatever ailed him had no effect on three successful orchestral concerts in the South Australian capital. The tour then turned inland, taking Willy to Bendigo and Shepparton, two Victorian country towns. At the first he played in a civic hall, at the second in the Star Theatre, which a decade later was demolished to make way for a bowling alley. A week before the Shepparton recital he cabled Bill James to say he had developed a 'leg' infection and could not prepare Beethoven's *Appassionata* sonata. Although programmed months before, this important middle-period work failed eventually to be included in any of his twenty recitals. Indeed, Kapell played no Beethoven at all on the tour. The *Appassionata* is an exquisite piece, dark and dense and characterised by anguished lyricism. Occasionally, a lovely shaft of optimism breaks through. Its short middle movement taken at walking pace is Beethoven at his best. The sustaining pedal, colloquially known as the 'loud' pedal, keeps notes sounding until they die. Normally, when a pianist lifts a finger from a key the note is immediately stopped by a damper. Beethoven instructed the performer – through his marks – to use the pedal sparely. A player as capable as Willy could have negotiated the *Appassionata*'s seventeen pages without pedalling at all. If, indeed, the infection was on his pedal leg.

A hint at Willy's feelings about playing new works – including the *Appassionata* – can be gauged from an earlier letter to Rhoads. In Perth, the Western Australian capital, he had played a Mozart sonata (A major) that was new to him. The keys were 'swimming in dew' because of humidity and his nervousness. He played carefully, he wrote, 'walking on egg-shells'. But he played it and he 'had a new Mozart now!' The *Appassionata* in three weeks was next. 'William Kapell tries the *Appassionata*!' he wrote Rhoads. It would be his 'first big Beethoven'. He was forcing himself to learn it – and learn it very quickly. Otherwise, he would never play it. Beethoven daunted him, and he promised himself that once the tour was over he would set aside time to study the master.

A day before he was scheduled to play the *Appassionata*, he wrote to Rhoads saying the work wasn't ready.

By the end of September, he was back in Melbourne, where he felt more at home, for four final orchestral concerts. On the afternoon of the first, Collingwood beat Geelong at the Melbourne Cricket Ground to win its first Victorian Football League (Australian rules) premiership in seventeen years. More than 89,000 spectators – in a city of a little more than a million souls – cheered on their clubs. A mile away at the Town Hall, far fewer Melburnians turned out to see Willy. In each of the last Melbourne concerts, attendances were such that the pianist was paid only his base fee.

Bill James's official report for the month heaped praise on Willy before commenting that 'his recitals have not had wide appeal and will probably be remembered as brilliant pianistic achievements rather than as profound musical experiences'. As well as being an administrator, James was competent at gaucherie. Early in the tour he had told a Sydney *Daily Telegraph* reporter that Willy himself had thought he had been immature in 1945. 'He said he would like to give Australian audiences a glimpse of [the] advancement he had made in the intervening … years.'

Was it just a glimpse, or was Willy feeling duty-bound to leave a testament, the sum of his life's work, a final and glorious exhibition of his greatness? Two letters to Anna Lou hint at answers. On 24 September, she returned alone to New York. (She told me recently she felt 'terrible' leaving him at Sydney Airport because 'it was the end of the end'. She had a premonition that she wouldn't see him again.)

Two days later, he mailed the first of the letters. He had come in from a concert, having just played Brahms's first concerto with Heinze. Despite hitting a few notes that Brahms hadn't written, the performance had a 'fantasy and beauty' about it that had caused 'dry throats'. He continues, 'I played to thee, to music, and I played for my honour and so that these people will know in years to come that they are missing someone, someone who can touch them and warm their hearts.' Despite the dull pain caused by his 'treatment here', he retained 'power and songfulness'. Referring constantly to Anna Lou as 'thee', he decides that music-making is really about 'singing', and singing must be of or for someone or something. 'Never in my life have I felt more passionately songful that at this time.' He sang his noblest songs to 'thee'. He had been very nervous before the concert. The 'curse' hit his hands and fingers and he needed ten to fifteen minutes to loosen up. 'I seem to become more nervous with the years.' He was playing better, he told his wife, and even the concerts in Sydney she had heard were fine and undeserving of the 'kick in the stomach I got as a reward'. Kiss 'our wee persons for their Daddy', he tells Anna Lou. He kisses 'their sweet Mommy, who is so young and pretty'. He signs himself 'Kuffle'. (Anna Lou was 'Kufflet'.)

The following Monday, his 'mood is getting more and more depressed'. In a letter that begins, 'Dearest treasurelet', he divulged that people were noticing. Heinze described him as being 'in the dumps a bit, my boy'. Before the concert, he'd been 'sick to my stomach, and dreaded walking out there' to cope with Brahms again. He played very well, he wrote, in spite of the critical blasts he had endured, 'dull' concert-goers, a brutal itinerary and the 'severest fatigue of my young life'. Somehow or other, he went on, he managed to 'carry my honor and my integrity like a valiant banner' and he felt proud and secure within himself. He competed with no one, he said, playing only 'to satisfy a deep inner desire for honesty and purity, mainly in a musical sense'. He played so that he could 'sleep without remorse and guilt'.

Despite a vote for his own self-awareness and integrity, the next paragraph revealed mounting anxiety. Practising was next to impossible, and even to look at a piano 'fills me with unwillingness'. He hadn't slept enough, he needed to rehearse the Rachmaninoff concerto, but the thought of even its first theme made him nauseous. He had spent the day walking around in a daze, barely getting two hours in on Brahms. He looked at the piano and looked away. He went out to buy music and everyone stared at him, which was irritating. He took a nap in the afternoon for thirty minutes, and during it dreamt about a 'rave-notice from the Great JOHN SINCLAIR about the wee William Kapell playing Brahms', he told Anna Lou.

The letter's handwriting is telling. 'JOHN SINCLAIR' is in capital letters, while 'wee William Kapell playing Brahms' is written in tiny lower-case copperplate. He was picked up for the concert in a 'hearse', he notes. The letter gives no hint as to whether the 'hearse' was part of the dream or an ironic term for an ABC chauffeur-driven car. He got in and riffled through the evening *Herald* to see if 'JOHN SINCLAIR HAD GIVEN HIS SOLEMN OPINION OF me'. He hadn't. Once again, it is unclear whether Willy is dreaming this or if it actually happened. Ditto, his remark that, at the Town Hall, he slumped into a chair and stared at Sir Bernard, who told him, 'My boy, you are overdoing it.'

★ ★ ★

Willy had eight concerts to play – a single recital in Canberra, the national capital; four with orchestra in Sydney; and three recitals in provincial centres. His last concert was to be in Geelong, the home of Ford, which set up a plant there in 1925 to make Model Ts. Its 70,000 or so inhabitants also shipped off bales of fine Merino wool to be woven into luxurious fabrics in Italy.

As at his Sydney recitals, Willy suffered both faint praise and very favourable notices. John Moses thought his reading of the Brahms (first concerto) was 'full of defiance and impetuosity and superb technique'. The *Sun* reviewer thought his playing of the Prokofiev third concerto was 'a marvel of clarity and precision'. At the same concert, T. F. M. in the *Telegraph* described it as 'dynamic, beautifully balanced and clear cut'. But M. L. in the *Sydney Morning Herald* described the penultimate Sydney show as 'rather prosaic music-making'. Prokofiev's third concerto was 'crisp and authoritative … but somehow one expected more voltage'. (Days earlier, he or she had described Willy's 'vigorously disciplined attack on the first solo passage' of Brahms's first concerto as the 'memorable event of the concert'.)

A small town, Horsham is a de facto wheat capital in the far west of Victoria. In its comely, beige-brick, art-deco Town Hall, Willy played Scarlatti, Chopin, Schubert and Liszt at his penultimate concert. The local *Wimmera Mail*'s Brendan Walsh dubbed him 'among the top group of world pianists'. A 'new world artist' had arrived. Willy's reading of Chopin's third sonata was 'inspired … lovely cantabile passages … like limpid drops of water'. His 'interpretative capacity and artistry … place him among the very first ranks of world pianists'.

The morning after, Eunice Gardiner, who was also a pianist, scooped her music-journalist colleagues. A long interview with Willy in Sydney's *Sunday Telegraph* began, 'William Kapell, visiting American pianist (and one of the world's greatest), swears that when he leaves Australia next week it will be goodbye forever.' Gardiner wrote that his words were, 'I shall never return.'

In a letter to Nell Fleming written three weeks later, Gardiner, who was a friend, revealed the origins of the interview. She had seen Willy only three or four times, but 'he talked to me, I felt, as though he were talking to himself in a mirror'. Gardiner remembers one special night. Willy was staying at Jo Fallon's harbourside mansion and was 'very burned up' about Browne. They went down to the Fallons' boatshed, where Willy practised on a 'not-very-good' upright. He played the Chopin first concerto, which came out 'fresher and more magnificent than I thought it could sound'. She said she decided that if Willy wanted to say what he thought about Browne 'I would get it into print'. It had, however, been a difficult article to write, she admitted, critic against critic.

Through Gardiner, Willy aimed both barrels 'almost wholly' at Browne. He said, 'It is time that a stop was put to the Madhatters' tea-party, which represents a large proportion of music criticism in Sydney'. He called Browne the 'mastermind of a precious coterie of gentlemen who all write, it seems, as he dictates. Much of what is written is uninformed, false and malicious; it is often even ridiculous.' Gardiner described Willy as 'good and mad', and it was just as well the 'days of duels are done'. She continued:

Kapell crouched lower in his armchair and glowered as he swung into the main theme of his interview with me. It might have

*been Beecham sitting there, spitting invective; it might have been
Beethoven spilling rage. The air was electric.*

*'Would these critics believe that I'm some sort of robot – a
machine – flawless technique and cool calculation in equal parts?' he
asked.*

*'"Dry Bach" … "cosy harmony", "aggressive approach",
"coaxing modesty" – Bah!*

*'They say my Mozart is elegant, decorative, impersonal,
unsmiling, well-bred, charming – aargh!*

*'They assert that I find a work like the great B flat minor sonata
of Chopin no more than "shallowly exciting".*

*'If Rubinstein or Horowitz or Serkin said such things to me I
would want to crawl into a hole and hide myself. But who are these
persons who so belittle my emotional capacities?'*

Willy berated critics who said he played with little effort. It was only
through hard work that he made it look effortless. He spat again,
'dry Bach' and went to the piano, giving Gardiner a mini-recital that
she described as 'liquid sound, mellow, golden, authoritative'.

Some critics had said that the warmth of his Schubert was
'surprising'. Why? It didn't surprise him. They spoke of tone as hard
as New York asphalt. 'That's a lie – a downright lie!' he stormed. 'Is
New York asphalt harder than any other, anyway?'

If one was being kind, he said, one might find the Sydney critics
not knowing any better. But this was not the case. Their utterances
came from 'unprincipled minds'. They were the words of men who
eschewed responsibility. 'If they chose their words with as much
care as I choose the tones I play, they, too, might claim integrity.
These critics want music to be as limited as their own little minds.

So that which is beautiful, that which is true, they damn it – they dismiss.'

Willy finished his tirade by calling Sydney critics 'evil' and a 'great danger to the future of music and young musicians in this city'.

Something was up. It would seem unlikely – almost impossible – that a professional musician of Willy's stature could have been so riven by negative critiques. After all, he had recognised that they were mostly the work of a single – if influential – person. What could explain his outburst? Had he reached – for unknown reasons – a breaking point, his usual acuity corrupted, skewed? Was he attempting to punish the ABC and its 'brutal' tour by arguing that it had thrown him like a carcass to Sydney's unschooled critical wolves and its chief attack dog? One thing is certain. His roiling against Sydney reviewers was sparked by rage, not by any reasonable reflection on his artistry's demotic appeal.

Two days after the Gardiner interview appeared he cabled Anna Lou. 'ALL IS WELL STOP AM EXHAUSTED STOP SYDNEY BLAST HAS APPEARED STOP MANY BRAVOS STOP AM BRINGING LITTLE BEARS STOP ARRIVING SAN FRANCISCO 29 WILL TELEPHONE = = WILLIE'.

He had only one more concert to play – within the granite blocks of the Plaza Theatre, Geelong. What he would play had been decided – Mozart's sonata Köchel 331, Chopin's *Funeral March* sonata, Debussy's *Suite Bergamasque*, two Schubert impromptus and Liszt's *Hungarian Rhapsody* number 11. But how he would play them was another matter. He had choices to make. Which Kapell would decide what his fingers and mind produced on the night? The good and kindly father who filled his plate with cocktail sausages and showed guests at an after-concert party photos of his children? Or the artist, the tortured and increasingly desperate aesthete, for whom only perfection was good enough?

Geelong was thrilled to be getting Kapell. In Geelong Grammar and Geelong College – top, chipped-stone schools where wealthy croppers, graziers and woolgrowers boarded their sons – boys were urged well in advance of 22 October to get excited. The day before the concert, the *Geelong Advertiser* ranked Willy's visit 'one of the musical highlights of the year'. It would become a massive understatement. In a seven-paragraph story, it applauded the ABC's 'innovation' of sending celebrities to the bush. Kapell's 1945 tour had 'left a lasting impression, and many people who gained pleasure from hearing his broadcasts are now able to attend actual performances'.

★ ★ ★

The Plaza Theatre emerged from the cramping onto a small block of land a Presbyterian church and a Mechanics' Institute hall. They had been built in the madness of a mid-19th century gold rush, which had increased the city's population twenty-fold. Destroyed by fire in 1926, the hall was rebuilt as a theatre. By the time a two-storey Florentine facade and an ornate interior that hinted of Art Deco and Spanish missions were added, Geelong had a venue to be seen in. Twenty years later, though, it had been let to run down. It was a shabbier and grubbier cinema than others in the city, but also the place where musical comedies and Gilbert and Sullivan operas played. Visiting musicians were also billeted to it. Its interior was said to maintain a low enough temperature to keep local fish fresh, and the lavatories were down a path behind the hall. Dressing rooms behind the stage were 'appalling', as one local put it. The Plaza was a fleapit, in truth, and its horsehair seats had wooden arms. It owned a piano – possibly a Steinway – that, at a recital the year before, a young Paul Badura-Skoda had himself tuned during interval.

Ray Humphries, one of the ABC's lesser Victorian bureaucrats, drove Willy to Geelong on the afternoon of his concert. Willy rested up in the spacious Victorian mansion of John Brockman, the choirmaster and organist of St Paul's Anglican Church, who also headed a family engineering firm. John was president of the city's ABC subscribers' committee – Geelong's chief music-lover. It was his and his wife Jean's job to receive Willy after the show.

By eight-o'clock, the recitalist was in tie and tails in the Plaza's decrepit green room and ticket-holders gathered. The *Advertiser* reported that the early-spring 'night was chilly and dressing was mainly guaranteed to keep the concert-goer warm'. Several of the audience were 'seen to be carrying rugs'. Good tickets were on sale at the door at 10s, 7s 6d, and 5s.

Promptly at 8.15 p.m., Willy emerged from the wings and, for the last time, strode to a keyboard to do what he lived for. And he played as few have ever played before.

At 10 p.m., the ABC broadcast only Chopin's *Funeral March* sonata, the last piece before interval. (The concert had opened with Mozart.) Its placement was perfect. Teams and individuals give their best once they have stretched, warmed up, parted cobwebs, gained confidence and shifted into top gear. The second quarter of an Aussie rules football match, say, or Willy's performance of Chopin's thirty-fifth opus.

Willy knew how sublime his feat had been. He had attained the summit he had been striving to reach all his artistic life. Perhaps gone beyond it, he must have thought, rising to interpretative altitudes where even he was short of breath. He had arrived, anyway, at the end of his quest, a mature artist, and we can only imagine his joy. He was banking on a permanent record of the concert. The ABC must have one.

No one saw him tune the piano at interval, and he returned to the keyboard and sat down to commence Debussy. The Plaza's black cat padded on to the stage from the right and approached Willy. It looked him up and down in the haughty way only black cats can, and sauntered off, disappearing into the wings stage left. The audience giggled and Willy – perplexed – blinked, failed to smile, and began the *Bergamasque's* 'Prélude'.

The following day the *Advertiser's* 'Comus' wrote that the cat had 'marred' the concert. A 'strikingly dingy' backcloth had also spoiled the occasion. Otherwise – and bafflingly – the recital was 'even more superb than the music which was played'. The only professional critic at Kapell's last recital wrote that the young American had 'captivated his audience with a web of enchantment'. It was a 'marvellously fitting climax' to the year's subscription series. Willy's 'brilliant interpretive ability' roused concert-goers, and he played three encores. He had given the national anthem 'an unusually elegant stature' at the start of the show, and 'struck a rich mood' with Mozart. 'Then, as if to show what could be done with a much lesser piece – for Chopin is notable more for effect than invention – Kapell stirred up the dramatically emotional strength of the Sonata, Op. 35 ... Here was turbulence and tragedy blended with the lovely sensitive strains of the *Funeral March*'. 'Comus' had nothing but praise for Willy's Debussy, Schubert and Liszt, concluding that the evening had been 'memorable'.

Spectres of turbulence and tragedy might have shared the wings with the Plaza's black cat, but Willy appeared not to have seen them. He returned to the Brockmans in a seemingly relaxed mood. Mingling with about a hundred Geelong concert-goers, he helped himself to cocktail frankfurters, savoury boats, asparagus rolls, pavlova and smoked salmon with white sauce. At one point he turned to Ray Humphries and said, 'Say, Ray, have you got those pictures of my kids?' He wanted to show them to someone.

But his joy and ease were short-lived. By next morning, his mood had changed dramatically. He was desperate. He stormed the ABC's Melbourne studios demanding a recording of the Chopin. According to John Sinclair, Willy burst in virtually shouting, 'The tape? The tape? I've never played it like that before.' None was provided.

And over his last week in Australia, his mood plumbed ever-deeper depths. Willy and John Sinclair visited Jascha Spivakovsky in Toorak and talked and played music all night. Sinclair left the pianist outside the Menzies Hotel at six in the morning, agreeing to correspond on the incidence of tragedy in the lyrics of Schubert's songs, Sinclair told Milton Stevens in 1983. Willy gave a reason. He had 'funny things going through his head', said Sinclair.[1] 'Three times before he left [Melbourne] he held up his hand and pointed to the 'Life' line and said, "You see, I should not be here."'

Bonnie McCallum waved him off from the Menzies hours later. 'He was longing to see the children,' she wrote. Willi Serkin's wife took a picture of Bonnie, her nine-year-old nephew Roger, Willy and Patricia Tuckwell outside the hotel. And then he was gone.

In Sydney for five days before boarding *Resolution*, Willy visited Joseph Post at home. He had been before – several times – to 'let off steam' about critics, as Post put it to Gemmell. The conductor and his wife 'gave him all the sympathy we could muster – and then he could have a cup of coffee and go home still muttering darkly about his enemies. We saw him for a short time on the night before he left on the fatal flight. He came out to, as he put it, "have a last plate of Australian strawberries". This being a reference to our having a patch of strawberries growing in the garden and Willie [sic] was quite intrigued when he visited us the first time, to go down with a torch at about 11 p.m. to pick and eat fresh strawberries'. Post finished his letter by saying Willy was possibly among the greatest artists he had partnered.

Gemmell dug deeper. He wanted to know if Post had heard Willy say that he doubted whether he had long to live. In a second letter, Gemmell wrote, 'Perhaps it was his frequent fits of depression, but on October 23 before departing from Melbourne he very clearly told several people (independently), including myself, that he felt he might not live to see home.' Post replied that he couldn't recall hearing Willy doubt his lifespan, but 'he was in a rather depressed frame of mind on the last occasion when I saw him, and muttered once or twice that he would never come back to Australia again.'

Only recently, Gemmell added to his earlier comments.[2] He thought Willy was tense to the point of 'being distraught some of the time'. He projected fanaticism. Gemmell said he gave him 'the impression of wanting to do nothing else but play forever'. The reporter saw several of Willy's Melbourne performances and was 'awestruck by [his] fluency'. He glimpsed him two or three times at the Ellerys, and 'he gave me the impression of being dedicated to the exclusion of interruption'.

Play forever? In a sense, Willy *had* played forever, or a fair portion of it: thirty-seven concerts – twenty recitals and seventeen with orchestra – in a little over three months. He made a percentage of profits over and above his guaranteed fee only four times. His gross return for orchestral performances was £2125, and for recitals £3320 8s 6d, a total of £5445 8s 6d. After he paid income tax and expenses, he banked £2806 2s 2d from the tour, an earning not hugely different from his takings in 1945. If he had played thirty-seven concerts in America, he would have earned around $55,000. The total cost to the ABC of staging the recitals was £2196 6s 8d or about £110 a performance.

At Sydney airport overseas terminal, he repeated to members of the press his promise never to return. I can imagine the scene.

'Hey, Mr Kapell. Can you look this way, please?'

The hacks swing their axes. Photographers want him full-face.

'Can you look this way please, Mr Kapell?'

'Did you mean what you said?'

'Hey, mate, this way!'

Flashes explode. Reporters scribble and scrum, and an elbow knocks off a chocolate-brown fedora. Willy quickens his curious forward-slash walk, the soles of his shoes treading the linoleum no one quite knows where. A cigarette wags on his bottom lip. His tweed sports jacket flaps open with each stride. (Eunice Gardiner has come to see him off. He's put on old clothes, he tells her.)

Outside the terminal, a prop on VH-BPE, a DC-6 of the Australian airline BCPA, an aircraft called *Resolution*, begins to turn. A second starts a lazy spin.

'Mr Kapell. Hey, Mr Kapell! Anything to say? Have you got anything to say?'

Willy stops and butts out the smoke. 'To say? To say?' he says. 'Well, there are a lot of things I *could* say.'

'What about not coming back to Australia?' says a reporter, pen poised.

'Did you mean it?' asks a second.

Willy buttons his jacket. 'I meant what I said.'

★ ★ ★

As a postscript to the tour, on 29 October the *Sydney Morning Herald* published its opinion of Willy. It began, 'Mr William Kapell, the distinguished American pianist, left these shores yesterday with a final malediction on the whole race of Australian critics. Mr Anthony Quayle, who should know better, has applauded his [Kapell's] earlier remarks'. The paper also cited Australian soprano Joan Hammond, who had recently damned Australian reviewers. But Sydney critics treated none of the artists badly, the *Herald* insisted. 'They were praised for what they did well; they were criticised for what they did less well. That, after all, is a critic's duty.' The *Herald* went on to acknowledge that musicians were more important than critics, but it did not mean 'that they were always right'. Kapell was among performers who 'come to Australia in the mistaken belief that they are conferring great honour on the rude colonials whose duty is to be grateful and applaud. They do not want criticism. They want undiluted praise.' Visiting artists needed to understand that Australian critics had heard and seen other performers of 'even greater distinction, and they have learned to acquire standards of their own'. In a 'homely phrase', the leading article ended, 'we are not as green as we are cabbage-looking'.

As Sydneysiders hear-heared the *Herald*'s rhetoric, Willy was over the Pacific. In fewer than twenty-four hours he'd be dead.

CHAPTER SEVEN

Roy's Recorder

'Roy ... had developed an unusual and somewhat sad-looking facial expression not conducive to serving the public. [He] bought a medical book with illustrations and soon found a picture that matched his face. Diagnosis, thyroid deficiency. The doctor agreed, and – thyroxine prescribed – his face improved and Myer gave him a job!'

From Maurice Austin's eulogy for his friend Roy Preston

'[You] cannot do better than install this standard overhead traversing gear ...'

From an advertisement for the Royce Senior Recorder

IT MAY BE safely presumed that cosmetics salesman Roy Preston was alone – his mother, Ruby, in bed – when he cut his most important recording. He usually made sure that no one distracted him.

No notes or photographs exist that describe how things were in Roy's living room that momentous night. (The inner-suburban worker's cottage in which he and Ruby lived has been radically renovated since 1953.) However, Roy's actions during the twenty minutes in which William Kapell played Chopin's *Funeral March* sonata in Geelong have turned out to be precious. We know now what they resulted in, but the writer is left to colour in the scene, reconstruct an event without which Willy might have disappeared altogether from the world's musical memory. I see it like this.

★ ★ ★

Roy Preston flung open the radiogram's doors just to sniff the air and cock his ear. He loved the odour. When those Radiotron valves – 'the world's finest', as the cover ad in *Radio and Hobbies* put it – warmed up, they produced a whiff of freshly buttered toast. Their tiny pigtail filaments glowed orange. Heated to red-hot in a vacuum inside a glass bubble just fancy, he marvelled. He loved to look at them. And listen to the whole apparatus, which hummed softly, like a barely sounding sixteen-foot pipe of a Wurlitzer. Always the same note. Perfect note. Constant. Who'd have thought a lathe and an amplifier and radio receiver could be so seductive. The Royce Senior Recorder, to give it its full name, reminded Roy of the girls in *Australasian Post*. It was a brazen hussy, as Mum might say. Seductive. And Royce was a nice name – almost his own.

He placed a blank 16-inch acetate disc on the transcription turntable, which twinned a playback counterpart alongside it, and swung the Royce's weighty beam into place. The metal parts had their own smell – light machine oil and cold steel. He bent to sniff them. What a contraption! Manufactured in Melbourne, it was worth every bit of the money he'd sacrificed for it. Look at the recordings he'd made, though. Hundreds already. Not just of theatre organs and jazz, but also the classics, which he was broadening his interest in. You had to compare the Royce's value with radiograms *without* cutting apparatus, too, with their three-speed automatic changers and French-polished cabinets. You couldn't *record* music on them. Only play it through their 'de luxe' speakers and 'de luxe' mahogany cases. What was the price of that one he saw the other day? An HMV? What was it? Over 200 guineas. Two hundred pounds plus two hundred shillings. Two hundred and ten quid.

They say the new tape recorders will be safer. He's read all the guff. He used to write the guff. Type it up, anyway. He knows what lies a lot of truths can tell. Sure disc recorders *can* be dangerous. There was the flammable swarf, of course. The tiny coils of acetate that ball-up when you make a record can explode. Curls of microgroove. Yeah, it's explosive. But it's worse if the disc is cellulose nitrate. Mine aren't. You'd have to be unlucky, too, for the swarf to catch fire. Perhaps light up while recording. And *he himself* brushes away, of course, the swarf as he goes. Don't let it mount up, that's the rule. They tell you that. It's obvious. That's why I bought the brush. He reaches behind the Royce, feels for a No. 4 paintbrush and props it behind his ear.

And, yes, your stylus could get wrecked gouging through the coating to the aluminium beneath. It had to be just light enough to ride from side to side and be faithful to the music. He was a stickler, too, for the right angle of contact. Exactly right. It was give and take, this recording stuff. A balance. You had to go to a lot of trouble. Correct force in the groove. The *microgroove*.

They were all the go, microgrooves. But perhaps not for much longer with all these tape recorders coming in. Even Myer's sell them. Can't imagine they'd be better than microgrooves, though. He cut them like Michelangelo chiselled marble, he smiled. Precisely. Like he shot during sniper-training. Accurately.

Roy fitted a heavy steel scroll to his recorder. It was the thickness of a broom handle and had a spiral groove that met a cogwheel at the centre of the apparatus. You fitted more music on each disc the tighter the spiral. Didn't it look the goods, the Royce. A real serious industrial machine. Innards from a warplane? Could be. Part of the landing gear. Or flaps winder-outer. It wouldn't look out of place in the wreckage he'd seen in New Guinea and Bougainville. Its teal-coloured stippled paint was the giveaway. It shouted cutting edge. Who'd have a new-fangled tape recorder when this did a better job?

He waded through his hoardings. Yes, he was a hoarder, he admitted to himself, even if Mum tidied up after him now and then. Recent editions of *Radio and Hobbies* waited in stacks. The *Argus* in piles. How he wished he and Mum had been able to keep the big house in Coburg. To think that they'd lived in the next best street to The Grove. Now they were in a tiny ... Well, to be honest, it was a slum, really, wasn't it? A bedroom each for him and Mum, a kitchen and a front room – Mum called it the 'lounge', like posh people do. Bother brother Ernie and his assault charge. Assault with a weapon. To wit, a blooming monkey wrench. And his skipping bail. Someone had to forfeit the money, didn't he? He and Mum, in their case. And they'd lost the big house because of it. Just as well he'd got into Myer's. Just as well he'd risen to run cosmetics. Mum and he could afford it. But only just.

Roy shook his head. Nothing should ever be thrown out, he'd told Mum time and time again. But where was this week's *Listener In*? Why was it always buried?

Roy sorted through concert programs years old. You never knew when the past might need verification. You couldn't rely on memory. Would *The Listener In* be in the boxes of secret reports, how-to-surrender leaflets and operations maps he'd brought back from the Pacific? He laughed. Lance-Sergeant Preston, intelligence clerk, had typed them and edited them. Why shouldn't he keep a few? Was it legal? Who cared? There'd always been a streak of Ernie in him. 'Spruso', his comrades called him, after his hair-oil.

Roy looked in the mirror above the mantelpiece. Not a bad-looking bloke, if I may say so myself. Now I've got the thyroid right, that is. He winked at the porcelain ducks flying above the mirror. Bullet-straight, their course. He put 'em up. He knew they were straight. Made sure they were. He smiled at himself. He did have a touch of the slick about him as well, though, he conceded.

Roy eventually found *The Listener In* near the top of a pile of *Women's Weeklies*. He turned to the listings for Thursday 22 October 1953 and ran a finger down the columns. 3AR – 484m and 620KC – was broadcasting a sonata played by William Kapell.

There it was: '10.00 William Kapell, piano; Sonata Op.35 (Chopin)'. Kapell? Who was he, now? Kapell? Ah yes, the American pianist touring for the ABC. Chopin. It wasn't the whole program, of course. Typical of the ABC. Bits and pieces. They were a bits and pieces mob, the ABC.

Roy went to the walnut bookcase he and Mum had bought from that fat second-hand dealer Mick who tap-tap-tapped his next smoke on his Ardath box. He scanned the shelves and pulled out Bacharach's *Musical Companion*. He looked up Chopin and turned to page 588. Opus 35 was the so-called *Funeral March* sonata. He knew that one. According to Bacharach, the slow movement's funereal motif was entirely personal. The whole piece was 'permeated through and through by the poignant, heart-stricken sense of tragedy for which the funeral march provides the climax'. Heavens!

Roy positioned the recording head – the size of a cigarette pack – above the disc. Just those two little wires there would take the broadcast from the radio and etch it on to the disc, he marvelled. He tickled the sapphire stylus, coaxing muffled scratches from his loudspeaker. The point wasn't pointed, he'd learned. Actually, it was round. Royce Ferguson had told him in the shop. But it was so tiny it gouged. At an angle of eighty-seven degrees precisely. He balanced the stylus's force against the counterweight see-sawing on the other side of the beam. Had to be just right, the right weight. Not too light. Nor too heavy. Just perfect. He took his time … A little lighter. Perfect. Ten o'clock start. He'd have time to take Mum a cuppa. 'Daa-daa-de-daa', he hummed, and put on the kettle.

★ ★ ★

Royce Ferguson, a pioneer of Australian recorded images and sound, appears to have cut few permanent grooves about himself. The Australian Film and Sound Archive has not a single reference to his recording device which, by the early 1950s, might have been in the hands of many scores of hobbyist Melburnians, according to the best estimates. No brochures appear to have survived showing how to install a Royce Recorder, how it worked, the care involved in using it to make the best recordings, the painstaking steps you had to follow to get superior results. As a device, the recorder itself was unremarkable, and similar apparatuses were engraving acetate discs throughout the music-loving world. That Ferguson classed his machine as 'standard' indicates, perhaps, the man's modesty. But it was a precision instrument, after all, and that its steel beams, worm drives and central rotating gear were lathed in Melbourne in a factory in St Kilda Road is – when Australian manufacturing had a broad spectrum but low volume – remarkable.

Ferguson himself comes across as someone so ordinary in manner and appearance that those who knew him struggle to describe any striking attribute. He was short, had brown hair, and was very helpful to amateur music-lovers who sought his advice about the art of trapping sound. And that's about it. He sometimes attended hobbyist recorders' meetings and spoke softly. He had a shop in Little Bourke Street, its window dressed with a turntable, a Royce machine dominating. Loudspeakers, amplifiers, stroboscopes and 'all accessories for the recordist', as Ferguson's advertisement stresses, were also behind the glass.

Born in the late 19th century or early 20th, Ferguson and a certain Ted Howell gained newspaper column inches in 1924 by inventing a device for counting the calls made on telephone exchanges. The implement also allowed callers to leave their numbers if they failed to get through. It was, in short, an early answering machine. Reports say that the young men had spent three years and £1000 to develop the device. They hoped to sell it to the Post Office but, if that failed, they would take it to the United States.

The call-counter-cum-answering-machine can't have besotted early telecommunications executives, because by the late 1920s Ferguson had moved on to celluloid. Royce Films Limited had a logo of a shaggy Australian terrier barking inside a circular frame on which the company's name flourished in arabesqued capitals. It mimicked the famous MGM lion, of course, forgoing its accompanying motto, *Ars gratia artis*, or art for art's sake. Just as well, because the company's one and only movie – a jerky silent comedy called *King Kut Comedy No. 1* – is hardly at the pinnacle of film culture.[1]

Disc-cutting was Ferguson's next obsession. By 1936 it had become popular worldwide among cognoscenti of captured sound, and Ferguson found himself a pioneer in the production of Australian machines. No one knows just how many Royce Recorders were sold, if Ferguson made more than one model or, indeed, if he had any major competition. (Roy Preston's machine was stamped with the serial number '101'.) But there appears to be little doubt that he led and others followed.

And those who used disc-cutters were convinced of one thing: in the hands of perfectionists they reproduced far more faithful and superior sound than could be captured on tape. The differences were huge. Audible. Moreover, the acetates would remain *permanent* copies if they weren't worn out by over-playing.

Such a thought was distant from Roy Preston's mind, of course, as he lowered the stylus and began engraving – for posterity? who knows? – William Kapell's version of the first agitated phrases of Chopin's thirty-fifth work.

Hog bristles flick away the accumulating swarf as the second movement, a scherzo that is more mournful than playful, follows the first. Roy etches the well-known funeral march – the third movement – in sad grooves. Willy takes almost seven minutes to play it; profound is the tragedy with which he invests it. Roy thinks it's exquisite.

He stands alongside his machine the entire time. He never sits when he records. He makes sure of that. He doesn't smoke, either. Attentive, he is. He brushes away a curl of swarf.

Kapell plays the final movement – marked *presto*, or as fast as you can play it – in eighty-seven seconds. The notes swell and fade in brilliant avalanches that shout and whisper, surge here, quieten there – eerie sound curtains that are sometimes gossamer-thin, sometimes rough as burlap. He is shaping with enormous clarity an urgent, mighty and emphatic climax to the work. It has a new economy and renewed beauty after this concert. Willy is seeing to that. There's a final definitive chord, which he barely gets out before applause explodes from the audience inside the cold bluestone shell of Geelong's Plaza Theatre. Roy is greatly impressed.

Even if they aren't clairvoyants, many concert-goers, too, know exactly what they've just heard. It's memorable – phenomenal. Immortal, if someone has bothered to record it.

Roy lifts the recording head off the acetate, runs fingers through his hair, props the No. 4 brush behind an ear and removes the disc. He slips it into its home-made plastic envelope and brown-paper sleeve. Volume on five, he says to himself. I'll write it down tomorrow. Amplifier six-and-a-half. Having unknowingly cut a morsel of recording history, he switches off his set-up and replaces the No. 4 behind the Royce. The valves' pig-tailed filaments fade to grey, and he turns off the lights and goes to bed.

CHAPTER EIGHT

Where Are the Tapes?

'DEEPLY GRIEVED TRAGIC NEWS PLEASE ACCEPT
OUR SINCEREST SYMPATHY.'
Cable from Saffo and William James to Anna Lou

'He kissed her [Anna Lou] over the telephone and said,
"See you Friday". Those were the last words she heard from
her husband.'
Frederic Mann, Willy's former patron, to reporters in New York

ANNA LOU AND the children were staying at the Meurice Hotel on 58th Street, Manhattan, waiting for Willy's return. She had spent the day with her husband's managers and Steinway executives discussing his next American tour. Some had known of Willy's death but had declined to break the news. Eugene Istomin and Constance Hope from RCA Victor met her in the Meurice's lobby. The pianist and the record-company executive did not know each other, and Anna Lou instantly grasped what she later called the 'terrible truth'. She said to Hope, 'He's dead isn't he?' Hope led her to the elevator and said, 'I'm afraid so, dear.' Her immediate thought, she wrote in notes for an autobiography, was that it was better thus than being 'terribly wounded' and unable ever to play again.

Her hotel suite was crowded with friends and family members. A friend, Margot Gumport, had taken the children – David, four, and Rebecca, two – to her home. Dr Bychowksi told Anna Lou that Willy wouldn't have suffered – his death would have been instantaneous. Willy's Aunt Olga sat on the bed and rocked back and forth, sobbing.

The following morning at the Gumports, Anna Lou took David and Rebecca on her lap and told them their father would not be coming home. His plane had crashed. David remembers his mother winding herself in window drapes and sobbing. Mark Rothko, the abstract expressionist painter, sat with her for an hour in the Gumports' library without saying a word.

Anna Lou's life without Willy had begun. And although she remarried, had two more children and forged a brilliant career, she told me, 'My life was nothing without him.'

★ ★ ★

Bob Kapell went to buy a paper at a newsstand in Manhattan's Pennsylvania Station and read 'in big black letters – "PLANE CRASHES: William Kapell Feared Dead".' Willy's patron Frederic Mann tried for hours to reach Edith and Harry Kapell in Florida, where they had retired. Their number was being changed, and the phone rang out. They were listening to the news while having dinner, and heard about their son's death that way.

Mann represented the Kapells when they were too grief-stricken to speak. He told reporters in New York that Willy had telephoned Anna Lou at the hotel as soon as he had touched down in Honolulu. Anna Lou had 'urged her husband to rest for a few days before coming home', he said. 'Bill [sic] thought it over for a few seconds, then replied that he was anxious to see his wife and his two children and would fly on. He kissed her over the telephone and said, "See you Friday". Those were the last words she heard from [him].' The Melbourne *Sun* corroborated Willy's almost cancelling his onward journey to San Francisco at Anna Lou's suggestion. An unnamed friend of the Kapells told a *Sun* journalist that 'he said he'd feel happier if he came home and relaxed with the children'. It was later revealed that Willy was supposed to rehearse and possibly record chamber music with two of the greatest string players, Jascha Heifetz and the cellist Gregor Piatigorsky, in Los Angeles on the way home. Bill Judd,

Heifetz's manager, told her the great violinist could never forgive Willy for dying.

Australian critics who had praised Willy now gathered to mourn him. On news of the accident, Sinclair wrote two long articles for the *Herald*. Late in his tour, Willy had got a name for resenting criticism, Sinclair said. But it wasn't the case. He hated what he thought was 'unfair criticism'. His 'annoyance' with Australia, the reason behind his saying that he would never return, 'sprang largely from a Sydney ... critic's remark that his playing was often no more than "shallowly exciting"'. Kapell's anger was understandable because he 'never felt that way about music – or anything else'. But if Sinclair's pen was at its most sympathetic, Willy's last remark to his friend was drenched in bathos: 'Could I come back to Australia and not play in Sydney?' he had asked. Sinclair was convinced Willy would return. For him, the New Yorker was 'one of the rare young musicians of his time', an 'unusual complex of qualities'. His technical mastery of the piano was of little interest to him, he wrote. 'He hated notes as such, and virtuosity when it was an end in itself.' He believed a musician should mature, and he believed he was doing it – seeing his own 'life aims clearly'. The kind of technique needed to play Rachmaninoff and Tchaikovsky concertos had inhibited finer performance skills and musical sensibility required for Mozart, Willy believed. 'So he ceased playing the Tchaikovsky and the first two Rachmaninoff concertos, and intended playing the third Rachmaninoff concerto for the last time during his next season in America.'

In the December edition of *Australian Musical News*, Linda Phillips emphasised 'the quality of his attainments, the dedicated approach to music, the mastery of his skill, the insight, the never ending search for perfection'. She said he gave joy to thousands and won many friends with a 'human, charming and unspoiled personality. His loss is everybody's loss … Let Shelley speak: "Forget the Past, his fate and fame shall be/ An echo and a light unto eternity!"' Phillips also castigated the ABC for failing to organise a minute's silence in remembrance of Willy at the Melbourne subscription concert following his death.

Heinze said he had held him in the 'highest esteem' since first performing with him in 1945. Juan Jose Castro, the Victorian Symphony's resident conductor said, 'With the disappearance of an artist of his kind, we know how great a loss his death is to the present world.' And Castro shone new light on Willy's mental turmoil. 'At every meeting I felt that a tragic destiny marked his way through life. A melancholy pessimism dominated all his thoughts. He told me once in a discussion that he asked himself sometimes if it were worthwhile for a musician to play in the present-day world.' R. G. Lamb, the ABC's federal concert manager, said Willy had been anxious to rejoin his family, 'which is why he did not stop over a day at Honolulu, although he had a room booked'.[1]

Even dead, Willy was at Lindsey Browne's mercy. It seemed as if the *Sydney Morning Herald* critic could not help himself. His obituary appeared two days after the tragedy. A few weeks ago, he began, Kapell gave Chopin's *Funeral March* sonata one of 'several beautiful performances' in an 'uneven concert season'. But then, no doubt reflecting, Browne recanted, set his vengefulness aside, and came up with one of the best snapshots of Willy's artistry in several hundred words of magnanimity. First, he called Willy's death – after those of Ginette Neveu and Jacques Thibaud in air crashes – a 'fearful blow' for music-lovers. Then, he assessed his fame. Kapell was a 'clever, disciplined and obsessed craftsman who knew what greatness was, knew the doggedness with which one had to fight for it, often doubted whether he had the little bit extra that greatness means, hated to be reminded where he might have missed it (for he probably knew already), and could yet be as great as some of the greatest we have ever heard'.

A sympathetic caricature followed. The American was a 'fuss-debunking little New Yorker, hard as Bowery kerbstone, half-choked with cigarette smoke, militantly full of battle against all the elements of East Side underprivilege in his background'. Browne noted Kapell's 'ruthless streak of sanity … He knew he had to work fiercely, to think fiercely, to burn himself up as a kind of furnace in which his music might temper itself. And he did that.' His Debussy was 'exquisitely trim in design' and he had the right tempered aggression to play well Prokofiev and Khachaturian. He might not have been the greatest musician to visit Australia, Browne opined, but he had been the 'most distinctively American … of all the musicians I have heard'.

Despite Browne finding some good in Willy's work, Eunice Gardiner – whom Nell Fleming called a 'sweet, warm soul' – was incensed by the obituary. On reading it, she had felt a 'disgust and rage that never will evaporate while I have the power to feel anything!' she wrote Fleming.

Dot Mendoza was a Sydney pianist, educator and composer who broadcast a regular ABC program called 'Handful of Keys'. She had a story. Having just finished a show – her first after a long and painful illness – she was about to leave a studio when Willy walked in to rehearse. He complimented her on her program, which he had been listening to outside. They chatted for a while about pianos. She had no idea who he was until a voice from the control booth interrupted, 'How long will you require the studio, Mr Kapell?' The famous Mr Kapell! Discombobulated, Mendoza must have appeared to Willy to have succumbed to the vapours. He noticed her fainting, anyway, and insisted on helping her out of the building.

The music universe sobbed. Nell Fleming reported back to Australia that Kapell's death had 'somewhat disrupted' the ABC's New York office. Staff were being besieged by reporters and friends of the Kapells. 'I don't believe anything for years has so shaken the music world of America.' Columbia Artists' Management had informed her that Anna Lou was 'bearing up most wonderfully'.

American tributes avalanched.[2] Claudia Cassidy wrote that 'to those who loved him as pianist and friend, [his loss] is irreparable.' She continued, 'When I say as pianist and friend, the words fall in that order by natural sequence. Willy was a pianist first, last and always. You had to understand that.' In him was the 'relentless, terrible and wonderful compulsion of genius'. Virgil Thomson wrote that 'few artists have ever battled so manfully with management or so unhesitatingly sassed the press. He was afraid of nobody, because his heart was pure.' He could play 'great music with authority; his readings of it were at once musically sound and genuinely individual'.

Eugene Ormandy wrote to Anna Lou after he had broken the news of Willy's death to the Philadelphia Orchestra. 'That evening we played [Beethoven's] *Eroica* symphony and before we began I told the audience of the irreparable loss the music world has suffered and of our love for Willy, and of his for us, and concluded with these words: "The members of the Philadelphia Orchestra and

I would like to play the *Funeral March* movement in memory of our departed friend." We did.' Aaron Copland penned a very long and loving letter to the young widow, much of it an analysis of his friend's approach to his art. 'Willie [sic], if he had lived, would always have remained a youthful artist, in the best sense of that term. The search for artistic growth, the ideal of maturity was a central and continuing preoccupation with him. Emerson once wrote that the artist is "pitiful". He meant, I suppose, that the true artist can never be entirely satisfied with the work he does. William Kapell was that kind of true artist.'

A perhaps unexpected homage came from the British-American broadcaster and journalist Alistair Cooke, who lived in New York and devoted his 'Letter from America' to Willy the day after the accident. (Cooke called himself Willy's friend, and the only film of Willy at the keyboard was recorded on 15 March 1953 for Cooke's 'Omnibus' arts program, which ran on the CBS network. Willy plays a Scarlatti sonata, a Chopin nocturne and an arrangement of an Argentinian folk song. He is straight-backed and undemonstrative, occasionally looking away from the keys, perhaps towards the film crew. At the end of the nocturne, he is unsure whether to continue straight on with the folk song and seeks assurance, gesturing towards people outside the frame. His sideburns are of rock-star length.)

In his twelve-minute tribute, Cooke says Willy 'held fiercely and unyieldingly to a view of his profession as almost a priesthood, which required unwavering devotion from dawn to midnight; unremitting practice, practice, practice; an almost trembling humanity before good music, ancient and modern … He died a lucky man. For not many men [coming] into middle age have been fortunate enough to go through to the end without, in some forgivable way, compromising their best.' Cooke contacted Nell Fleming, suggesting that the ABC should broadcast his encomium. It did.

Willy's playing, character, and the way he met his death had created in an instant an American legend as enduring as the granite blocks within which the pianist had performed his last concert. Recordings of his last performances would fix his genius for the ages. If they could be found. Where were the tapes? Melbourne surgeon C. Bernays Melville asked in a letter to the 'manager' of the ABC a day after Willy's death. He thought the broadcaster might 'plan to do something for the benefit of Mrs Kapell with the recordings that it must possess'. He too, his letter ends, would like to obtain 'some tangible memento of that brilliant pianist'.

Anna Lou had heard many of his Australian concerts. She knew the bullion – the worth in artistic gold – of any permanent recordings that might exist. Three weeks after *Resolution* clipped the redwood tops, she telephoned Nell Fleming to ask if 'any and all recorded tapes' made during the tour could be sent to her, as Nell put it to her superiors in Sydney. To reinforce the request, Fleming cabled next day, 'MRS KAPELL AND R. C. A. VICTOR GRATEFUL LEARN WHETHER OR NOT KAPELL TAPE RECORDINGS AUSTRALIAN TOUR HAVE BEEN ERASED, APPRECIATE EARLY REPLY ...' She followed up the telegram with a letter saying that RCA had heard that the ABC erased tapes of broadcast performances. It continued, 'RCA finds this difficult to believe, and would greatly appreciate learning whether or not this is true in the case of the Kapell performances'.

Unfortunately, it was, as Bill James explained to Bernays Melville and Fleming. To the surgeon he wrote, 'Mr Kapell, like the majority of our visiting celebrities, was under contract with commercial recording companies, so that of necessity, any recordings made by the ABC during his tour were purely of an ephemeral nature, made for one broadcast only after which they are subject to compulsory destruction.'

Nonetheless, an all-points bulletin was despatched to the broadcaster's field stations. 'ADVISE URGENTLY WHETHER YOU HOLD RECORDINGS ANY AUSTRALIAN PERFORMANCES RECITAL OR ORCHESTRAL BY WILLIAM KAPELL.' Replies arrived promptly: 'NO RECORDINGS', 'REGRET NOT HOLDING', 'NOT HERE'. Head office cabled New York, 'KAPELL RECORDINGS APPEAR ALL ERASED ACCORDANCE NORMAL PROCEDURE BUT MAKING FINAL CHECK'.

So that she could advise RCA Victor, no doubt, Fleming was sent a long explanation. Tapes were made when broadcasts had to be delayed 'owing to other programme commitments'. Contracts between touring musicians and the ABC stipulated that the recording be broadcast only once. Staff were 'instructed to erase these recordings as soon as they have been used, in the interests of the artist'. It continued, 'We do not think it is fair to the artist to permit such recordings to remain in existence any longer than is essential.' However, there was a chance that two tapes of a Sydney performance sent to Port Moresby in Papua New Guinea might still be intact. They were made on 'portable machines, and it is therefore very unlikely that their technical quality would be such as would be suitable for conversion to commercial recordings'.

Soon after Anna Lou enquired after tapes, Bill James had great news. The Port Morseby tapes *had* been recovered. They were of

Kapell's 10 October performance of Prokofiev's third concerto with the Sydney Symphony under Joseph Post. It had been Willy's last engagement with an orchestra, and the transcription appeared to be in 'excellent condition'. Charles Moses was delighted. 'I think we should try to arrange for commercial discs,' he memoed James, 'as the project should be well worthwhile both for publicising our Orchestra and from the point of view of the royalties.' James later told Moses that, although the acoustics of the Sydney Town Hall had resulted in a certain 'cloudiness', the performance was 'alive and brilliant'. RCA Victor had already released a Kapell Prokofiev third with the Dallas Symphony and Antal Dorati, but 'Kapell's performance on our tapes appeared more mature and varied'. James recommended that the ABC arrange with RCA a royalty agreement or an outright sale of the performance. If the company wasn't interested, then 'we should consider gaining necessary authority from the Estate [of William Kapell] and RCA to make our own local pressings. We have adequate funds available for this purpose.'

No record exists of the elation Anna Lou or RCA must have felt at the news. (RCA had earlier shown interest in chasing transcriptions from the Australian tour; in particular, a Mozart concerto with the Sydney Symphony under Eugene Goossens, and Willy's version of Copland's sonata.) But it was short-lived. Nine months later, Nell Fleming told head office that RCA had returned the tapes 'with no comments attached'. Three months after that she sent Sydney official confirmation that Willy's recording company had decided not to use the Australian tapes 'for commercial purposes'.

Four years after Willy's death, Anna Lou prompted the ABC to ransack its archives yet again in the hope of finding a Kapell performance. None was discovered.

★ ★ ★

No finer musician than Isaac Stern ever drew a bow across strings.[3] If people asked, he would tell them that he played the workhorse violin concertos – by Brahms, Beethoven, Tchaikovsky, Mendelssohn and Sibelius – the hundredth time with the same respect for their composers and their pieces as he had had as a student. Stern's playing had unique conviction. Experiencing it involved intimacy – a kind of three-party wedding of listener, player and music. Playing Bach's chaconne in D minor for solo violin, Stern would lead you on an eight-minute guided tour of the human soul. (Equally fascinating on television was to watch his slaughterman's hands, the right bowing so sweetly, the left nimbling the fingerboard.)

With pianist Alexander Zakin, he toured Australia for four months in 1954 and moved into top gear as soon as his feet hit the tarmac. He wanted to play a memorial concert for the New Yorker. The ABC agreed to broadcast its first half for £150, the money to go into the kitty. The performers were paid their fees, which were also tipped in. In conjunction with the Jewish National Fund of New South Wales, he and Zakin played the Sydney Town Hall on 27 July. T. F. M. in the Sydney *Telegraph* reported that Stern 'seemed to be emotionally upset after he had played the Bach Chaconne'. His conception of the work was 'as thorough as everything else he does', but it seemed to lack 'some of the boldness and tonal grandeur usually expected in this mighty … music'. The rest of the program included sonatas by Beethoven and Tartini.

Three months later, Stern clarified what the fund would buy – half of a little over £2000 would provide a Kapell memorial grove of eucalyptus trees in Israel. The other half would be spent to send

TOP LEFT: A rare photo of Willy, who never smiled for the lens. Taken on tour in Vancouver. *William Kapell Collection, International Piano Archives, University of Maryland*

TOP RIGHT: Early publicity photo. *William Kapell Collection*

RIGHT: Willy and Anna Lou begin a South American tour in 1949. *William Kapell Collection*

TOP LEFT: About to tour Israel only weeks before his Australian commitments in 1953, Willy with Anna Lou, David and Rebecca. *William Kapell Collection*

TOP RIGHT: Alan Gemmell's photo of Willy taken in Melbourne. It was used on at least one American record cover. *William Kapell Collection, and courtesy of the photographer*

LEFT: Detail from one of Willy's seascapes. *Author's photo*

Crossword-puzzle setter and *Sydney Morning Herald* music critic Lindsey Browne. *Courtesy of Fairfax Media*

The Royce Senior Recorder.
From a brochure

Brass ruler from Roy's machine, showing serial number (top right) 101.
Author's photo

Bruce Dickson in a BCPA cockpit with his son. *Courtesy of Chris Purcell and the Queensland Air Museum*

Wreckage of *Resolution* at the crash site. *Author's photo*

ABOVE: An Athol Shmith photo of
Cliff Hocking at Thomas' in the 1950s.
Courtesy of David Vigo

RIGHT: Sketch of Roy Preston on active
service in New Guinea. The artist's caption
is 'Spine Drill'. *Courtesy of Maurice Austin*

Maurice Austin at Essendon Airport's Airways Museum. He holds one of Roy's acetate discs. The Civil Aviation Historical Society, which runs the museum, devised and produced the BCPA 'panel' behind Maurice. *Author's photo*

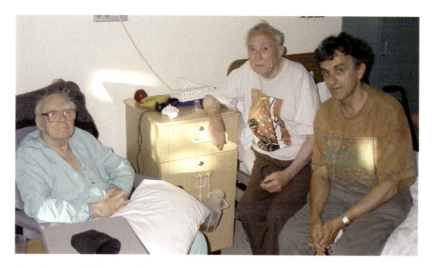

Roy Preston (left) near the end of his life. His brother, Vic, and Vic's son, Russell, sit on the bed. *Courtesy of Maurice Austin*

Ernie Bonyhadi and Shirley Gittelsohn hold Maurice's package containing Roy's precious acetates. *Courtesy of Maurice Austin*

Bob and Ann Kapell in
their studio apartment
in Manhattan.
Author's photo

Anna Lou at the celebration
dinner at Brasserie 8½.
Courtesy of Josh Kapell

Recording engineer Jon Samuels.
Author's photo

an Australian music teacher overseas for fifteen months for further training. He or she would study for a year in the United States and about three months in Europe. Stern had noted several musical shortcomings in Australia: the quality of string players in the ABC orchestras, the lack of 'decent' concert halls and an abyss where music education should be. His original idea was to spend the money on a student who, as Stern told Max Keogh of *Tempo*, might not return. Those who won Kapell awards would be contracted to come back. The fund was being managed by an expert panel that included Bill James, Charles Moses, Bernard Heinze and Eugene Goossens.

Following the Stern–Zakin concert, at least two more benefits topped up the prize pool. Australian musicians Ernest Llewellyn, Robert Pikler, Lauri Kennedy and Hephzibah Menuhin (sister of Yehudi, she was born in San Francisco but lived much of her life in Australia) put on a concert. Irish tenor Patrick O'Hagan performed another. And the first Kapell winner was finally announced – Ernest Llewellyn, leader of the Sydney Symphony. When he left Australia in September the following year, he remained out of pocket. Ever the percipient commentator on things musical, Eunice Gardiner in her *Telegraph* column wrote that it 'does not reflect credit on us ... that the full sum required is not yet available'. In particular, she was critical of the ABC's music department. Its bureaucrats' salaries never ceased when they went abroad but Llewellyn, who was, like his fellow ABC musicians, not even on the broadcaster's permanent staff, would not get paid. The ABC would save money as soon as he left.

Lack of further mention in the press suggests that the scholarship lapsed.

★ ★ ★

As well as grief and tributes, eerie coincidences ultimately followed Willy's death. Within five years, the trio of young keyboard virtuosi that had embarrassed the ABC with its riches in 1945 were all gone, all dying at the age of thirty-one.

Noel Mewton-Wood's career had flourished. Despite having been born in Melbourne, he had remained in England to significant acclaim. The English conductor Sir Henry Wood, who had performed with the finest musicians for decades, said Mewton-Wood reminded him of 'all the greatest pianists ... including Rubinstein, Liszt and Busoni'. German composer Paul Hindemith believed that if you wanted to hear his piano works played properly hire Mewton-Wood.[4]

The pianist was homosexual, and in 1946 his partner was Bill Federicks, a British Council bureaucrat. They set up house in the London borough of Hammersmith, and Mewton-Wood's mother, who had taken the boy to the British capital, did not approve. Indeed, she and the family in Australia were reportedly ashamed.

A hypochondriac, Federicks became the pianist's agent. Late in 1953, he complained of a pain in his torso. Mewton-Wood ignored the grizzle. The pain worsened, and Federicks was rushed to hospital. His appendix had burst. Operated on successfully, he died, however, on the eve of his discharge. Inconsolable, Mewton-Wood blamed himself and overdosed on aspirin. A surgeon friend found him and took him into his care. Convincing his rescuer that he was well, Mewton-Wood returned home a few days later. Just over a week after his first attempt at suicide, he swallowed a cocktail of gin and hydrogen cyanide. This time, there was no mistake.

Kapell and Mewton-Wood were born – and died – two months apart. And in May 1958, Richard Farrell was one of three killed when a car left the road in Sussex, England, hit a tree and overturned. Neville Cardus wrote in the *Manchester Guardian* that the New Zealander was 'one of the most promising pianists in Britain'. His death was a 'grievous loss to the concert world'. It was a 'sad irony' that his career had been 'cut short by accident, a fate that was shared by William Kapell, who was largely responsible for developing Farrell's gifts'.

Farrell had hewn for himself considerable fame. He had toured the United States, played Carnegie Hall, and the new Festival Hall and Royal Albert Hall in London. He had performed with Beecham, Sargent and other important conducting knights such as Adrian Boult and John Barbirolli. He had toured his home country several times, and played more Beethoven than Willy. At one point, Rubinstein is alleged to have remarked that the music world contained three pianists – Kapell, Farrell and himself. The New Zealander's ultimate objective was to conduct.

Kapell, Mewton-Wood and Farrell – all lost to violence and tragedy. Not to mention music.

CHAPTER NINE

True Gentleman

'Roy did not waste words, and … spoke ill of no one.'
Bruce Ardley at Roy's funeral

'I have a customs declaration of Roy's that itemises twelve records and two tins of needles that he imported from England in the 1930s.'
Maurice Austin

GIVEN HIS CHANCE, Roy Preston might have played music well. It was his life. It swallowed him whole. But instead of becoming a musician or composer he turned to listening, the obligatory third person in the appreciation of organised sound. The French writer Maurice Blanchot claimed a reader is as important – as pertinent to meaning – as the writer who penned the words he or she is reading. While an obvious idea, it urges those who consume the arts to approach them with intellectual rigour. Roy gave Blanchot's claim a musical dimension. He took listening seriously. The joy he derived from music's endless styles filled his days and gave significance to his existence. He loved almost all music without discrimination – he took pleasure in theatre organs, brass bands, jazz and classical. Some performers and performances he preferred over others. Pop music left him cold.

The eldest of three sons, he was born in the inner industrial suburb of Richmond, Melbourne, in May 1915, seven years and a few months before the birth of Kapell. His father Tom was a professional cook and his mother Ruby kept home. Like Willy's parents, they were resigned to membership of the lower-middle class. But Roy's father did well, and when Roy was an infant the family aimed high, moving to a home in Coburg, a suburb with bourgeois enclaves of new and generously proportioned dwellings on the enlarging northern outskirts of the city.

No sooner had things turned for the better than fate had its say for the worst. When Roy was seven, Tom stepped off his morning cable tram into the path of an oncoming car and was killed. Roy's mother was seven months pregnant with third son Victor. Already tough enough, times got tougher. Relatives helped the family through, but there was no question of Roy studying for a profession. As soon as he was legally allowed to leave school he would be sent to work. A curious child who loved word-play but faced the bleak prospect of never being required to apply his mental acuity, he could not be blamed for retreating into music. He built himself a crystal set and heard theatre organs for the first time through the hiss and pop of redundant army headphones. He knew church organs. His family were Methodists, after all.

Mother and sons regularly attended the city's Wesley Church, a small steepled abbey built in 1858. Its pipe organ – Melbourne's first – was installed the year the church was consecrated. A pious congregation maintained it, and Roy would have heard it at its best. Good Methodists, in fact, devoted Sundays to their faith, children attending divine service in the morning, Sunday school in the afternoon and a second session of worship in the evening. For twenty minutes before the evening service an organist gave a small recital. Roy listened. Ruby Preston and her boys would have sung the consummate hymns of Charles Wesley and Isaac Watts, John Hughes's tune 'Cwm Rhondda' lent to *Guide Me, O Thou Great Jehovah*, and John Henry Newman's *Lead, Kindly Light*. Walter Smith's *Immortal, Invisible, God Only Wise* was a Methodist favourite, and Haydn's sublime slow movement from the *Emperor* string quartet, which hymnals co-opted, was often sung.[1] Roy could have had no better grounding for a profound love of music.

Like the Kapells, the Prestons had a piano and Roy received early lessons from an uncle who also brought to the sessions a wind-up gramophone and records. Roy appears to have advanced at a fair pace in his piano studies, but he stumbled at Sinding's agitated and arpeggiated *Rustle of Spring*. Verdon Williams was the son of the conductor of Wesley Church's small orchestra. He also played its tympani. (The church held 'Pleasant Sunday Afternoon' concerts.) Verdon, who later met Willy Kapell, was a boy his own age and already a competent pianist. After one PSA concert, Roy began to tell him the problems he was having fingering the popular Sinding piece. Verdon intimated that he had never learned it, and he should bring it in and they would work on it together. Next Sunday Roy propped the music in front of Verdon, who rattled it off note perfectly.[2] Perhaps, as his friend played, Roy decided he'd be a better listener than performer.

His first job was at an uncle's blinds factory in Surrey Hills, an eastern suburb fifteen kilometres from Coburg. At the Royal Melbourne Show, the bicycle manufacturer Malvern Star had a stand, and Roy bought one of the machines on display – he couldn't wait to pick up a new one. But he quickly got sick of pedalling to and from work and moved to a job in the centre of the city. A messenger boy for the Student Christian Movement, he was paid fifteen shillings – less than two dollars – weekly. But his position had an appropriate bonus – it was close to theatre organs, which were becoming the love of his life. He quickly discovered where all six were. He loitered at an exit door to the dress circle seats of the State Theatre to listen to players practising. He found a vent up a lane beside the Lyceum Theatre that 'let the bad air out', as he later described it. Disregarding the stale oxygen, Roy stuck his ear to the vent to listen to rehearsals.

He also went to Friday lunchtime recitals by William McKie, who played the Melbourne Town Hall's Grand Organ. McKie was born in the working-class suburb of Collingwood, separated from Richmond by an intersection. He won a scholarship from Melbourne Grammar School to study the organ at the Royal College of Music in London, and by his late twenties had become a revered and masterly performer. In 1930, Melbourne City Council invited him back to take up the dual roles of music consultant and official organist. At the age of thirty, McKie began a series of free weekly recitals. The organ, which occupied the rear wall of the main auditorium in the basalt-grey, faux-classic city seat, had been refurbished two years earlier. The concerts ran for seven years for half an hour from 12.15 p.m., repeated at 1.15 p.m. (Kapell was to play several times at the Melbourne Town Hall.) The lunchtime recitals exposed Roy to Bach toccatas and transcriptions of such pieces as Wagner's *Ride of the Valkyries* and Sibelius's *Finlandia*. In 1932, McKie organised a Bach festival – its program enormous – and two years later a Bach–Elgar festival. We can assume that Roy attended both. McKie returned to England in 1938 to become Westminster Abbey's organist, a post he held until his retirement in 1961.[3]

At home, Roy tuned the radio to frequent theatre-organ broadcasts by musicians such as Reginald Dixon, who commanded the Wurlitzer[4] of the famous Tower Ballroom in Blackpool, and Sidney Torch, another virtuoso.

He changed jobs, becoming an assistant hosiery knitter at Beau Monde's inner-suburban factory. An increase in salary meant that he could at last buy records, which he played on a wind-up gramophone. He discovered the Eastern Market's record stalls, which sold discs for a few pennies. His tastes broadened, but he loved theatre organs above all. He walked to work to save money to buy 78s. Many were imported from Britain along with tins of needles for his gramophone. An invoice from November 1936 shows that he imported a dozen records and two 'Pkts of needles' from Alfred Imhof Ltd of New Oxford Street, London. It fails to detail the music on the records, but Roy's outlay was two British pounds and a shilling, probably a week's wages.

He qualified as a hosiery knitter, overseeing complex mechanical warpings and weftings, and in subsequent years learned the temperaments and complexities of knitting machines so well – worked them so meticulously – that he was in demand at Melbourne's biggest mills. He took on a series of jobs in several factories and was paid well. It is easy to imagine that – as Roy adjusted a knitter for optimal output and best quality – he might have imagined he was playing an instrument that produced sound. Despite a devotion to theatre organs, he was too shy, he said late in life, ever to introduce himself to the city's star performers. He had no girlfriends and never married, and beyond music, his only pastime was cinema.

When war broke out, Roy was barred from enlisting because he was the family's main breadwinner. In November 1941, though, he 'got in first', as he described it, somehow bent the rules, and enlisted in the Second Australian Imperial Force (volunteers). His hands were of no great size or strength, but in body-type and height he was a wirier version of Willy Kapell. He was so 'very reedy', as he put it, that at enlistment the medical examiner marked him 'temporarily unfit'. Private Preston VX65652 was ordered to undergo 'corrective treatment (underweight)' and for ten months he was bulked up at a special camp in the northern suburbs.

After basic training, he defended Australia's western shores near Geraldton, north of Perth. He was one of thousands of troops dotted along the coastline. There was no music. He returned to Melbourne and was selected for intelligence training, completing several courses – including a three-month clerk's course. Next stop was New Guinea. For a fortnight, he joined a sniper unit, even if by now few Japanese were fighting. A deadly shot with an Enfield .303 rifle, Roy sprayed bullets all over the place when he was issued with a Bren gun, which stutters at five hundred rounds a minute. 'I couldn't keep it steady,' he said. Fighting out of his division, he was drafted to deskwork in a unit providing topographical intelligence – largely issuing reports on troop positions and movements. A confidential report on his abilities describes him as 'reliable, quiet and hard-working'. He was also a 'good typist'.

Roy typed orders and telegraphy and eventually drew up surrender leaflets to disperse by air. Despite his apparent frailty, he did the impossible and avoided tropical diseases such as malaria, which almost all his comrades contracted. But he caught something of a musical infection from American servicemen – jazz. Ending his war service on Bougainville Island, he edited, wrote and published a little newspaper for troops, the *Torokina Times*. He was by now Lance Sergeant Preston, responsible for the writing and distribution of the most secret documents. He even drilled junior ranks.

He was never scared, describing his war years in Port Moresby and other tropical theatres as 'great fun'. At one of the weekly concerts of recorded music amplified for troops, he met a comrade who was to be important later in life: Eric Wicks.

Three pencil portraits drawn by another jungle compatriot are among the few images of Roy that exist. Willy and Roy have an eerie resemblance; both had meditative, brooding good looks, defined features and dark, swept-back hair.

On 12 November 1945, discharge certificate number 305103 shows that Roy had served his country for 1498 days, 845 of them overseas. He would never again leave Australia. He had won no medals for gallantry or courage under fire, but he was demobbed with a 1939/45 star, a 'Pacific' star and a 'war medal'.

On his return to Melbourne, he went back to the mills. Music, however, was more important than ever. Late in 1947, an acquaintance who lived two streets away invited Roy around to listen to his Airmaster Radiogram. A modified chiffonier, it boasted a power pack, amplifier, radio tuner and two large turntables. A Royce senior recorder straddled one of the turntables, a high quality pick-up the other. After Roy's third or fourth visit, his new friend said he was bored with the whole set-up. He wanted to buy a Leica camera. Roy offered him £100 – months of wages – for the whole caboodle, and lugged it, piece by piece, to his place. His first recording was of a theatre organ concert broadcast from Adelaide. Others quickly followed. 'I was making records … At home!' was how he expressed his untypical glee. By the early 1950s, he had cut hundreds of 16-inch acetates – mainly of theatre organs and jazz, but also of symphony concerts and recitals. He remained a 'pretty solid' concert-goer, later holding a Gold Card to the Victorian Symphony Orchestra's winter seasons. He had also got over his shyness, becoming friends with some of Melbourne's best jazz musicians and, at last, his heroes: the city's theatre organists.

If the *Torokina Times* was his first stint as an editor, the *Rhythm Review* was his second. A small magazine of the Melbourne Rhythm Society, a jazz club, it detailed the usual news and happenings in a lively scene. Roy copied discs for the society's members and began his own private label – 'Crosbyana' – which duplicated pirate recordings of Bing Crosby that were unavailable commercially.

Riding home one wintry night after a late shift in 1951, sleet in his hair, as he put it to a friend, he'd had enough. With these hours, he'd never get to the concerts he wanted to attend, he reasoned. He turned around his Malvern Star, cycled back to the factory and handed in his resignation.

He knew a lot about the garment business – at least textiles, and making them – so he had a shot at joining the Myer Emporium, Melbourne's biggest and most elegant department store. Rejected, he looked in the mirror and wondered why. Was that a sad face or what? Bother! There was a slope to it, too, he reckoned. You can't confront the public, encourage them to buy goods, with a face like that. He referred himself to a comprehensive treatise on pathology, finding a photograph that looked somewhat like the visage in the mirror. It was thyroid deficiency, he decided, and tests by a GP, his next port of call, confirmed the self-diagnosis. Prescribed thyroxine, which contains the active thyroid hormone, Roy was soon able to smile at will. Myer put him on.

Within months, he'd gone from men's and boys' wear in the basement to men's overcoats on the first floor. But perhaps his attention to detail and his new brimming look got him promoted to the cosmetics department on the ground floor, just inside Myer's tall front doors. Melbourne's nicest and richest women shopped at Myer, and Roy charmed them. Soon, he was in charge of more than a dozen girls, whom he loved, and thirty-three cash registers. He stuck to the task for the rest of his working life.

Recitals by Stanfield Holliday, the 'Featured Organist' at the Capitol Theatre, were often broadcast. How he and Roy met is unknown, but he valued Roy's recordings of his playing. He could not only hear himself perform, but Roy's advice became invaluable. Stan would write to Roy, telling him of an upcoming broadcast, detailing the program and playing times. He nominated the performances he'd most like to hear if Roy was 'running short of time'. He ends one letter, 'Hope you get a good cutting of it'. Another is chatty. 'Mrs Holliday thanks you very much for your kind invitation, but has already made arrangements to see a sick friend in hospital. She is Madam Horowitz, a sister or cousin of the famous pianist (Vladimir Horowitz). She herself was famous in her day, as a pianiste also.'

Bruce Ardley, a teenage pianist then, has become a renowned Wurlitzer exponent. He witnessed some of the post mortems conducted by Roy and Stan on Stan's broadcasts. Bruce worked on Saturday mornings in a relative's shop beside the Capitol and eventually got to meet Holliday, turning his pages. After a broadcast, Stan said there was a bloke in North Fitzroy Bruce should meet. They went out to Roy's. Bruce describes Stan as a 'consummate artist' perhaps a few years older than Roy. But he listened as Roy played back what he had performed just an hour or so before. Reginald Dixon of Blackpool's Tower Ballroom was the benchmark performer then, and Roy would put on Dixon's recordings and explain to Stan how Reg used ornaments and injections of tiny phrases to maintain the music's momentum. He'd compare the Tower's master with other organists, including locals such as Horace Weber, Aubrey Whelan and Charles Tuckwell, father of the great French horn player Barry and the violinist and mannequin Patricia. And Stan Holliday undoubtedly returned to the Capitol with new insights and ideas.

Bruce lived near Roy, and the teenager began dropping in, often to hear a fresh recording or something new in music. He'd ring him at Myer to okay it – Roy and his mother had no phone – then 'get on the two-wheeler' and be around that night. Only Roy and Ruby were ever there. Even slighter and shorter than Roy, she'd have her hair in curlers and a net. She was a paragon of hospitality, bringing out cups of tea and biscuits. Roy was in his early thirties and Bruce was fifteen, a 'fairly impressionable' age, as Bruce puts it. Yet there was never the slightest erotic insinuation in their relationship. Bruce thought Roy had *no* particular sexual preferences. He didn't think he was homosexual, and he never saw Roy with a female friend, even if his salesgirls at Myer adored him.

Bruce cannot remember a single outstanding remark Roy made. He never discussed politics or sport, an Australian craze, but devoted his full attention to you in conversation, especially if you were talking music. 'I think Roy was unable to see beyond music,' he says. At home, 'he probably wouldn't have been marvellous company.'

Roy never spoke about his father or himself, never swore, dressed casually sometimes, but looked the part – often wearing colourful bowties – at Myer. He told neither jokes nor war stories, and lapsed from Methodism. As was fashionable, he smoked, but not excessively, and carried a matchbox into which he'd butt out his cigarettes. Bruce never saw him drink alcohol. In dredging his memory for an outstanding reminiscence, he can remember only one. To save them, several of Melbourne's theatre organs were removed pipe by pipe and rebuilt in other venues. Roy happily worked all night with a gang of enthusiasts on the Capitol's Wurlitzer. Something needed cutting one time, and Roy pulled out of his pocket a razor blade, one edge of it wrapped in brown paper for grip. The opposite edge had been uncovered in his pocket.

★ ★ ★

Engineer Julien Arnold was one of a handful of founding members of the Theatre Organ Society of Australia's Victoria branch. Roy attended a pilot discussion to plan the society's setting-up, but missed the first official meeting in September 1961 because he had to go to a symphony concert. He got along to the second, and never missed one after that. He did much more than pay his dues. When TOSA decided to buy the Capitol organ, which was moved to a suburban cinema ten kilometres distant, he put up his home as security and lent the society the required funds. In the committee's early days, he'd simply empty his pockets of coins and notes. (If one of his Myer girls needed lunch money or a loan, Roy dug it out. His boss once noticed and reprimanded him.) He was for a while TOSA's secretary (honorary, of course) and with speed and accuracy typed its regular newsletter, *VOX*.

Julien has fond memories of pulling out the Capitol's Wurlitzer. Roy would turn up straight from work and change into a boiler suit. The pipes and their connections were tucked away in confined and grimy spaces. A team of usually four enthusiasts began at about 8 p.m. and, one night, Roy left twelve hours later 'as black as the ace of spades' to be at Myer when the doors opened. Julien saw him that morning walking the store's buffed floors, shaven, a bright bowtie blooming, his suit fine and fitting as if bespoke, black shoes polished and hair slicked back with a little dab of Brylcreem.

The Capitol was rebuilt in the Dendy Theatre in suburban Brighton. TOSA was broke, but by the late 1960s it needed to splash the opening with a brief series of concerts by a star attraction. Roy put up $3000 (Australia changed to decimal currency in 1966) required for English organist George Blackmore to play the series.

For nineteen years, Julien edited *VOX*, and for most of them Roy wrote its record reviews. In the November 1961 edition, for instance, Roy wrote – perhaps heretically – that there were 'several minor weak spots' in a Reginald Dixon performance. While Dixon's musicianship was of a 'general high quality' what you didn't hear was 'subtlety, nor do his dynamics ever drop below mezzo-forte'. The Tower's Wurlitzer was 'splendidly recorded, with a most happy acoustic to the sound, the feeling of a large enclosed space'. Emptiness enhanced organ music, he wrote, because this was how it is 'naturally heard', unlike in many American recordings, which were 'more often than not "studio-fied"'.

In the same issue, he assessed Chicago organist Leon Berry at the Hub (Roller) Rink in Chicago playing an instrument in which 'percussions have been removed from the swell boxes'. Perhaps, Roy surmised, the Hub people had heard about 'Reubert Hayes in Brisbane', because the city was 'thick with American servicemen at the time Reubert tried this out'. Berry's rhythms were 'slow and deliberate'. In other reviews, Don Baker offered a 'continually changing kaleidoscope of tonal variety, which is fully caught by the clarity of the recording, and he couples this with considerable animation and a frequently dazzling technique'.[5]

While married to music – a kind of romantic near miss – Roy remained at a listener's distance from art's coalface, its making. Close, and yet so far. Through *VOX* and eventually newspaper reviews, however, he no doubt saw himself communicating, telling others what he knew about the music he loved.

CHAPTER TEN

Bootlegs Kick

'One of the sad stories is that, in collusion with a friend of mine, tapes of Kapell's performances had been kept – illicitly I may add – and these were of high quality done on big EMI recorders … [All were] wiped by the engineers of the Post Office.'

Clifford Hocking in a letter to American music writer, Joe Salerno

'People just don't give me extra money because things go well.'

Blues guitarist Stevie Ray Vaughan to Clifford Hocking

I HAD LEARNED from several sources that well-known Melbourne entrepreneur Clifford Hocking had met both Willy and Roy. Moreover, Cliff had understood the value of Roy's acetate disc of William Kapell's most important performance.

Cliff Hocking died in 2006 but his business partner, David Vigo, a younger man, was presumably still about. Some sources suggested that he continued to run the firm Hocking and Vigo and bring out acts to the antipodes. He might, I thought, be able to fill me in on Cliff's role in the story of Willy and Roy.

Vigo's profile was virtually invisible. I looked for a website to no avail and tried a couple of telephone numbers. They rang out or got me to leave messages that provoked no responses.

My wife and I were dining one night in a small restaurant in a remote mountain valley pretty much as far from Melbourne as you can go without leaving the state of Victoria. The owner-chef and his wife, whom we knew, joined us after I'd paid the bill. We talked about all this and that, and à propos of nothing, the chef said he and his wife had recently made friends with a local couple. He was a music promoter, and they'd taken a skiing holiday together. He mumbled the name. My ears flapped. I got him to repeat it. Not David Vigo? Yes, that's the bloke, he said. He'd brought out all kinds of stars to Australia over the years and lived in a nearby village. When I'd caught my breath, I said I'd been chasing him for months. Really, said the chef, who rang

Vigo immediately, even though it was after 10 p.m. He passed me the phone.

I told him about the Kapell project – that I wanted to nail Cliff's part in a mystery. Cliff knew all about Willy, he said – even decades after his death, he used to rave about him. David had a vague idea what had happened, but he was still going through many of Cliff's 'boxes'. They might hold relevant papers. Others were already being archived at the Performing Arts Museum. He'd be happy to help.

We met him and his wife, Kitty, over coffee at his house the next day, the first of several meetings, phone calls and exchanges of emails.

★ ★ ★

In the 1950s, less than half a mile separated Myer's lipstick counters and Thomas' record store, where Clifford Hocking sold vinyls. Pronounced 'Thomas's' – with the terminating possessive 's', but always written without it – the store billed itself 'Australia's leading record shop'. Occupying a small corner of Melbourne's central city grid, it probably was.

In the 1950s, the shop had grown out of a 'piano, organ, phonograph and musical warehouse' set up by Donald McBeath, an Australian violinist who had toured the world with the famed Irish tenor John McCormack, whose voice wept. In 1921, McBeath married Eleanor Thomas, and a son, Kevin, was born to the couple in 1924. By the mid-1950s, Kevin had left school and completed a suite of occupations – messenger boy at a classical music radio station, backstage hand in a Melbourne theatre and announcer and producer for BBC radio in London. But he needed a new challenge and decided to develop the family business into Thomas', a specialist retailer of recorded sound.

Eight years younger than McBeath, Clifford Hocking had grown up in a similar, lower-bourgeois environment. He, too, had left school early to take up clerking, first for the State of Victoria's electricity commission, then the ABC, where he found his colleagues a great deal more interesting. Like McBeath, he had studied music. An ornate London College of Music testimonial decorated with two Grecian nymphs strumming a lyre and playing a violin is dated December 1949. It certifies that seventeen-year-old Clifford Henry Hocking has gained honours in 'pianoforte playing elementary section'. He is the pupil of 'Mr E. Truswell', it says.[1]

Hocking's father Fred had fought in World War I, a veteran of the failed Gallipoli campaign, which has become a trope for Australian courage under fire. He brokered bakeries, and married Olive. The couple had five sons, Clifford the youngest. When Clifford was twelve, Fred's business partner told him about a friend who pursued what Cliff imagined was the perfect profession. His name was Archie Longden, and although he was an Australian, his home was in the south of France. David Vigo believes that Longden might have been distantly related to Hocking. At any rate, Longden arranged tours of his home country for unspecified European musicians. For Cliff, this seemed Utopia. He was even more impressed when he learned that Longden travelled everywhere by taxi. The impresario appeared to lead 'just the most wonderful life', as Hocking once put it.

But there were neither appropriate qualifications to obtain, nor a beaten path to tread, that would lead towards the career of concert promoter, and by 1954, Cliff had become an ABC publications manager. It was also the year he first went overseas. With a couple besotted by classical music, he visited Britain, Italy, Germany, Lebanon and India. Later in life he said it had opened his ears and eyes.

Full of ideas, he returned to an 'actually rather small' Melbourne, as he described it, and joined McBeath as a shareholder in Thomas'. The pair accelerated the store's fame and profits, making it Melbourne's top record shop. McBeath was especially interested in serious contemporary music, and Hocking loved the classics, in particular, piano repertoire. According to Vigo, Cliff 'fancied himself as someone who knew about piano players'. A record would turn and Hocking would say, 'Oh, that's Byron Janis' or 'That's Emil Gilels.' Hocking and McBeath hired David Hills, who was a jazz buff, and when a potential buyer came through Thomas' front door all bases were covered. One of them would sound out him or her, introducing the customer to the best person to handle the inquiry, and a sale would usually result. McBeath, Hocking and Hills – they were supported by other sales assistants – would show the shopper into a booth, regale him or her with headphones and lower a needle onto a track. A weekly ABC radio program McBeath and Hocking presented also promoted Thomas'. They played any and every kind of music, enhancing sales. 'They broadcast … Indian, Japanese, classical, Ol' Blue Eyes, the whole bloody lot,' as Vigo put it.

By 1961, the McBeath family wanted to make changes at the record store. Hocking didn't like them, and he decided at last to follow Longden's footsteps. He sold his shareholding back to the firm and headed overseas. In particular, he envisaged bringing to Australia the best players of Indian classical music, and he began by tracking down the distributors of their recordings. He found

Sharan Rani and Chatur Lal, who were esteemed players of the sarod and tabla, a heavy stringed instrument and hand-beaten drums. Less than a year after leaving Thomas', he had organised and managed his first tour. He also quickly gained a business partner, Rod Timmins, scion of a wealthy Melbourne Jewish family.[2] Rod was a cellist who had never worked much, and his mother was only too happy to see him occupied for gain.

In London, Cliff had several drinks one night with a young Australian actor and satirist who was at the end of a West End run of the musical *Oliver!* Barry Humphries had only a small comic role as an undertaker, but after long discussions, Hocking felt that he had the potential to perform a one-man show back in his home town of Melbourne. Humphries was, in those days, a heavy drinker who was not the easiest person to organise. But Hocking got him back from May to September of 1962 to perform in two small halls, the Melba, which is on the University of Melbourne's main campus, and the Assembly, adjoining a church in the central business district. (He also played a season in Sydney.)

Humphries and Hocking called the show *A Nice Night's Entertainment*, a typically Methodist title for a Melbourne welded to conservatism, and Humphries introduced the audiences to Edna Everage, a modest Melbourne suburban housewife. (She had had a few less significant outings already.) During the first show, Rod Timmins sat in a small back room behind the Assembly Hall's stage, as David Vigo puts it, 'wearing a green eyeshade and counting the money'. The enterprise grew pleasingly, and in February 1965 Vigo joined Hocking and Timmins.

Interested in books and music, Vigo had left school to become a survey draughtsman. Because career opportunities were few, he moved to selling books, laboured in landscape gardening, then landed a job at Monash University library. To become a full-fledged librarian, he was told, he would need qualifications. The idea of studying subjects 'as boring as batshit' dissuaded him from sticking around literature. He had first met Hocking at Thomas', where he had gone to buy a jazz disc with birthday money. They had stayed in touch, and when Hocking confessed one day that he needed an assistant, Vigo jumped at the chance. He, Hocking and Timmins – and usually at least one other person, whether he be a 'Russian guy, an art teacher, Paco Peña, or a bloke who came and went' – shared a big house in Richmond. The office was David Vigo's bedroom because there was space in it for a filing cabinet. On what Vigo calls a 'fearfully hot' day in 1969, Timmins died of a heart attack. Hocking and Vigo worked on to establish a unique and profitable business.[3]

Assembling a jigsaw of clues, Vigo and I confirmed the strong possibility that Roy met Cliff at Thomas'. Again, there are no notes. But Roy was addicted to music and bought hundreds upon hundreds of records. And Thomas' was arguably the best place in town to buy them. The temptation to reconstruct their meeting – based on what later transpired – was enticing. I succumbed to it.

★ ★ ★

Roy Preston has skittered up Bourke Street hill to Thomas'. It's just after noon, and preparations for the 1956 Melbourne Olympics are all over the newspapers. He's told the sales girls he'll be back in thirty minutes. Some lunch-break browsing for records. He can't think of anything better.

He smiles, his glance taking in Thomas' ceiling, tiled with signed publicity portraits. Tom Lehrer. Bit too clever for him. Victoria de los Angeles. He'd go to one of her concerts. How did they scribble such big signatures?

'Can I help you?' says Cliff Hocking.

'Just browsing, thanks,' says Roy, smiling.

'Any particular interests?'

'Theatre organs …'

Cliff drags on his sculpted chin, a kind of prow to his acorn face and its bonnet of black hair.

'Anything else?'

'Well, I do go to all the concerts. Symphonies. Recitals.'

Cliff waves an arm at Thomas' walls. From floor to ceiling they're lined with shelves of records. Covers stare from many. 'Plenty of that here,' he says. 'Any particular music … musician?'

No, says Roy, but they begin chatting about the ABC and its concerts. Cliff says that while we, here in Australia, are fortunate to get some of the world's best classical performers, many types of music are never heard. *Their* people never tour. Indian classical, for instance. Has Roy heard it? No, he says. Wonderful stuff, Cliff tells him.

'But we *do* get some amazing talent, you're right about that,' says Roy.

'Who's impressed you lately? We might have some of their discs.'

Roy adjusts the Windsor knot of his paisley tie. 'I actually cut my own records at home.'

Cliff's eyebrows arch.

'On a Royce traverser. Onto acetates. Off the radio.'

'Oh,' says Cliff. 'Perhaps you don't need Thomas' then.'

Roy stares at Cliff. 'No, no. I buy lots of LPs as well … *And* make my own.'

'Who've you recorded?'

'Just about everyone. Off the radio. Theatre organists. Jazz. ABC concerts. Recitals.'

'Who've you got?'

'Well, one that comes to mind is that poor chap Kapell, you know, who was killed in an air crash?'

Cliff Hocking's eyebrows rocket up, knocking askew Tom Lehrer's spectacles.

'Kapell?'

'Yes, William Kapell. You know, the young New York bloke who was killed going home. Plane crash.'

Cliff shakes his head. 'I loved the guy. His playing was magic.' He pauses. 'I met him once.'

'Really!' says Roy.

'Yeah, I used to work at the ABC. I knew the woman who looks after visiting artists, Bonnie.'

'Well, I never.'

'Yes, I met him after a concert at the Town Hall. Bonnie took me backstage. I was twenty-one, and we shook hands, and he says, "Pleased to meet you." And then he says, "Did you like the concert?" And I said how *marvellous* it was, how much I loved his playing, and he got out of a satchel, there and then, a publicity photograph. Signed it on the spot for me. Bill.'

They're both smiling now. Cliff nods at the shelves, tells Roy that Kapell recordings are few and far between. He might have one or two.

'I recorded his last concert,' says Roy.

Someone in Thomas' jazz section fumbles a 12-inch long-play. A stack of Louis Armstrong covers crashes from its shelf, horns glinting, brows sweating, white kerchiefs aflourish. Lips puckered.

'The last he ever gave?'

Roy nods.

'Here in Melbourne.'

'No, it was in Geelong.'

'You recorded it in Geelong?'

'No. I recorded it here. At home in Fitzroy. The *concert* was in Geelong.'

'The last one?'

'Yes. Chopin's *Funeral March* sonata. That's what 3AR broadcast.'

'The last time he ever played in public?'

'That's right.'

'It's historic.'

'I suppose so.'

Cliff hunches his shoulders, tilts his head sideways. 'What's the quality like?'

'Well, I take a lot of trouble. With the counterweight and so on. If you get the weight right, the recording's good.'

'What are you doing with it?'

Roy shrugs. There's a long silence. David Hills is restoring Satchmo to his shelf.

'What do you mean *doing*?'

'I think you should get it copied. So there's more than one. Just in case.'

Roy glances at the ceiling, consults Victoria de los Angeles on the idea. She thinks it's a good one. An indispensable one, really.

'That's a *good* idea,' he tells Cliff.

'I know someone who could do it. Not to sell or anything. Just to have more than one copy. For safety's sake.'

'Yes. For safety's sake.'

'What's your name?'

'Roy Preston.'

'Hang on, I'll get some details.'

Cliff leaves Roy to get a used docket and a biro.

★ ★ ★

What Cliff didn't tell Roy was that he had already recorded Kapell. In a 1976 letter to American music writer Joe Salerno, Hocking revealed that 'in collusion with a friend of mine, tapes of Kapell's concert performances had been kept (illicitly, I may add) and these were of high quality done on big EMI recorders'. Hocking's friend worked for the broadcaster's 'Recorded Transcription' department. After the secret tapes were made, she was posted elsewhere in the ABC. On her return to the transcription service, Hocking continued, 'all the Kapell tapes had been wiped by the engineers of the Post Office'. In 1953, he explained, the government's postal bureaucracy was in charge of supplying outside lines for ABC broadcasts.

In the letter, Hocking revealed how hard he had fallen for Willy's playing. The feud with Sydney critic Lindsey Browne was 'the pygmy attacking the giant – perhaps he found the passion of Kapell's playing threatening!' Two paragraphs later, he wrote, 'Kapell used to come [into] the ABC studios and play and, with another Kapell crazed fan, I used to listen through the glass of the broadcasting booth as [he] rehearsed Schubert, Chopin and Debussy.' During his concerto performances, 'one could feel the control move swiftly from the [conductor's] podium to the piano stool'.

Exactly when it occurred is unknown, but Hocking was quick to copy Roy's acetate of Willy's last show. In view of later events, it may also be presumed that he copied recordings of two other works Roy had etched of Willy's Melbourne performances – Mussorgsky's *Pictures at an Exhibition* and Rachmaninoff's third concerto. He told Salerno that 'we' – presumably he and Roy – had the 'Chopin processed and about 35 copies were pressed'.

Cliff would have gone to someone like Bill Armstrong at Armstrong Studios to execute what was a routine procedure. Armstrong cannot remember if he did or didn't do the work, but Roy's acetate (or acetates) would have been placed on a transcription turntable connected to a Byer tape recorder running 'full track' at fifteen inches per second. (Armstrong says Max Byer's Melbourne-manufactured machines were the best going then.) From the tape, a master disc would have been cut. While several other studios would have made the master if he hadn't, says Armstrong, W&G – a branch of a local precision engineering firm called White & Gillespie – would have pressed the copies. Where they are is anyone's guess.

Before travelling to New York in July 1971, Hocking made out a brief inventory headed 'List taken by C. H. on trip 3/7/1971'. Down the page is the reference, 'Gregor Benko, Vice President, International Piano library, 215 West 91st Street, N. Y. 10024'.

Gregor Benko and Albert Petrak founded the International Piano Library in Cleveland in 1964, a year before Vigo joined Hocking. Like Hocking, Benko had worked in a record store but was only twenty-two when he and the like-minded Petrak established their not-for-profit organisation. Its key aim was to archive material relating to classical piano music – to answer the following question. Who are the major performers? What is the music? Are there unknown recordings of great pianists of earlier years? Are there unrecognised composers? A year after setting it up, Benko took the institution to New York City and became its managing director – for twenty years. In New York, he was required by law to change the name to the International Piano Archives, and within a few years IPA had established a world-renowned collection. It was lauded for its policy of sharing what was uncovered. Benko was collector, musicologist, author, concert presenter, reviewer and record producer. Later, IPA was to have a bias towards Romantic music.

The cost of husbanding IPA's collections was always far greater than any earnings, and in 1978 Benko donated the complete archive to the University of Maryland just outside Washington DC, where it remains today. IPAM (IPA at Maryland) gratefully accepted what it calls Benko's 'audio treasure'. It also notes Benko's acclaimed diligence '*in releasing reissues of historic piano performances*'. (Author's italics.)

Hocking's 1972 diary notes show that he arrived in New York on 22 September for Cleo Laine and John Dankworth's debut at Alice Tully Hall, which Cliff felt wasn't grand enough for them. Three days later he contacted numerous people, including 'accountants and solicitors' for Rosalyn Tureck, the American Bach pianist.[4]

Following the reference to Tureck's connections in Hocking's diary comes a single entry 'International Piano Library'. In his letter to Salerno just four years later, Hocking wrote that he had 'delivered some years ago' to Benko a 'sonically atrocious' recording of William Kapell playing Rachmaninoff's third concerto and

Chopin's *Funeral March* sonata. For Vigo, 'some years ago' could easily have meant 'say, four years ago'.

We can do no more than speculate about what Clifford Hocking had in mind for Roy's recordings. Vigo says that Hocking knew well Australian recording executives and might have handed them over to a company such as EMI had he desired their commercial release. Indeed, Hocking and Vigo made several commercial discs of Cleo Laine and John Dankworth performing in Melbourne Town Hall. Perhaps Roy Preston had not wanted their release to record buyers, and he and Hocking had decided that they would be best preserved.

Benko lives in upstate New York and declined my invitation to meet. He was brief on the telephone, suggesting that I email him with the questions I wanted answered. He said he could remember little about his dealings with Hocking. Cliff visited him at least twice at the IPL/IPA office, which was his apartment on 91st Street. Original acetates were handed over, as far as he could recall, and IPA used, first, the Rachmaninoff third concerto as a 'membership premium LP'. It was given as a bonus to those who paid an annual fee of $10 (later raised to $15). Benko had no idea just how many new members the offer would have attracted. But more joined for the Kapell recording than those who signed up for Australian pianist Percy Grainger's disc of the Grieg concerto. In his email responses, Benko said that Anna Lou 'graciously allowed us to issue this material' without payment. Percy Grainger's widow, Walter Gieseking's daughters and Josef Hofmann's sons had acted similarly with other releases.

The Chopin sonata, by contrast, was later put out on an OPUS RECORDS – IPA's label – twelve-inch LP. Century Records of

Springbrook Road, Saugus, a small community forty miles north of Los Angeles, struck sixty-five examples of a 'test pressing' of the Chopin in March 1977, coupling it with Roy's cutting of Willy's *Pictures* rendition. It is a reasonable assumption that OPUS released the disc soon after. A rectangular green label on a brown sleeve announces 'WILLIAM KAPELL' and on a line underneath, 'FROM HIS LAST RECITALS'. 'OPUS 83' is in the bottom right-hand corner.

Benko said that IPA 'existed continually on the edge of extinction, with almost no money to support existence and collection and publication'. He made commercial decisions according to the circumstances of each recording, he said, trying 'to do what I thought was the right thing'. Saving and publishing important recordings such as the Kapell acetates was his policy. And he would have returned the acetates if Cliff had wanted them back, he told me.

* * *

Take off his steel-rimmed glasses, wrap Maurice Austin in a tunic and cowl and he could walk on to a film set as a medieval monk. His eyebrows pale to invisibility, and a monastic crown of straight blond hair rings his baldness. His gaze is direct, a faint smile at times turning up the corners of his lips. Although much younger than Roy, he was his friend. In the last years of Roy's life, he was also his carer.

He was born in Hobart in the 1940s but grew up in Melbourne, one of several children of former motor mechanic Jack, who had become a Baptist minister. He made crystal sets and single-valve radios as a teenager, loved photography and was captivated by music, especially the sound of pipe organs.[5] School didn't suit him – he couldn't 'come to grips with' mathematics. His father had friends in the printing industry – churches provided a lot of work for printers in those days – and Maurice left secondary studies to become a trainee compositor, setting type by hand. As the industry changed, he operated linotype machines, which produced lines of type from pots of molten lead-alloy, then learned to cut and paste copy for 'offset' printers. At the end of his career he was, by his own account, pretty handy with a Mac computer. An 'unashamed left-winger', he has never drunk alcohol.

The aisle seat next to him was vacant at a theatre-organ concert at the Dendy in about 1988. An elderly TOSA member – perhaps in his seventies – took it. Roy and Maurice became immediate friends. Maurice thought Roy was a 'personable, friendly bloke', the sort of character who would sit next to anyone who appeared to be new to the society. He was also astounded that Roy could name the stops an organist was using.

Roy had given up driving, he explained, and he had trouble getting to TOSA events because most of them were in theatres and town halls miles from where he lived. He was, he explained, about to take public transport home. They lived on the same side of town, said Maurice, Roy's inner-suburban cottage on a convenient axis with Maurice's outer-suburban home. He offered to pick up Roy and take him back to North Fitzroy after meetings. Roy loved the idea.

Maurice was rewarded each trip with four or five of Roy's sixteen-inch acetates. At that stage, Maurice had no idea how many discs Roy had recorded, just that his friend worried about what would happen to them. He supposed, he told Maurice, that they would 'end up down the tip'. Maurice replied, 'Over my dead body.'

Maurice well recalls a particular wintry night he picked up Roy. As usual, Roy was huddling under a tent of weak lamplight at the end of his street. Maurice couldn't be sure, but Roy was probably wearing a calf-length grey gabardine raincoat, collar turned up against the chill. He's holding acetates for Maurice, and gets in the Subaru's front passenger seat.

Even before they're in Michael Street, Roy shows Maurice a CD. He waggles it, bouncing streetlights off the cover into Maurice's eyes.

'You'll never guess what I found in Batman's,' says Roy.

'No idea,' says Maurice. 'But you're shining it in my eyes.'

'One of my recordings. Sorry.'

'What d'you mean, one of *your* recordings.'

Roy places the CD on the acetates in his lap.

'You never made CDs,' says Maurice. 'Only acetates.' He smiles at Roy.

'One of *my* recordings,' insists Roy.

'What's it of?'

'William Kapell, the American pianist. You know, the bloke who died in a plane crash. He'd just played the *Funeral March* sonata.'

'Gee, that's years ago.' Maurice points at the CD. 'How'd your recording get on there?'

'It's off an acetate.'

'Yeah, I know. But that's a CD.' He stabs at the discs. 'How'd it get from being an *acetate* to being a *CD*?'

'I gave it to a bloke.'

'Which bloke?'

'I can't remember his name. It was a long time ago. The entrepreneur bloke. You know. Cliff ... Cliff ...'

'I don't know any Cliff.'

Maurice shrugs. Silence.

'I'm quite pleased about it. Wonderful, isn't it?' says Roy. 'My recording. For the whole world to listen to.'

★ ★ ★

When they reached their destination – a town hall with a Wurlitzer – Maurice took a closer look at the CD. It was called *William Kapell Plays Chopin*. Sonatas two and three follow a dance-hall of *mazurkas*. In parenthesis on the back cover under the *Funeral March* timings is a footnote. The record came from an ABC broadcast of Kapell's last recital, it says. It continues, 'Recorded on acetate, the sonata was not transferred to tape until many years later. Extensive restoration has not eliminated all the defects of the acetate recording, however it has made it possible to perceive the musical qualities of this historic performance, and for that reason it is being issued here along with studio recordings.'

The CD's total playing time is over seventy-three minutes, and it was made and distributed by BMG Music (Bertelsmann Music Group Entertainment) in New York. The copyright date is 1987, and BMG owned and distributed the RCA Victor label, the company for which Kapell recorded, which is also mentioned on the back.

It is quite possible that Anna Lou herself alerted BMG to the existence of Roy's recordings of the Geelong Chopin. Gregor Benko had, after all, told her about it. And many other people – especially IPA subscribers – by now knew about the performance and might have contacted the record company. In an email, Benko told me he didn't know how BMG acquired the recording. It is unclear exactly when Cliff heard that Roy's cuts had been released commercially.[6] But it annoyed him.

Irrespective of who owned its transcription, the Geelong Chopin is arguably Willy's most important performance. It is the supreme testament of his late playing, epitomising his art. When Jerome Lowenthal wrote in *Clavier* magazine of being a Kapell student, he said he had also detected what he called a 'discernible shift in [the pianist's] musical thinking' over the years. Two years after first playing the *Funeral March* sonata for Willy, Lowenthal brought it to him again. He tried to play it the way Willy had told him it should go. This time, Kapell's reaction was harsh – almost angry, Lowenthal reported. Willy said, 'Actually I used to play it that way, but I think now that I was wrong.' Following Chopin's instruction *'agitato'*, Willy wrote 'and *dolente*'. Agitated but sorrowful.

Lowenthal wrote in *Clavier* that, on the evidence of his 'last recorded performances … his playing was undergoing an inner metamorphosis. Nothing had been lost – the celebrated drive and brilliance were undiminished, the lyrical passages were still molded by a beautifully controlled *cantabile* (singingness), and the overall pianism was still masterful and punctilious – but everything seemed now to go deeper into the soul and further towards the limits of expression. Kapell was fully aware of this, and his awareness made the situation in Australia doubly ironic and doubly painful.'

On tour in Australia two decades after the disaster, Raymond Lewenthal also heard tapes of the Geelong Chopin and Rachmaninoff's third concerto. He wrote that 'I can't imagine that there has *ever* been greater piano playing than this.' It was note perfect but also warm, poetic and controlled, the harvest of a 'colossal temperament and complete integrity'. In remembrance of Willy, Lewenthal played the *Funeral March* sonata on the same stages and in the same halls as his more esteemed countryman. The feeling had been eerie, he said.

★ ★ ★

Kenosis – from the Greek verb to empty – has several religious definitions. One is a description of Jesus's relinquishment of divinity to become a man, to interact totally with other men, to force their acceptance and understanding of him and, finally, to suffer and die on their behalf. At its base is the idea that to empty oneself to achieve the miraculous requires total sacrifice. Willy's artistic kenosis in Geelong was complete, radical. Lowenthal was right. The pianist had managed in those last concerts, if we are to measure them by the Chopin recording, to renounce his artistic otherworldliness and come down to earth to perform in a way that encaptured anyone who listened. In this case, the ears of the audience belonged to Australians, and whether or not they appreciated what they heard was not Willy's concern. Baring his musical soul might summarise what happened but fails to capture the dignity with which he did it, the Herculean effort he had invested in producing the sounds he made, their transcendence. But that is what he did, and we shall never know precisely why.

In his letter to his friend Shirley Rhoads early in the tour, he said, 'It seems to me that on the highest levels of achievement … there is inherent … a kind of agony that results from the inability to cope successfully with the material.'

As in any martyrdom, Willy had suffered knowingly. Achieving the best you can possibly do, reaching the limits of your capabilities then putting a shoulder to them – to see if they'll give – defines agony, which might be seen in this case as a conflict between great art and an attempt to perform it as the player believes it deserves to be performed. Willy endured it.

CHAPTER ELEVEN

Lost Litigation

'You fly [with radio aids to aerial navigation] across the oceans, across the mountains, across the polar regions, across the continents, in times of storm, fog, cloudiness, extremes of heat and cold, wet and dry, and they work. That is all, they work. And airline crews and passengers alike depend upon them, fly by them, live by them; and, if there is any evidence that they ever die by them, the Court hasn't heard it in this case.'

Judge Willis Ritter, directing **non obstante veredicto** *(notwithstanding the jury's verdict) in 1963 that BCPA (trading as Qantas) was liable for damages*

'We reverse both the granting of judgement n.o.v. and the conditional granting of a new trial, thus reinstating the jury's verdict in favour of defendants and setting aside the judgement entered upon the second jury's determination of damages ...'

United States Court of Appeals, 1965

KAPELL'S KIN LOSE $924,396 AWARD

New York Times *heading, 6 June 1965*

LESS THAN A year after the calamity that had claimed Willy's life, the pianist's executors filed a claim in the American Federal District Court in San Francisco for $750,000 (£335,000) damages against Qantas, BCPA's 'successor'. They alleged that the airline had demonstrated a 'disregard of known safety standards'.

In fact, the Kapell estate also pursued actions in the Supreme Court of New South Wales and the Supreme Court of the State of New York. A 1956 article in the *Age* says that Qantas, which took over BCPA's assets two years earlier, had 'fought service of the summons'. (Writs for damages delayed BCPA's formal liquidation until 1967.) T. Roland Berner, a solicitor and executor of the Kapell estate, said that Willy was making about $100,000 a year in 1953, and the amount to be claimed would be based on his potential income had he lived. By 1959, Berner had decided on a figure – just over $7 million – and because of legal technicalities the Federal District Court had taken over the entire action. The Sydney *Sun Herald* reported that several damages cases arising from the disaster had been settled before going to court. It claimed that the Kapell side had declined a Qantas offer to settle out-of-court for $82,000 – a paltry sum, bearing in mind Willy's earning capacity.

Like many American legal sagas, Anna Lou's struggle to win compensation for the death of her husband was a legal rollercoaster that soared and dipped over many years. Lawyers began arguing the case in March 1961, and a final ruling on costs was made in June

1966. For a while, the estate of William Kapell was represented by Melvin Belli, the brilliant Californian counsel who dropped the brief to represent Jack Ruby.[1]

But I wanted to look beyond sketchy news clippings, presuming that transcripts of the proceedings would be fairly easy to find. I tracked down a couple of relevant judgements, which had been published online, but what was said in court was nowhere to be seen. I called across the Pacific. District court officials were unfailingly courteous and helpful. But they didn't have transcripts of cases heard so long ago. I would have to try America's National Archives. Here, too, the engagement of those who fielded my calls was earnest and polite. But there was no guarantee, said Tricia of the archives, that I would find every word of the hearings. They were so long ago. She would get up the boxes, which were in storage off Manhattan, she said. I made appointments to look at what they contained late in 2011.

Three big cartons on a trolley confronted me when I settled into a chair on the archives' twelfth-floor offices in Varick Street. I'd be exaggerating if I said you could write 'Kapell' with a fingertip in the dust that had gathered on them. But they looked as if they hadn't been opened for a very long time.

Inside, I found treasure. Tied up with string and thin ribbon appeared to be every word spoken during Anna Lou's efforts to win compensation. The bindings had cut grooves into thousands of pages of legal folios that had been typed, in many cases, on what appeared to be tracing paper. And when I undid the knots, it seemed as if I was the first person to have touched them since they'd been tied. Over three days I sharpened many of the archives' pencils and filled copious sheets of its sulphur-coloured notepaper.

★ ★ ★

At the first trial, the judge was Willis Ritter,[2] who had recently and successfully navigated America's legal estuaries on behalf of the wife of Janos Feher, a Sydney watchmaker who also died in the *Resolution* crash. An influential jurist, he made brave − some said controversial − decisions, and liked to drink and carouse. The *Herald* in Melbourne had reported the day after the crash that Mr Feher was en route to America with his seven-year-old son John. They were to seek treatment to save the boy's paralysed arm. A jury in California had decided against compensation, but Ritter set the verdict aside. In a second trial, Mrs Feher was awarded $35,000, and in a parallel proceeding, another appellant from the BCPA accident who had been initially rebuffed was awarded the Warsaw Convention limit of $8300.

The convention's decree was crucial to the hearings. Invoked in 1929 after thirty-one aviation law experts had hammered out what they believed was just compensation for death by airline, the convention settled on a figure of $8300, expressed originally as 125,000 French francs. Many nations, including the United States, ratified the edict. The relatively low compensation figure was struck to avoid hampering the growth of a fledgling industry − air travel. (The convention has since been superseded.) Appellants could succeed in a claim for higher amounts only if it could be proven that an accident was caused by an airline's 'wilful misconduct'. (Article 25 spelled out that an air carrier could not 'avail himself' of the provisions of the convention 'if the damage is caused by his [sic] wilful misconduct'.)

So over the thirteen days in which the first Kapell trial was argued, much of the evidence attempted to prove or reject the notion that the BCPA crew had shown 'wilful misconduct' in its approach to San Francisco airport. It was a crucial toss to debate, the focus of Belli's case on behalf of the plaintiffs, and ultimately the hinge on which the irascible Judge Ritter swung open the door to compensation.

Representing Anna Lou and her children, Belli[3] was as flamboyant as Ritter. Born in the Californian gold rush town of Sonora, he became known either as the 'King of Torts' (civil wrongs) or 'Melvin Bellicose'. Though he was constant in the pursuit of justice, he was less than steadfast about marriage, having six wives, five of whom he divorced. Among many of his celebrity clients were Zsa Zsa Gabor, Errol Flynn, Chuck Berry, Muhammad Ali and the Rolling Stones. One source claims that he won more than $600 million for litigants over his lifetime. He made important contributions to consumer-rights law, and pioneered the use in court of graphs, charts, photographs, films and expert witnesses. When he won a case, he reportedly flew a pirate's flag, the Jolly Roger, above his offices in Montgomery Street, San Francisco, and fired a cannon from the rooftop. He wrote many books – including the definitive text *Modern Damages* in six volumes – and appeared in several films and television programs, not always as himself. (He fancied himself as an actor, and once appeared in a *Star Trek* episode.) As a thespian, however, he was a better barrister.

He opened the Kapell case guns blazing. 'The first sentence to you in our proof of this lawsuit is that we shall show you that this BCPA airline, whose plane our plaintiff was in, our deceased was in, had violated the landing instructions, landing orders, and had violated its own prescribed landing orders and landing pattern and was so violating them at the time of the accident'. The evidence would show that Kapell was 'one of the three greatest pianists in the world at the time of his death – and then a young man – and we will also show that Mr Kapell was developing tremendously; he was more of an artist-pianist'. He was going to lay over in Honolulu 'for a couple of days' rest. But the violinist Jascha Heifetz had asked him to come to Los Angeles to do a couple of records with him, and that is the reason he took this airplane instead of laying over in Honolulu.' Well-known musicians would give evidence about Kapell's qualities, and Judge Ritter would instruct the jury on the 'narrow issues of this case'. Then Belli asked jurors to 'fasten your seat belts and relax, and see if I cannot give you something of what happened in the early morning, 8.30 or thereabouts, on October 29, Thursday, 1953'.

He asserted that the 'ground facilities … upon which airplanes … must rely for safety … were in good and perfect operating condition'. He would put on the witness stand 'a Mr Jacobs', a safety officer for another airline, who would tell you he had seen BCPA aircraft come in to San Francisco airport low over his house. 'We will show that [*Resolution*] … was attempting … to sneak in low in a way that he shouldn't have attempted to come in on that morning'. The complainant's legal team had worked out an amount of compensation based on Kapell's potential earnings and expected lifespan, and the 'considerable sum of money that we are praying for … [is] $3,150,000 for the death of William Kapell, one of the world's greatest pianists, along with Rubinstein and Horowitz'.

On the key point of whether Bruce Dickson took a shortcut – and therefore thought he knew where he was – or whether he was simply lost, Qantas's defence stated in its opening remarks that 'it is our contention that he was conducting an approach; had been led

astray; was in the midst of his approach and crashed into the hills …
[We] say that this pilot did not deliberately let down into a fog in
the mountainous areas'.

In quick succession, Belli produced his musician witnesses.
Some took the stand; others had provided depositions outside court,
including José Iturbi. He said Willy had reminded him that they
met when Kapell was a child, and that Iturbi had presented him
with an award. 'As a matter of fact, I think it was a turkey and
it was when he was about nine years old in New York. He was
already outstanding.' Kapell, said Iturbi, was 'more than excellent'.
There were excellent pianists and magnificent pianists, but there
sometimes arrived 'the touch of a sort of magic'. Kapell hadn't
reached the peak of his career, was still very young. Pianists didn't
retire, he told the court. 'The general public, they retire us.' He
had seen Paderewski play at about seventy-eight, and had recently
attended a Rubinstein concert. The pianist was seventy.

Edith Kapell told jurors about her son as a boy. She had got him
early piano lessons, but after a while 'we couldn't hold him back.
We weren't too interested in making a career out of a child prodigy,
but at ten we couldn't hold him back, so we started him, and he
went like – they called it like Jack and the beanstalk. After three
months he overran children that were studying five years.'

The peerless Jascha Heifetz said he had chosen Kapell from 'quite
a selection' of pianists to accompany him in recordings of the three
Brahms violin sonatas. They had put down one, and were supposed
to be recording the other two in California. 'I was waiting for
the arrival …' Pianist Rudolf Serkin, almost twenty years Willy's
senior, said Kapell had asked to play for him. He ended up learning
as much as he could have taught him. He had heard most of the

young pianists, and Willy 'was for me the greatest of the talents I had ever encountered'. Belli asked Serkin if Kapell had reached his peak. He played magnificently, replied the witness, but he was 'so expanding, expanding his gifts, developing his gifts, that I believe he would have gone on in many new fields which he hardly had touched in music'. Belli excused the witness and, as he was stepping down, said to him, 'That wasn't so bad, was it, sir?' Serkin replied that he wished his examination could have gone on longer because 'I loved [Willy] and admired him.'

Frederick H. Jacobs told jurors that he had been with United Airlines for thirty years. He had been a flight engineer for almost the past twenty years. He had also been an air safety instructor who had made about 750 approaches to San Francisco airport. The correct procedure was to come in over the outer marker at the base of the San Mateo bridge and make a clockwise turn before lining up the runway. But he had seen several aircraft of two airlines come in low over his house, which was to the south of the usual route. Belli asked him which companies owned the aircraft. 'British Commonwealth Pacific and Philippine Airlines,' he replied. He could read their names and even lettering on the fuselages. In his opinion, they were flying too low. How low? asked Belli. Jacobs judged that if he could read twelve-inch lettering on the sides of the aircraft their altitude was about 600 feet. Hills nearby were 400 feet high, so the BCPA and Philippines planes were 'cutting in too close'. From June 1953 until the accident four months later he saw each week several of the companies' aircraft flying low approaches. Sometimes the wheels were up, sometimes they were down or beginning to emerge. Belli asked Jacobs if United would ever try to land in a similar way. 'Never have,' he said.

Van Cliburn told the court that when he was studying the piano he had as his 'wonderful young symbol Mr William Kapell'. He was of such standing in the small towns of America that in some of them 'the local restaurants that had jukeboxes even took portions of the very famous [Rachmaninoff Paganini] *Variations* and would have a little record made up and would play this'. He said that in October 1953 Juilliard's dean asked him if he would like to meet Kapell. He was 'so thrilled, terribly excited'. Two nights later, friends told him that Willy had been killed in an air crash. 'I was overcome with grief.' Cliburn told the court that Kapell was not at the peak of his career – he was about to play more chamber music and more of the truly classical composers Beethoven, Mozart and Bach. His earnings from concerts and records were bound to increase greatly.

Leonard Bernstein, arguably America's most famous musician, was soon on the stand. The composer of *West Side Story*, pianist and conductor of global renown summarised his achievements. But he spoke so softly that several jurors complained that they couldn't hear him. He said, 'It just seems immodest to say such things loudly.' Belli asked him not to be too modest. He would stop him if he got too modest. Asked to rate Willy, he said the task was easy. Some pianists were the 'sheer virtuoso, the acrobat', musicians who were often unable to play more serious music such as Beethoven sonatas and Bach suites. The great players of Bach and Beethoven, on the other hand, were sometimes incapable of pulling off Liszt's Hungarian rhapsodies, for example, and failed to have 'that flash, dash that is associated with virtuosity'. Kapell was well on his way to becoming that 'very exceptional pianist, both aspects rolled into one'. Moreover, he was extremely popular with other musicians.

Conductor Leopold Stokowski said Willy was 'one of the greatest talents of our time'. He was in immense demand. What set him apart was 'greater talent'. Cellist Gregor Piatigorsky said that he and Kapell had rehearsed in Los Angeles before he went to Australia and he was supposed to stop over for a further session when he returned. (The evidence failed to clarify whether the recordings would have been made in Los Angeles.) His musical talent was 'very great', and he was 'very strongly' on his way up. His potential was 'unlimited'. Isaac Stern said Willy was 'probably the most brilliantly successful pianist to appear on the scene since the day of Horowitz'. Indeed, he was considered to be the natural successor to Horowitz and Rubinstein. He was a 'fanatically dedicated' artist. He made no allowances for errors; he had 'an inner fire, a drive that was remarkable', and he could communicate his excitement to audiences. He was simply the 'most exciting talent to hit the American scene in several generations', and he was reaching a 'particularly fruitful period'. He was always searching for 'musical truth'.

Rubinstein, the doyen of American pianists, said that he heard Kapell play as a boy of thirteen. Someone asked him if a patron should give young Willy a piano. Rubinstein said he deserved two. He told the court that Kapell was fast approaching a musical summit – that he was considered 'the best American [born] pianist'. (Rubinstein himself, he reminded the jury, became a citizen only in 1945.) He was very ambitious and worked probably a little too hard. He was prepared, for instance, to tour Australia – 'so far off'.

Anna Lou had remarried, but for the District Court of the Southern District of New York, she revealed the intimacy and love that characterised her marriage to Willy. He wanted more children, for example, but they had decided that they didn't 'have the right' to have them because they travelled so much. He was a 'devoted father, in every sense of the word' and kept in touch when he was away. He loved having David and Becky around him.

Ada Graziano was the employee at Columbia Artists' Management who booked Willy's concerts. She told jurors that '[we] were selling him for $1500 and up' a concert. She had once got $4000 for a pair of concerts. He rated among the top artists in terms of demand, and he had 'certainly not' reached his top earning capacity. (Rubinstein had earlier told jurors his own fee was $5000 a concert.)

And frosting on the plaintiff's cake was Willy himself. For jurors, Belli's sidekick Richard F. Gerry screened the *Omnibus* 'kinescope' and played recordings of Liszt's *Mephisto* waltz and a Schubert impromptu. As the last notes faded, Gerry said, 'That, your honour, is the … case.'

★ ★ ★

The defendant's lead counsel Austin P. Magner was quick to respond. He moved for Judge Ritter to direct a verdict in Qantas's favour. The plaintiffs, he contended, had introduced 'no evidence by any witness, document, deposition or other' of wilful misconduct. Nor had they introduced any evidence of 'intentional' reckless conduct or violation of regulations by BCPA, its 'agents, servants, or employees'. Magner sweetened his strategy with a cop-out. Qantas was prepared to pay $8291.87 for Willy's death, $497.40 for the loss of his checked baggage and $331.67 for the loss of personal effects carried in *Resolution*. The total came to $9120.94. Judge Ritter threw out the proposal.

The complexities of flying into San Francisco on instruments formed the bulk of the defence. The implication was that something in the ground systems that guided aircraft on to the runway must have erred on that drab morning. Dickson, it was implied, must have thought he was in the right place to descend when clearly he wasn't. Magner assembled days of testimony on navigation signals, 'markers' of various sorts – fan, middle, outer, 'Z' and 'Belmont' – intersections in the air, topography, the differences between instrument and visual flight rules and the signals pilots received when they descended correctly: blue lights flashed, bleeps sounded in pilots' earphones, needles swung from pointing ahead to pointing backwards. A reasonable inference is that twelve ordinary men and women might easily have become confused by the expert witnesses, and that confusion could have led to doubt that the navigation systems were working properly.

Debate on what exactly 'wilful misconduct' amounted to was also extensive, and counsel on both sides argued repeatedly for the admission or denial of legal precedents and citations.

In summing up, Charles Parker for Qantas stressed how long the legal action had been going on; the complaint was filed in 1954 and here it was, 1961. And, crucially, the plaintiffs had led 'absolutely no evidence of wilful misconduct on the part of this pilot or the crew members'. The burden was on the plaintiffs to show 'by a preponderance of the evidence' that misconduct had been wilful. The two people who could tell the court what happened – the pilot and the co-pilot – were unavailable. But if they were here today, Parker continued, they probably couldn't tell us what happened. He told jurors what he thought 'wilful misconduct' meant. The pilot would have had to have executed an 'intentional act ...

knowing that in all probability it is going to result in injury, and with complete and utter disregard of that probability'. Then there was the question of the ground facilities aircraft relied on to land. The 'preponderance' of the evidence had shown that they were not working properly.

Parker reiterated a theme. The plaintiffs were out to confuse jurors. (By any judgement, the defendant's testimony carried the most confusing ballast.) In essence, his tactics were a legal version of a distilled Br'er Rabbit strategy. Uncle Remus's bunny pleaded with Fox and Wolf to save him from being tossed into the briar patch. They decided otherwise, of course, and once among the thorns Br'er Rabbit escaped. Parker said that 'Mr Belli is going to get up here … and tell you to put your thinking caps on, and in those thinking caps there is going to be a lot of confusion'. All jurors needed, he contended, was 'good common sense and valuation of the testimony'. Time and again, he stressed that Dickson must have thought he was in the right place to begin his descent. Time and again, he asked jurors not to let Belli confuse them.

For ten days, Belli had been in no position to ask jurors to wear any thought-provoking headgear at all. He had been out of court – in hospital with hepatitis. Richard Gerry began summing up the plaintiffs' case without him. The evidence showed that Dickson had descended intentionally into the clouds. The plaintiffs did not have to prove that he knew he would hit a mountain. Their case was only that Dickson descended intentionally when he knew – 'or should have known' – that there was a probability of harm. He was reckless, he knew mountains were close and he had not flown over the instrument-landing-system outer marker before deciding to land. He had 'disregarded the danger' of his actions. The plaintiffs didn't have to show that Dickson wanted to commit suicide or murder anyone. They merely had to show that he intentionally went into the clouds when he was told not to.

Towards the end of his address, Gerry referred to documents that counsel had tried to obtain from the other side. One was a report alleging that the director of civil aviation in New Zealand had complained about an approach and landing Dickson had made at Whenuapai airfield near Auckland. The same report, said Gerry, showed that on another occasion Dickson had failed to carry out his duties as a BCPA captain. Despite Judge Ritter ordering the defendants to hand over the report, the plaintiffs had been unable to check these allegations.

Apparently having arrived by ambulance, Belli took over. He had been motivated 'to crawl down here today' and sum up, he told the court, on the theory that each legal side was 'entitled to one invalid'. (One of Qantas's counsel had a heavy cold.) It was, he added, long past his bedtime. Standing near jurors, he assured them that he was not 'pathologically contagious', but he hoped that, logically, he might be 'somewhat infectious'. He wanted to talk about damages owing to the descendants of a man 'whose brush was dipped in the pot of celestial fire'. He would put up figures on the blackboard, and he hoped that the jurors wouldn't retire and say to themselves that lawyers always ask for more than they should. The sum he sought – over a million dollars – would be supported by sound facts and figures. He was asking for neither a handout nor sympathy. He reminded the jury of his opening address weeks before – his contention that Dickson had 'sneaked in [to San Francisco airport] and violated the pattern'. He reminded jurors of Jacobs's testimony, of the two airlines, BCPA one of them, that 'sneaked in all the time so low that he [Jacobs] could read the numerals on the side of the plane'. He was so concerned that he talked to his superior about it. 'He made that charge against BCPA ... and ... against Qantas at that time, and then he said after the accident they didn't do it any more'. That BCPA took shortcuts into San Francisco had never been denied, he said. After 118 flights into the area, Dickson saw a hole in the clouds and thought he could sneak into the airport. He knew better than the man in the control tower; Dickson was a pilot who 'sets up his own traffic signals ... to save three turns, save three minutes'.

Belli moved on to discuss what might be fair compensation for Willy's death. He turned lyrical. Which people make life worth living? he asked jurors. He had been in Russia last winter and the most highly regarded people were ballet dancers, pianists and conductors. They couldn't be jealous of Kapell's earning potential because he was dead, and 'we would not hear a Kapell again'. In what amounted to about ten years of public performances he had 'crowded the treasures of a lifetime'.

Based on a lifespan of a further forty years and figures tendered in court, a reasonable gross sum of compensation was $12 million, said Belli. But removing taxes and the cost of living and his own costs would cut the sum by more than half. Over several minutes, he worked through the numbers, précising amounts that Willy would have spent on himself, and the interest on a lump sum that his widow and two children might be expected to live on. The target shrunk, and counting compensation for property damaged in the crash, he finally settled on asking for $1,154,257.

Fairly late in the trial but before he charged the jury, Ritter had – inadvertently – revealed his feelings. They should never have shown, of course. Dickson had flown the plane into the mountain, even if he hadn't intended to, he said. He had skippered *Resolution* 'in a path he was not instructed to follow' and had 'failed to follow his instruction from San Francisco tower'. Dickson intended to go down into the clouds before he had passed over the instrument-landing-system's outer marker. Although it was later criticised by appeal judges, his charge to the jury nonetheless canvassed arguments on both sides and attended to the law of the matter. His favouring the plaintiffs, though, was unconcealed.

It was his duty to explain, he eventually charged the jury, what was meant by 'wilful misconduct'. It was up to jurors to decide on the evidence whether 'any act or omission of the pilot or flight crew … amounts to reckless disregard of the probable consequences of the safety of the passengers'. Because of the nature of air travel, he said, it might be that a jury 'would feel justified in coming to the conclusion that some relatively minor breach of a safety regulation amounts to "wilful misconduct", although it would not do so in places and on occasions when the consequences of such an approach would be much less serious'. He asked jurors to consider the circumstantial evidence and to draw inferences by using their 'good common sense and sound judgement'. This was a civil case and not a criminal one 'and less proof is required'. A mere 'preponderance of the evidence' was needed to find in favour of the plaintiffs. By preponderance, he meant the greater weight of the evidence or the evidence 'which to you has a more convincing force and effect'. In spite of all this, he wanted jurors to agree unanimously on their verdict.

Just before lunch on 3 April, Ritter sent them to their room. By 4.50 p.m. they were back with a verdict. The jury foreman announced that it was unanimously in favour of the defendants. Belli asked that the jurors be polled. One by one, each told the clerk that he or she had found for Qantas.

Doubtlessly suffering the sequels of his illness, Belli nonetheless moved immediately for the judge to determine the verdict, ruling in favour of the plaintiffs, notwithstanding the jurors' decision (*non obstante veredicto*). A new jury should rule on compensation. The defendants had admitted negligence and there was also – as a matter of law – 'wilful misconduct'. Closing arguments had 'completely and utterly' confused the jury, he contended, especially references by counsel to 'a mistake on the part of the ground equipment'. It was 'absolutely without the evidence', and therefore the defendant's counsel had misled the jurors. That the jury had failed even to award $8300 under the Warsaw Convention showed that it had misunderstood Ritter's charge to it, said Belli. It had been given a 'way out' through the defendant's 'speculative evidence' about a purported drop in electricity to a piece of ground equipment and the lack of a fail-safe mechanism at the Half Moon Bay marker.

Ritter asked for Belli to put his motion in writing, and arguments were eventually heard three months later in Salt Lake City. He was to rule on them two years later, on 28 June 1963.

Ritter expounded his decision over more than eighty pages. It is impossible not to wonder what he was thinking – how he weighted the case in his loneliness and alcohol in Salt Lake City, how he assessed the arguments.

He began by recapping why he was making a decision. The plaintiffs, according to court rules, had the right to – and asked for – either a new trial to look at all the issues, a 'directed verdict' in their favour followed by a new trial that would consider damages, or an overruling (*non obstante veredicto*) of the jury's decision and a new trial limited to the issue of damages. He then recounted details of the fatal flight, noting that a new crew came on board for the Honolulu to San Francisco sector. Exchanges between *Resolution* and air traffic controllers are spelled out before Ritter notes that at 0845 a 'call to the flight was unanswered as were all subsequent calls'. Evidence showed that the aircraft crashed 'at approximately 0844 on King's Mountain, about ten and one-half miles from the ILS [instrument-landing-system] outer marker'. Ritter stresses that the flight was thrice ordered to maintain *'at least five hundred feet above all clouds'* (his italics). Contacts were by voice, and no one, writes Ritter, could seriously 'urge that the crew did not receive or understand these three clearances. And there could have been no doubt in this pilot's [Dickson's] mind as to what he should have done.'

Ritter makes a lot of the aural and visual navigational cues *Resolution* would have received if it had descended over the outer marker. A continuous series of bleeps would have been heard, a blue light would have flashed and a needle on the instrument panel would have swung from pointing forwards to pointing backwards. He decided that the 'BCPA plane could not have received the ILS outer marker signals in the vicinity where he [sic] crashed'. Moreover, a United Airlines flight had landed from Honolulu ten minutes before *Resolution*. 'Everything was normal.' And another flight left for Honolulu over the marker fifteen minutes after the crash. 'Everything was normal.' He cites the evidence of an airline captain who agreed that Dickson could not have descended into the clouds before passing over the marker if he had followed his instructions from the ground on 29 October 1953.

He quotes many pages of courtroom exchanges before deciding that the defendants had 'exhausted ingenuity' attempting to prove that Dickson might have been confused by navigational signals. They had 'totally failed to prove it'. The defendants had not shown a single instance of another pilot's mistaking the Half Moon Bay fan marker for the ILS outer marker, which were miles apart. He concluded, 'It is obvious the flight did not maintain at least 500 on top of all clouds. Neither did it fly from the Half Moon Bay … marker … direct to the San Francisco ILS outer marker. Nor did it … cross the outer marker initially at least 500 on top. The pilot did not fly that aircraft to the ILS outer marker at all.'

He examines the jury's decision. It had failed to award 'the widow and children' even the capped amount in the Warsaw Convention of $8300. Drawn up as a single copy in French, the convention was authentic and binding, he decides. Article 25 orders an exception to the capped amount if the damage derives from the airline's 'dol'. Ritter dwells on what 'dol' means for several pages, concluding that it has no exact equivalent in English in common law. It could mean various things even in France, and comes from the Latin *dolus*, which can mean trickery, deceit, evil intent and many other shades of wrong. He plumps for a British rendering of the word as 'wilful misconduct', taking a passing shot at the Convention itself. It was supposed to subsidise the '*then* infant' air-travel industry, but it was a 'strange concept to us in the United States that the subsidy should be taken out of the widows and orphans of passengers'. He notes that the 1955 Hague Protocol had revised article 25. Although it had not yet been ratified by the United States, he notes that it removes the limit on damages if an airline or its agents has acted 'with intent to cause damage or recklessly and with knowledge that damage would probably result'. He notes that the Hague Protocol requires 'knowledge' that damage would probably result. 'The Second Circuit [his jurisdiction] does not,' he insists.

Then follows the crux of his thinking. He interprets article 25 in the present case *not* to mean that 'BCPA or the pilot had to have a deliberate intention to kill William Kapell, to wreck this aircraft, or to commit suicide'. If the pilot was instructed to stay above the clouds but flew into them, 'the requisite intention is present if he intended to violate his instructions and do what he was doing. In order to be "wilful misconduct" he need not have intended to cause the harm which resulted.' Put simply, Dickson was knowingly doing the wrong thing by flying into the clouds, even if he had no intention of harming himself, anyone else, or *Resolution*. It was the axle on which the whole legal see-saw rotated. And it could hardly be disputed, Willis added a little later, that Dickson didn't know what he was doing. Moreover, 'what the BCPA pilot did involves an easily perceptible danger of serious bodily harm, or death, and the chance that it would so result was very great. There was a high degree of probability that it would result.'

He turns to uncontradicted testimony that 'all summer and early fall' before the crash, it was the 'custom and practice' of BCPA to 'come in around King's Mountain and down into the airport just about on the course this one seemed to be heading on'. He refers to Melvin Belli's summing up. 'You see, Mr Parker [for BCPA] didn't ask one of their witnesses, and they didn't bring a witness, to deny the accusation [against] this established airline – Quantas [sic] is involved – that they shortcut'. (On the bench, Ritter had noted to himself, 'The silence of defendants on this point shrieks.') Belli continues, '[Eight] years since the air crash, and not one witness to refute the custom and practice of BCPA to take that so-called shortcut'. Belli says the only mistake the BCPA flight made was not flying over the proper instrument-landing marker. And it could be characterised as 'negligence', but it has to, 'under the law ... be wilful misconduct because it is up in the air, where a second makes 50 times the difference of a slow-moving boxcar'. It was never rebutted that the pilot 'violated a navigational order'.

For Willis Ritter, he concludes, 'it is enough that he [the pilot] realises or, from the facts which he knows, should realise that there is a strong probability that harm may result, even though he hopes or even expects that his conduct will prove harmless. The circumstances must be such that the risk created is unreasonable. Can anyone doubt it?'

The final sentences of the judgement must have filled Anna Lou with endless hope. Relying significantly on Belli's dogged specificity and his own discretion, Judge Ritter decided that the verdict should be overturned, and that Anna Lou should win. 'Judgment will be entered for the plaintiffs on the issue of liability, and a new trial is granted on the damage issue only.' Qantas was liable for the accident, he decided, and a new trial would decide only the amount of compensation the young widow and her children would receive.

* * *

TIME magazine reported that Belli had not been able to argue the compensation trial because he was preoccupied with Jack Ruby's defence. The next instalment in Anna Lou's quest for compensation began on Monday 27 January 1964 and ended three days later. Magner and George Tompkins represented Qantas, and Harry S.

Gair, Robert Conason and M. Victor Leventritt, Anna Lou. Hearing the matter – again in New York's southern district – was Judge Edward C. McLean.

Gair began by asserting that Willy was the greatest American-born concert pianist. Again, he promised, eminent musicians would testify to Willy's greatness, but not too many for fear of contravening court rules about 'cumulative' evidence. The court would hear of his 'consummate artistry', in any case. And it would hear that he was coming back from fourteen weeks in Australia to San Francisco and then to Los Angeles to make recordings with Heifetz and Piatigorsky for RCA Victor.

His first two concert fees – when he was nineteen or twenty, said Gair – were $75. From there, the climb was steep: '$200 for a contract, $400, $600, $800, $1000, $1200, and we will show that in June 1951 … his … minimum fee [was] $1500 …' Concert pianists' expenses were high, and early in their careers they could expect to lose up to seventy per cent of their gross earnings. Nonetheless, Kapell's net earnings for 1951 were $17,000. In the ten months in which he lived in 1953, the counterpart figure was $20,000. He had been already booked for forty performances in 1954. If he had lived, his 1964 fee would be '$3500 or more', Gair explained. Anna Lou's counsel took jurors through painstaking calculations based on projected earnings and life expectancy.

For the plaintiffs, Stern took the stand again. Willy had 'hands touched by God'. He was the only American pianist 'automatically included amongst the five great names in piano playing in the world'. There were parallels in his and Willy's careers, but Willy's rise was 'more meteoric' than his had been. They were the best in their fields, but the piano was more popular than the violin, the violinist remarked. Stern said he played 125 to 160 concerts a year, and although Willy was paid in 1953 up to $1500 a performance, his 1964 fee would have been as much as $4000. As a rule of thumb, more than half an artist's income went on expenses early in his or her career. But once established, outgoings dropped. Eventually a 'tour director' would maximise the musician's fees for the minimum expense, largely by arranging the highest-earning itineraries. Willy would have had 'more offers than he could physically fill'.

For Qantas, Magner interrogated Anna Lou about her husband's background, work habits and health. He seared her with questions about the number of doctors the family saw, naming them, wondering what they did. One was psychoanalyst Gustav Bychowski. Anna Lou said Willy had 'severe problems … of nervousness going on the stage'. The aim of seeing Bychowski was to help him with this specific difficulty. She agreed that her husband had been turned down for the draft because of allergies, but she believed his only allergy was to cats. Magner named the doctors that appeared on family bills – fifteen, in the end. But several, he discovered from Anna Lou, were paediatricians, obstetricians and gynaecologists. (None was a specialist in lung diseases.) At a later re-examination by Gair, Anna Lou estimated that Willy would have spent about ten per cent of his income on himself and the rest on the family. Early in his career, he had bought his parents their Upper East Side house in 94th Street. She and Willy and the children had rented two floors of it for between $225 and $250 a month and paid the rent whether they were there or not.

Alan Kayes, a recording executive, had been with RCA Victor for seventeen years. The company was about to sign Willy for an annual minimum guarantee against recording royalties of $20,000. If he had lived, his annual income from discs would have been between $25,000 and $50,000. It was a 'conservative' estimate, he said.

William Judd was vice-president and a director of Columbia Artists' Management. Gair asked him about Kapell's 'stature'. Back in the early 1950s, he said, 'Kapell established something that people in the profession were not sure would be possible at all'. At times choked with emotion, Judd went on, 'No one was sure that there could be an internationally famous and established American concert pianist, American-born, American-trained.' It was like running the four-minute mile, which many thought was impossible. Kapell's career was that kind of breakthrough. '[He] absolutely blazed the course that no one was sure could be blazed.'

Gair and Magner summed up stirringly. The great tide of evidence was against the defence, but Magner reminded jurors that Willy's friends had said he was going to make a fortune but in 1950 his net income was only $13,110. The following year it reached $18,259, but in 1952 – the last full year of his life – it had dropped back to $16,655. He asked jurors to take into account Kapell's allergy to cat fur and the number of doctors the family consulted.

Gair had it easier. He needed only to cite Stern's hands-touched-by-God quote and he was well on the way to heavenly compensation. While there were perhaps 'twelve billion people on Earth' – Gair was a lawyer, after all, not a demographer – there was only one Willy. We were dealing with not just the wreckage of *Resolution*, but the 'wreckage of a career'. And based on all the figures the court had heard to do with life expectancy, concert fees, record royalties, expenses and Willy's growing reputation, Gair computed a sum of $1,726,505. That was what the plaintiffs were asking for.

At 4.40 p.m. that afternoon, the jury awarded Anna Lou $924,396 and Magner immediately moved for a retrial on the grounds that the sum was 'excessive' and the court had 'erred in various respects'. Qantas appealed also on relatively petty grounds, quibbling, for instance, about how much of the award Kapell would have spent on his wife and children. Judge McLean threw out all the defendant's contentions. The decision stood.

This was not the kind of denouement Qantas, in its head office in Sydney, wanted to live with. It had settled for very much smaller amounts on behalf of victims without celebrity status. But it could not afford the publicity of losing to Anna Lou; although Willy didn't die in one of its aircraft, the shame and notoriety of losing was bound to blemish Qantas's excellent safety record. Along with other newspapers, Sydney's *Daily Mirror* reported in January 1964 that the 'Commonwealth' [Australia] would apply for the decision to be reviewed by the United States Court of Appeals, the second-highest jurisdiction in the American legal hierarchy. In New York, George Tompkins, for Qantas, said the airline would also appeal against 'a ruling by the judge finding them guilty of wilful misconduct'. In American law, deep pockets are – if not everything – a *sine qua non* for success. Wholly owned and backed by the Australian government, Qantas's pockets were of ocean-trench profundity. And in the long run, Qantas's management would have seen the airline's reputation as being vastly more important than paying out less than a million dollars.

★ ★ ★

Circuit Judge Leonard P. Moore and Judges Waterman and Kaufman brought down a unanimous decision some eighteen months later, on 9 June 1965. They reinstated the original jury verdict favourable to Qantas – the one Ritter had overturned – and set aside the second jury's determination of damages. Not only did Anna Lou and the children get nothing, their mountainous legal bills were their business to pay. Court costs alone came to $5312.50 and Belli's fees were estimated by one newspaper in 1964 to have been about $150,000. Anna Lou said recently that the money involved was the most she had ever seen. It had cost her scores of thousands of dollars.

Over fifty-seven paragraphs, many of them long, the trio of appeal judges castigated Ritter. They found his charge to the jury 'most favourable to plaintiff' in that it defined 'wilful misconduct' as it might occur in a series of 'hypothetical situations in the operation of the airplane while attempting to land, including the comment that "it may be that a jury would feel justified in coming to the conclusion that some relatively minor breach of a safety regulation amounts to 'wilful misconduct', although it would not do so in places and on occasions when the consequences of such an approach would be much less serious"'. Ritter's court had 'substituted itself for the jury and drew its own inferences from the facts'.

Moore and his benchmates cited a case that clearly showed, in their eyes, that a jury judges the facts, a court the law: 'It is the jury, not the court, which is the fact-finding body.' The court was not free to 'reweigh the evidence and set aside the jury verdict merely because the jury could have drawn different inferences or conclusions or because judges feel that other results are more reasonable'. They referenced another case that defined 'wilful misconduct' as 'intentional with knowledge that [it] was likely to cause injury to a passenger ... and likewise, if it was done with wanton and reckless disregard of the consequences'. They concluded that there was no justification that the 'only permissible inference from all the evidence was that the pilot had been guilty of wilful misconduct – whether under Judge Ritter's standard or under that stated by the prior cases'. Once the case went to the jury, they said, 'its verdict should not have been upset if reasonable men could find in defendant's favour, as they certainly could here'.

Moreover, they agreed with the defendant's claim that Judge Ritter's overturning the jury decision was an 'abuse of discretion'. He gave 'no reason' for granting a new trial. Viewed against 'the proper standard', the judges were unable to agree that the original verdict was 'against the weight of the evidence', which was 'almost entirely circumstantial'. Their last paragraph was a baseball bat to the skull: 'Judgment reversed with instructions to enter judgment upon the jury's verdict in favour of defendants.' Anna Lou's lawyers sought a rehearing of the evidence in the Supreme Court, but it was refused.

Obscured by thousands of pages of evidence and argument – a judicial juggernaut – was the simple truth that Anna Lou had lost. Moreover, everyday notions of fairness and justice in this case might easily appear to have been taken hostage by a legal obligation to attempt to define the ambiguous notion 'wilful misconduct'. What exactly it was depended on who was doing the defining.

Closed to doubt, however, was that Willy probably had an immense and lucrative career ahead of him. (Provided, of course, that he was not dying of terminal cancer.) His death was caused by a pilot and cockpit crew that had committed a fatal error. There was the evidence that BCPA pilots often used a shortcut into San

Francisco airport that began more or less where Captain Dickson had started his descent into the clouds. He was told *not* to fly beneath them. Yet he did. But because it may be presumed that he had no intention of injuring or killing anyone – let alone himself, in all probability – his behaviour was deemed, in the end, not to have been 'wilful'. (Other jurisdictions have wider definitions of the term.) His act might have been negligent or crazy or even both, but he did not, we may surmise, intend to hit a mountain. And whereas other passengers killed in the *Resolution* disaster were compensated in courts of law, Anna Lou and her teenage son and daughter were not.

The ABC could be said to have run Willy ragged with a brutal tour that ended in his depression. (Many artists, it must be added, played similarly long and arduous seasons.) An airline half-owned by Australia had hurtled him into a mountainside and Qantas, wholly owned by the government, had persisted, one imagines for commercial reasons, to defend a cause that might have been seen as morally indefensible. (Qantas archives told me that they have no records of the litigation with Anna Lou.)

The actions of government bodies in this instance were in irony of Australia's alleged moral platform. The young nation and its people emphasised equality – that in this most virtuous and democratic country, all and sundry got a 'fair go'. In truth, for many categories of Australians – Aborigines and unmarried mothers, to name two – and immigrants, especially scores of thousands of underprivileged British children who were forcibly removed to Australia, often into slavery and abuse, life was far from just. And it might equally be argued that little was fair about the 'go' the Kapell family had received.

CHAPTER TWELVE

Roy Retires

'The cover picture evokes a memory of your carrying an almost three-year-old Wendy up all those steps in 1951!'
Eric Wicks in a Christmas card to his friend Roy Preston

'Roy never spent a needless penny.'
Maurice Austin on his friend

WHILE ANNA LOU raised children, fought to keep her husband's memory alive, built a career and endured the torture of failed litigation, Roy Preston lived an unremarkable life. His devotion to music remained constant. But beyond his life's passion, there were few highlights. His last invoice for blank acetate discs was dated April 1960, and we may presume that he stopped cutting them soon after. He graduated to taping music, and he collected thousands of LPs, cassettes and CDs as each fresh wave of technology broke. He attended concerts of many kinds and was a resolute member of the Theatre Organ Society. He had several excellent friends, but none was intimate.

As an organist played a recital at the Plaza Theatre in Melbourne one night in the late 1940s, Roy was distracted by the back of a head a few rows in front. He thought it might belong to Eric Wicks, a former jungle comrade he hadn't seen since the war. At interval Roy and Eric had a joyful reunion. (Eric rose to sergeant and was in army education. He was also responsible for programming recorded music for troop concerts.)

For the next fifteen years Roy and Eric were close. Married to the astute Essie, Wicks had four children.[1] Roy holidayed with the family at least once, carrying Eric's daughter Wendy up hundreds of steps in the Blue Mountains. He went on Wicks family picnics. He was often invited to dinner or lunch. Their common interest was music, but they traded strong views on many topics. Eric –

like Roy – was unafraid to voice his opinions. They would have enjoyed their direct and uncompromising verbal rallies over this or that pianist, conductor or composer. It is not known if they ever discussed William Kapell.

Eric wrote – about music and community concerns – and eventually graduated from being a paymaster in a plastics company to editor of the local fortnightly *Heidelberg Mirror*. By the late 1950s, Eric had got Roy to write the *Mirror*'s record reviews. It is not known just how many Roy wrote, but they are forceful, sometimes funny, analytical and committed. In July 1959, he reviewed Vox discs of the London Symphony playing the seventh and eighth Beethoven symphonies under Edouard van Remoortel. The eighth, wrote Roy, 'emerges most triumphant, and even allowing for a couple of instances of unusual phrasing, which fail to completely please probably because they are unusual, it is doubtful if a thoroughly more enjoyable version … exists in the catalogue'. By contrast, the seventh had a 'different acoustic', and its 'tonal depth is rather less than on the Eighth'.

In October of the same year he reviewed records of a Bach Brandenburg concerto and Welsh voices. The Stuttgart Soloists performed a 'superior version of this most animated and flowing concerto' (No. 3 in G), and the Morriston Orpheus Male Choir presented 'superlative' music in terms of 'control, tonality and expression'. The singers' 'enunciation' was wayward at times, a 'rather minor point seeing that so much of the programme is in Welsh'. Roy recommended playing the Decca disc with 'a bit of treble boost'. On the same page, he damns the Melechrino Strings and Orchestra's *Music for Reading*. Cover notes were 'inanely occupied in justifying the title. What ridiculous twaddle they are!' The playing itself was fine.

Roy reviewed Haydn symphonies and brass bands, Satchmo and Sibelius. Mirror Newspapers published Roy's opinions in four editions that circulated in an arc across Melbourne's north-eastern suburbs. They might have been read by tens of thousands.

But by 1960, new owners had taken over the papers, Eric had left to edit a country weekly, and Roy appears to have written some forty-four reviews that were neither published nor paid for. In March 1962, he sent a letter to the Mirror group and attached an invoice. He hadn't been paid for almost three years, he wrote. Before then, Eric had arranged to fix him up in company shares. It is not known whether he received the £60 he was requesting.

The dispute soured his relationship with Eric, and they were to meet again only infrequently. Roy sometimes told those closest to him that he and Eric had been 'such good friends'; he clearly missed their mateship. But in either 2001 or the following year, Eric sent Roy a Christmas card, its face a photograph of the Three Sisters outcrop in the Blue Mountains. He wrote inside, 'The cover picture evokes a memory of your carrying an almost three-year-old Wendy up all those steps in 1951!' Forty years after their falling out and in the last years of their lives, they were to resume their friendship.

Roy also continued reviewing discs for *VOX*, the Theatre Organ Society's newsletter. But a reader once complained that he had omitted 'In My' when reviewing a version of the Duke Ellington classic 'In My Solitude'. (The first two words are often dropped in casual references.) Roy couldn't stand that degree of nit-picking, and he gave up criticism altogether.

By 1970, Roy and Ruby's cottage was tumbling down. It belonged to Roy by now, and he hired Kevin Borland to draw up a renovation. Borland was one of a small team of young modernist architects who designed Melbourne's Olympic swimming stadium. Its cross-section an inverted triangle, it balances – still, half a century later – on an apex like a diamond on a ring. Borland drew something almost as captivating for Roy's home auditorium, which was the cottage's front room, running the width of the house. Roy instructed Borland to come up with perfect acoustics. Between exposed beams more than a yard apart, the architect installed brown-stained plywood panels that made lovely catenaries towards the floor. Calculations appear to have been done to the sixteenth of an inch to achieve the best sound.

Ruby died in 1976 and Roy retired four years later. He was sixty-five, and financially comfortable. While music remained his greatest love, he read in many other subjects, including architecture, art, science and astronomy. An interest that surprised those closest to him had a sudden onset. He had never driven a car. But for unknown reasons he decided he wanted to get a driver's licence. The Red Cross needed blood couriers, offering to take on even the unlicensed and pay for them to learn to drive and pass the test. Roy jumped at the chance. Once he had gained experience and confidence with his sanguine deliveries, he bought a Honda Accord in metallic 'Tudor red' from former motorcycle champion Maurie Quincey, who had dismounted from two wheels to sell four.

Roy was not especially fond of his brother Vic, but they were 'blood', says Maurice Austin, and Roy and Vic began to tour Victoria in the Honda. Roy drove and drove, visiting most towns and hamlets. Although he travelled interstate – to Adelaide, for instance, for theatre-organ meetings – he was a real tourist for the first time. But not even Maurice ever discovered much about Roy's itineraries or the highlights of his trips. Roy never owned a camera, and there are no photographs.

Driving occupied Roy for three or four years. The miles flew by; some 350,000 kilometres were on the Honda's odometer the day it broke down in Benalla, not far from Shepparton, the small fruit-growing town where Willy had played a month before he died. According to Maurice, Roy had worn out his car. He had had a few minor accidents and near misses, and he believed his time as a road warrior was up. He sold the car on the spot, dropped his driver's licence in to a police station, and caught the train back to Melbourne.

★ ★ ★

Maurice ferried Roy to TOSA concerts and meetings for almost a decade. In return, Roy had given him, he realised later, perhaps a third of his acetate recordings. They rarely discussed what was on them, occasionally mentioning William Kapell, whose death touched them both. The trigger was, of course, Roy's Chopin recording and its curious appearance on a commercial CD. Roy ultimately remembered that he'd given the original to Cliff many years before. Maurice believes Roy would have said to Cliff, 'Just take it.' He wouldn't have wanted it back. And he had no idea on what winding path the acetate travelled to end up in the hands of BMG Music. And if he'd recorded Willy, he never mentioned ever having attended his performances in the Melbourne Town Hall.

This was unusual for someone who became a regular ABC concert subscriber. Very occasionally, Roy would delegate a friend to go to his home and record a broadcast if he was at a concert. But he was wary of doing it because he thought he worked the Royce cutter better than others. His results were superior. And a question begging an answer is his opinion of William Kapell's artistry. He never gave it, only ever mentioning Willy in the same breath as the pianist's tragic end.

He recorded many famous musicians. He mentioned to Maurice the pianists Solomon and Gieseking. He had been in the Melbourne Town Hall in March 1952 when two youths released pigeons during a Gieseking recital. Born in France the son of a German doctor, the pianist was tainted after performing in Nazi-occupied France. On this mild Melbourne night, he had got halfway through a Beethoven sonata when the men each released a bird. The pigeons were caught, and they and the youths were ejected from the hall. Roy told Maurice he remembered the flutter of the wings and the murmur that rippled across the audience.

Into his eighties, Roy was still walking, but a little slower. His dress standards were also slipping. Suited and bow-tied in Myer's cosmetics department, 'Spruso' had looked impeccable. But by now he attended TOSA meetings in worn – if sartorially appropriate – garments. Maurice failed to recognise him at Batman Records one Friday night. He saw a slight, elderly derelict enveloped in an army greatcoat thumbing through CDs. His hair was awry, and he was unshaven. Maurice thought he looked 'peculiar' – like a hobo – until he realised it was Roy. They said hello and Maurice left, intrigued and worried. The greatcoat, he learned, was Roy's, issued in the 1940s. 'Roy never spent a needless penny,' says Maurice. He would have walked on a cold night to the record shop, another five-mile return journey. The obverse of this thriftiness was his generosity to others, whether they had been his young female colleagues at Myer, TOSA members or Maurice himself.

Not long after, Maurice got Roy a mobile phone. He was to use it in an emergency, he told him. And he did.

Maurice hadn't been in touch with Roy for several months and was at a bicycle show at the Royal Exhibition Building. He decided to give Roy a call, partly just to say hello but also to make sure his phone was switched on and working. Roy answered. He was in the Caritas Christi aged-care unit of St Vincent's Hospital, a couple of hundred yards from where Maurice was admiring the bikes. He'd felt ill and rung the triple-zero emergency number, he told Maurice.

Maurice found Roy sharing a small ward. There were worse things than being in hospital, said the older man: he wasn't allowed to go home. There were too many objects to trip over, too much dangerous clutter for an old man, inspectors had told him. It worried Maurice, Roy's being 'doddery'.

Maurice knew about the mess. Roy had made no attempt to tidy it when he had gone twice to Roy's home in the late 1990s to interview him on tape: aural history of a TOSA foundation member seemed too important to miss. Roy had agreed to be taped only after much deliberation. 'I suppose you'll have to visit me,' he complained. He hadn't wanted Maurice in the house. Maurice understood why. Inside the front door, there was scarcely space to move. Piles of newspapers, magazines and programs were everywhere. Floor-to-ceiling metal shelves held acetates, LPs and tapes. String from a shelf to a bracket on a wall supported coat hangers of shirts. Shoeboxes and fruit boxes brimmed with magazines and sundries. One was simply labelled 'Tubes'. Others held broken shoelaces and pencil stubs. Saws hung on hooks, clothes spilled from half-opened drawers. An upright piano supported heavy volumes on astronomy, mythology and the universe, as well as boxed sets of Béla Bartók and Brahms. A globe of the world balanced on the books, a print of van Gogh's *Irises* behind it. LPs – led off by harpsichordist Wanda Landowksa – faced out.

Work had got Maurice down. The digital age was undermining many industries. Printing was one of them, and firms often changed hands. He was one of the last men standing, as he puts it, and to save money his company got him to train juniors who were more or less dragged off the street. His employer was bound for bankruptcy, he reckoned, just another of a series of outfits that knew little about the printing industry. And he was fifty. 'The whole thing became too much to bear,' he says. So he decided to quit. He'd look after Roy and pursue his own hobbies. He had a small superannuation and – like most loners – he had learned to live frugally.

A problem of his own – and one of Roy's – was solved, and Roy never again lived in his worker's cottage. Nor did he live with Maurice.

At first, Maurice signed on casually as Roy's carer. But as soon as he had declared himself, he was told Roy could not stay in hospital. St Vincent's gave Maurice a list of nursing homes that might admit Roy. They numbered around thirty, and Roy spent short periods in two before moving to a third – Cambridge House – where he would spend the rest of his days.

He was not yet seriously ill, just a man nudging eighty-six in decline. In his discharge notes written in February 2001, Caritas Christi's Dr Sam Hume reported that 'Mr Preston is a very thoughtful, highly intelligent man who ponders his symptoms and their treatment extensively – he is capable of understanding fairly complex explanations … and this is generally more reassuring for him than pharmacologic assistance'. Words, not drugs. A month later, he felt that Melbourne University should have his body for whatever purpose it decided. The offer was declined, the university wishing Roy 'many years of good health and prosperity'.

He had several ailments – his chronic thyroid complaint and compressed vertebrae in the neck among them. (He had surgery for the latter.) His health would never be good, and the project of caring for him – Maurice visited every other day – should become official, he and Maurice decided. Maurice became Roy's power of attorney, and would sign the paperwork for his important decisions. Care would be costly in the years ahead, and Maurice discovered that Roy had only $9000 in cash reserves. He thought he'd spend it on CDs, he told Maurice.

An obvious first move was to sell Roy's house. The property's title was at home somewhere, Roy told Maurice. Just where, he couldn't say.

On and off, it took a year to sort through what Roy had stored in his house. Maurice had help, and some fifteen cubic yards of rubbish filled each of two skips. Broken furniture, worn carpet, old curtains and cartons were dumped. Maurice remembers hefting Roy's typewriter over the edge. Behind a curtain were shelves containing stacks of newspapers. Rubbish prevented entry into a small shed in the back garden. Maurice imagined Roy threw stuff into it from the open door. He found American editions of *LIFE* magazine bound in New Guinea wartime tent canvas. A carton contained what must have once been secret intelligence documents, aerial photographs, orders, maps and surrender leaflets.

Then there were the recordings. Maurice took home twelve milk crates of Roy's LPs. About another six were sold. In all, some seven to eight thousand recordings. The acetates numbered fifteen hundred. There were several hundred reel-to-reel tapes, even more cassettes, and three thousand CDs. Maurice sold many of the LPs to collectors and got $1000 for a 19th century Australian copy of an English antique chest of drawers. One of the LPs appeared to be fat, and Maurice pulled out a small envelope containing a pound note and half-a-dozen ten-shilling bills. They hadn't been currency for thirty-five years. The title to the property was never found.

Of all Roy's possessions, Maurice thought the acetates were the most precious. Apart from giving permanence to rare and beautiful performances by many great musicians over several musical genres, they distilled the man. Roy's cuttings were a trope for him, what he was about. Maurice promised himself to go through them one day and impose some order – when he wasn't so busy. It couldn't be that hard because Roy had numbered his home-made discs, the numbers correlating more or less with years. There were also Roy's fat folders – half-a-dozen of them – containing hundreds of typed indexes of details in red (headings) and black (content) of all the recorded sounds he had made.

'L' must mean LP, Maurice surmised. 'C' for cassette. 'TS' must be 'tape spool' – reel-to-reel – and 'A'? 'Acetate', of course. On each of the acetates, Roy had scratched a number and an 'A' and 'B' on alternate sides. He would have tailor-made a plastic sleeve for each of his discs, too, running a hot knife or somesuch around the end to make and seal the curve. Each had its own brown-paper envelope – probably Myer's wrapping paper. And to each envelope was glued a list of the music inside and at what speed it had been recorded. On the same acetate, Maurice noticed, there might be performances recorded at several speeds to optimise the space on the disc. He remembered Roy telling him that he had wound cotton around one of his spools so that he could get an accurate twenty revolutions a minute for some of his less important cuttings.

I'll look at all this later, Maurice told himself, as he carried boxes to his car. Never know what I might find.

CHAPTER THIRTEEN

Digging for Treasure

'I became convinced in the 1990s that there had to have been other recordings because of broadcasts. Logic said so … It was needle-in-haystack stuff.'
Record producer, Jon Samuels

'Rediscover a legendary American pianist, whose tragic early death cut short a brilliant concert and recording career.'
Back cover blurb, WILLIAM KAPELL EDITION

ANNA LOU MARRIED Gaston de Havenon in July 1955.[1] He was a *parfumier* by trade and of French and Jewish forebears. Twenty-two years older than she was, he had divorced his first wife and had two sons, Michael and André. Anna Lou thought Gaston was 'very seductive and attractive'. He would provide her with financial security, love and a happy home. In autobiographical notes, she wrote that Gaston 'infatuated me and offered me a very different life from the one I had had with Kapell'. Willy's death had 'totally devastated' her, as she put it in a 2005 television interview, and marrying Gaston could easily be seen as a way of bringing light and stability to a life already blackened by tragedy. There would be 'no music to remind me of my loss'.

Once Gaston and Anna Lou had had two children – Alexander and Sarah – the family's rent-controlled Upper East Side apartment bulged; four children and two adults. (Gaston's sons were either at boarding schools, college, or living with their mother.) Anna Lou cooked – no mean task, because Gaston wanted his food properly done. In return, he supplied a considerable income. The exclusive American distributor of Weil perfumes from France, he also owned Ann Haviland, which made scents, soaps and cosmetics. Eventually, he sold out of both and set up a gallery specialising in primitive African art. Anna Lou had helped him with the collecting, and now she wanted to work alongside her husband in the shop. The idea was too much for Gaston. It was out of the question, in fact, and her offer was refused.

Until the age of sixteen, she had adored visiting a grandfather who was a farmer in Washington State north of Bellingham near the Canadian border. He had been a teacher and was one of the first chroniclers of the north-western Indian tribes and the lumbermen and sealers who had pioneered the region. Anna Lou recalled having worked on the farm, weeding onion plots and finding Indian arrowheads. Her interest in anthropology – the study of how man goes about living – was sparked at an early age.

So when Gaston declined to use her intellect she went back to school, entering the prestigious School of General Studies for adult undergraduates at Columbia University. The marriage had become 'pure boredom', as she put it, and she could have immersed herself entirely in study. (The couple divorced in 1974 and Gaston died in 1993.) But she was well aware of her family responsibilities, and for several years took only a single subject each semester.

Soon, her anthropological studies found a focus, and she was among a team of researchers that had begun to use video cameras to record poor New York families in their environments. She discovered that the median age of a homeless woman in the Bronx was twenty-six, and that many of the women had two dependent children. In 2005, she told the *New York Times* that the statistic had resonated with her: she was widowed with two children at twenty-six. She said, 'I'm thinking, my God, that's one of the reasons I'm so concerned. Freud would have had a wonderful time with it.'

She was awarded a PhD in 1978 at the age of fifty-two, and was at the forefront of advocacy for more affordable housing and improved welfare payments into her eighties.[2] (She died at eighty-five in February 2012.)

And although she had seen marriage to Gaston as an escape from music and all that it reminded her of, she remained devoted to Willy. As the years passed, her efforts to keep his name alive redoubled, becoming as important as her family and profession. She often said that she was nothing without Willy.

A consummate networker, she attracted a coterie of Kapell fans and those who were involved in recording or chronicling art music. Among them were Gregor Benko, Tim Page, IPAM's curator Donald Manildi and Allan Evans, who founded the Arbiter Recording Company, which saved performances by important musicians. Record producer Jon M. Samuels calls them the 'Kapell underground', and includes himself among those who aimed to make Willy better-known. I found him easily online and arranged to meet him for two long interview sessions in his cluttered basement recording studio on the Upper West Side of Manhattan.

He is adamant that Anna Lou led the group in its efforts to 'get the word out … She encouraged, cajoled, assisted and used her personality to convince people over the years that he [Willy] existed'. If she hadn't been so determined, his name might have disappeared altogether, he claims. He had met her at Willy's eponymous piano competition and a handful of memorial events. It was he who telephoned her to pass on the news that Jack Pfeiffer, the senior RCA Victor producer who had largely managed Willy's recording career, had died in 1996. Subsequently, they became close friends and, in Jon's words, he was 'something of an adviser to her' on Kapell matters. They met many times a year in various places, including her apartment and his Upper West Side brownstone.

Their chats usually included discussion on Willy's position in the pianistic hierarchy and how they could ensure that he would never be forgotten. She was, he says, 'indefatigable'.

Closing in on middle age, Jon is a roundish man of pale skin and straight black hair. The son of a banker and business analyst, from an early age he had a passion for music. He learned piano for five years, but not with any great intentions. He dropped out partly because his keyboard skills were incapable of reproducing the way he wanted music to sound. At Columbia University, he studied American history but also volunteered at its FM radio station, WKCR. He commentated on sport, broadcast the news and engineered a jazz program. For six years from the late 1970s into the 1980s he produced and hosted classical music shows and festivals, and for two years was a WKCR board member. He had fallen so deeply in love with music, however, that he thirsted for it.[3] The more he knew about it, the better.

Recordings are of several types. The vast majority are made by record companies with a view to releasing them for sale. Most of these are made in anechoic studios in an attempt to minimise the gap between the music and its capture. Others are done professionally at concerts and are released on the commercial market once they have been edited. Then there are many amateurs who capture performances at concerts or from the radio for their own pleasure.

Musicians, music-lovers and record companies had been looking for new Kapell recordings since the day the pianist died, says Samuels. He began hunting for all the Kapell he could find, and in 1993 made an astonishing discovery. BMG possessed, in its vaults, unlabelled tapes of a concert Willy played in the Frick Collection's Music Room in New York in March 1953, not long before he left on his last tour. Jon told Jack Pfeiffer of the discovery – also that there was other unreleased Kapell material about. Jack liked the idea of a comprehensive Kapell boxed set. Decisions about such things take time to make, and Jack tended to wait until he felt he could get a 'yes' from senior executives, says Samuels. Boxed sets for other greats – Heifetz, Stokowski and Monteux, for instance – were due to come out, and Kapell was seen to be less known and therefore less marketable. None of his performances was on stereo, too. Jon continued to argue hard on behalf of Willy and Anna Lou. His artistry was peerless, he told BMG management, most of his recordings 'had been out of print for decades', his 'backstory' was tragic, and the press and public would love it. But only after Jack Pfeiffer died was a decision made to go ahead, mostly because 'there weren't too many other collections of that size left that hadn't already been issued'.

In Kapell's case, Jon had small fortune on his side. Many fine musicians who died in the 1930s and 1940s had left little of a recorded legacy, but at least Willy had lived into the 1950s, when amateur equipment was becoming more affordable. There was a greater likelihood, too, that music-lovers had cut Kapell because he was often broadcast. But most amateur recordists were American. In Europe they numbered few, and in Australia, where he had played last, there was 'almost none', as Jon puts it.

Buoyantly optimistic, however, he was convinced that many recordings were waiting to be found. 'Logic said so.' He was unsure of how many might turn up, of course, but they would be bolstered by several pieces from the archives that might be sonically satisfactory. Initially, the Kapell recorded legacy was to be released on eleven compact discs but, from the project's start, Jon was under pressure to complete it. First, though, he wanted to find everything that had been registered.

He describes his quest as 'needle-in-haystack stuff'. He beat the jungle drums among Willy's 'underground', contacting Evans and Page, Benko and Manildi. He wrote letters and made long-distance phone calls. In its infancy then, email was not so useful or widespread as it is now. He spoke to every Kapell collector, every archivist, every related family member who might have recordings. 'I was trying to find literally everything that hadn't been unearthed.' He contacted Clifford Hocking, who couldn't remember who had etched the original acetate. But he did have a tape of an Australian performance of a Schubert impromptu (D. 935 No. 2) that was, in the end, too scratchy to use. (A better recording from a New York Town Hall concert in March 1953 made the collection.) Nonetheless, Jon was convinced that other amateur Australian recordings by Cliff's unknown hobbyist had survived, and with sufficient time and effort he would track him down. 'There was a good chance [he] was still alive.'

Australia was, however, a problematic source. The BMG budget didn't stretch to an air ticket for down under, and time differences between New York and Australia made long and sensible conversations difficult. He contacted the Australian Broadcasting Corporation (the word 'commission' was replaced in 1983, a cosmetic change) and got nowhere. He estimated that he needed three years to complete a project he was given nine months to do. His painstaking work also meant that he was spending longer than planned to remaster what he found. The studio budget got overshot, possibly by tens of thousands of dollars, and Jon's employment was on the line. In 1998, he 'reluctantly stopped looking ... I didn't finish, and I didn't expect to finish'. He adds, 'There are limits to chasing a phantom.'

When the guillotine fell, he had found some twenty-odd new recordings of varying lengths. Some had had a small distribution among collectors and fans, and the numbers are elastic. He describes the result as 'fairly successful'. Arguably his most important find was of the Frick recital, which was performed on 1 March 1953.

The Geelong Chopin is in the set, and Allan Evans's liner notes about it begin by describing the difference between Willy's studio and concert performances. He writes that to the 'poise and focus of his studio recordings was added risk-taking and an exciting energy, which this live recording captures'. Something of an understatement, Evans's endorsement fails to mention, of course, who cut the disc or how it got in the set. These sorts of details were incompletely known. Its date – 22 October 1953 – is noted, but not that it was the last time Willy played in public.

Called the *WILLIAM KAPELL EDITION*, the nine CDs suggest how steadily Willy was soaring towards an inevitable, peerless artistry. Audible beneath the fireworks is a fresh way of interpreting the repertoire with its own pair of lungs.

Samuels believes Kapell's playing can be separated into early, middle and late periods, much like many of the painters and composers Willy so admired. The recordings go some way towards demonstrating this. Only about half of them were 'commercial' – taped in a studio and intended for release. The other half consists of concert performances, which might have been taken off broadcasters' tapes and not specifically intended, at least at first, for sale. Included in more than ten hours of music are a Bach partita and suite, Beethoven's second piano concerto, a Brahms intermezzo, Chopin's *mazurkas*, two of his sonatas, the legendary Khachaturian recording, two Mozart sonatas, Mussorgsky's *Pictures at an Exhibition*, Rachmaninoff's second concerto, Liszt, Schubert and Schumann morsels and four Shostakovich preludes.

Examples of early Kapell date from 1945. Chopin's nocturne Opus 9, No. 1, was taped at a Carnegie Hall concert on 28 February. Willy is playing one of Chopin's many melodious and inspired takes on a genre originated by Irishman John Field. Its first section is a very long lyric that rises momentarily before wandering beautifully, aided by a perfect left-handed musical landscape. This early piece also has a restrained and largely untroubled middle section, unlike some Chopin nocturnes. The twenty-two-year-old playing it is known for his ferocity with ivories and ebonies, and it is easy to imagine he is having to restrain himself. In the main, though, the playing is delicate – so delicate, in fact, that he strikes some notes in the melody too softly. Just before the main theme is reintroduced, Willy handles a counterfoil in the bass with great sensitivity.

A month later, he entered RCA's Studio 2 in New York and interpreted the most famous of Liszt's *Mephisto* waltzes and three Shostakovich preludes. The first prelude is just over two minutes of mournful – if melodious – chords, and the second a slightly shorter waltz. Willy dances the dance with a straight back, accompanying it with demur trilling as the piece draws to a close. But it is the final prelude – less than half a minute long – that demonstrates a superhuman technique. A melody bounces about in the left hand against a continuous skittering of scales. It is scarcely believable that a human being can play the piano so fast, can plait notes into skeins of sound at such speed.

The *Mephisto* performance is legendary, what Samuels calls a 'spectacular' show, a 'devil-may-care interpretation' in which Willy demonstrates that the terror of the technical mountains Liszt challenges pianists to summit are no higher than a cigarette pack for him. His playing stupefies and dazzles – it can't be the work of man, but it is. More pointedly, Willy structures the piece's quite different sections – typical of Liszt's best piano music – into an artistic entity lasting almost ten minutes. The performance asserts that a phenomenal musician is emerging, not just a pianist. Evans's liner notes quote a Kapell jotting: 'Right now I battle the *Mephisto Waltz* daily … From now on, I will see nobody at all, go nowhere, and have nobody here. Charming eh? If I could play beautifully after this fuss, perhaps it might be worth it?'

The following year he produced with the NBC Symphony a recording of Beethoven's second concerto that fooled even Schnabel. Legend has it that the Austrian heard it on the radio and thought it was *his* recording. Artur and Willy owned matching strings of pearls.

If the mid-point of Kapell's recording career is taken to be from 1947 to 1951, the collection offers Liszt's *Hungarian Rhapsody* number 11, Schumann's F-sharp *Romance*, a Schubert *Musical Moment* and the Rachmaninoff showpiece, *Rhapsody on a Theme of Paginini* with the Robin Hood Dell Orchestra, Fritz Reiner conducting. Evans calls Kapell's playing of the Paginini and Rachmaninoff's second concerto 'mature conceptions of works he often played'. He quotes Claudia Cassidy: 'Age has nothing to do with talent, but plenty to do with the opportunity to develop talent. So while it was provocative a year or two ago to discover that Mr Kapell had a rare gift for Rachmaninoff, it was astonishing to discover what strides he has taken to bring that gift to maturity.' And Willy himself is cited on learning of the Russian master's death in 1943: 'Today I worked a couple of hours on the Paginini *Rhapsody*, and cried all the way through it, because I realised that the great master was no more. The towering Russian whose music I loved so much was gone forever … He loved romantic music, and he wrote it as no one else did. When the announcement of his death came over the radio, I had under an arm his third concerto, just having learned all the notes. I have a reason to personally grieve his loss, but I am comforted that every day I can open the covers of some wonderful and magic world that he expressed in music. He shall never die.'

Recorded in RCA Studio 2 in January 1947, the short *Romance* shows more confident shaping of melody than in several earlier performances of similar music. The middle section unsettles the listener by a modest − and correct − degree before Kapell lets the melody take care of itself right to the ending of soft repeated bass notes. Recorded four years later in the Town Hall, Willy's version of the *Hungarian Rhapsody* is among the most mature examples of his consummate musicianship. For most of its five minutes or so, the piece is a set of variations based on magisterial chords, which Willy plays quite stridently. But towards the end he unleashes shimmering staccato scales faster than a firefighter zipping up to join his crew. They fade and swell and are unsettling and otherworldly, casting doubt again on the pianist being one of us. And the Paganini *Rhapsody* is twenty-two minutes of virtuosity, apart from the entry into the exquisite eighteenth variation, which Willy converts into one of the most sublimely lyrical moments in the history of recorded sound.

His last tapings are less well represented. There is Copland, Chopin, Schumann, Scarlatti and Mussorgsky from the Frick recital. The gallery's Steinway is out of tune, and Willy gives the impression that he can't wait to finish the show and walk the few blocks north up Fifth Avenue to his home. Perhaps he was distracted by preparation for the tours to Israel, France and Australia. More likely, he hated the Steinway. Frick had hired it direct from the maker – it wasn't one of Willy's chosen instruments.

A better gauge of the quality of his musicianship towards the end of his life is a disc not in the collection. Six weeks after the Frick recital, Willy played Brahms's first concerto in Carnegie Hall with the New York Philharmonic, Dimitri Mitropoulos directing. Notwithstanding the deficiencies of a sleepy and at times ragged New York band, Willy executes his melodic lines with masterly clarity and shape. Amazing is the facility of his runs, the equality of notes meant to be of equal length, and his sovereignty over the score, the certainty with which he states it. He wrestles to the canvas both music and the orchestra in the 'Maestoso' (majestic) opening movement. His slow movement is meditative, poetic, poignant, passages exquisitely etched, the lyrical architecture balanced and solid. Not a note is sounded too loudly or softly, too harshly or weakly. Here is a master. Who knows, a genius? Curiously, Willy gives in to the Philharmonic in the final movement ('Rondo'), a rushed and, at times, we-came-we-played-we-got-paid discharge of duty.

A young Willy plays on the front of the boxed set. His head is bowed slightly. He concentrates on his hands. His haircut is fresh, his silk tie striped, the collar beneath it pinned at the neck. A blurb on the back says, 'Rediscover a legendary American pianist, whose tragic early death cut short a brilliant concert and recording career.' Then follow quotes from Claudia Cassidy and Virgil Thomson.

Thomson's begins, 'He was a great musician and a great fighter. He did not fight for himself or for just any music. He fought to play well and to play the best music.'

Willy's legacy was at last available to all, his artistry in permanence. The work was done. Anna Lou and her 'underground' had completed a long and difficult task, collecting and publishing most of the Kapell worthy of immortality. Jon Samuels, in particular, was disappointed that the original plan for an eleven-CD set had not been stuck to. (The Rachmaninoff third concerto with the Victorian Symphony, for instance, was slated for inclusion but omitted.) They deserved to be satisfied with themselves, proud. There might be crackles and pops in the archive, but superlative pianism overwhelmed them. More than eleven thousand units were sold worldwide, and BMG also had reason to celebrate.

Little of the music had previously appeared on CD, and the *EDITION* was applauded. Typical of adulatory assessments was Michael Kimmelman's in the *New York Times*. He wrote that this 'landmark' among piano collections 'should come as a revelation to many'. Kimmelman suspected that anyone who was hearing Kapell's playing for the first time would find it 'mind-boggling'. He noted the pianist's transcendent technique but insisted that 'he was in the end a poet'.

The set presented, if not a 'radically new vision' of the pianist, a 'truer sense of his legacy, a moving portrait of a young musician in the midst of change'. In 1998, Kapell would have been seventy-six, Kimmelman wrote. What would his playing have been like? The set showed an 'evolving sensibility', one that had not yet been fully formed. Movements of a Mozart sonata, for instance, were charming but 'precious and unsteady'. Kapell didn't yet wholly 'inhabit' Mozart. The nine CDs revealed that he was an 'artist in progress', that he thought about interpretations, took risks, yet was spontaneous. (He was also 'sometimes impatient'.) And when Kimmelman heard the usually 'hackneyed' slow variation of Rachmaninoff's Paganini variations he wept.

Writing in *International Piano Quarterly*, Donald Manildi began by saying that 'genuine heroes' in the world of pianism were rare. None deserved the epithet more than Willy. 'Had he not met with such a premature death, it is entirely conceivable that during the last 45 years Kapell would have ascended to the summit of the pianistic scene, deferring to no one in the quality and scope of his accomplishments.' On the other hand, he warned, the 'relentless intensity' of Willy's quest for perfection might have led to his total physical and mental collapse. Manildi analysed the highlights in each of the CDs and finished by saying that the *EDITION*'s musical significance could not be 'overestimated'. Willy's greatness was evident in everything he did, 'and we can only speculate as to what further heights he would have lived to conquer'.

In the *Washington Post*, Tim Page also used the word 'revelation' to describe the playing. To have 'more or less complete access' to Kapell's legacy was 'staggering'. He pointed out that by 1960 'there wasn't a single Kapell recording left in the catalogue and second-hand stores began to charge up to $250 for the scarcest titles'. Among the recordings was more than an hour of previously unreleased tracks, and the Frick recital was a bonus. He nominated the Geelong Chopin as 'one of the very greatest performances of the sonata – a reading of fury and, in retrospect, almost unbearable poignancy'. Page hoped that the CDs – a 'massive, beautiful reissue' – would win Willy a whole new audience.

Page's description of Willy and Roy's *Funeral March* sonata no doubt compelled music-lovers, Kapell fans, Anna Lou, the 'underground' and musicians to regret not having more recordings of his last concerts. If only they had been made. If only the ABC hadn't deleted theirs. An evolving genius, a superlative musician accelerating towards Olympian artistic realms … Who knows what more evidence of his genius might have revealed? It was the question the *EDITION* posed. Just how good had been his best? Because his best seemed to have happened in exotic and peculiar places with funny names such as Bendigo and Geelong. Could there be … Was it possible that … Were there other performances to match the Plaza Theatre's Chopin?

Willy was the greatest pianist America had produced, the *cognoscenti* told themselves. That was agreed. And all those who loved him and his artistry would have to leave it at that.

CHAPTER FOURTEEN

Treasure Found!

'How can we possibly describe the thrill we experience reading and re-reading your E-mails [sic] to Joshua?'
Anna Lou, on Maurice Austin's first contact with her

'These are the discs I looked for five or six years ago …'
Jon Samuels

'It's as if somebody were to find a dozen new paintings by Rembrandt or a lost film of Charlie Chaplin.'
Daniel Guss, director of the classic catalogue for BMG music

'He closed his eyes. We knew he was listening, and that was it.'
Maurice, describing Roy Preston an hour before he died

IN EARLY DECEMBER 2011, I hired a car and drove east on Long Island, leaving Manhattan – which always seems to me like life on an exercise bike – behind. I was heading for Greenport, a former fishing village about as far east on the North Fork as you can go. Even beyond the vineyards. After World War II, Greenport dived into half a century of decline. Then along came Willy's son Dave, who turned it into a delightful tourist town and summer escape that has been widely recognised as a model for small-urban redevelopment.

The spit is narrow here, perhaps a mile wide, and low and flat. The narrow straight road into town passes through patches of scrappy forest on either side until it hits pretty, tree-lined streets and houses. And at street level on a corner on the left is Kapell Real Estate, with a red sign hanging out the front. A big, bright and airy shop under a gabled building clad in dark, softwood shingles, it has a couple of old desks and filing cabinets. Landscapes, seascapes and portraits hang on its whitewashed walls, and antique models of ships rest on stands.

Dave and Eileen Kapell greeted me like an old friend, telling me not to mind the dog and introducing me to their son Matthew. Wearing a navy-blue baseball cap, Dave looked like a younger Steven Spielberg. Pretty and russet-haired, Eileen confirmed her Irish stock. They live in a modest vintage bungalow in the town.

Dave studied the piano for ten years and the cello for six. He sold cars, worked as a construction labourer and, in 1968, replaced his cello with a bass guitar. Sly Stone (of Sly & the Family Stone) taught him to play it, and for five years he was a freelance muso, performing rock, bluegrass and country and western. He had day jobs as well, ascending through hospitality from nightwatchman and dishwasher to general manager of distinguished Manhattan restaurants, including JP's and Marvin Gardens. He married Eileen in 1975, and Joshua was born three years later. (Matthew and Caitlin were to follow.)

Dave and Eileen decided to raise Josh 'outside the city', as Dave puts it, and they moved to Greenport in 1979 to invest in the restoration of old houses 'and to fish'. But very quickly he got involved in Greenport's restoration, administering federal grant programs then heading its planning board. In 1994, he was elected mayor, a post he held for thirteen years. The winner of many local-government honours, he was awarded in 2002 and 2003 fellowships to attend the Kennedy School of Government at Harvard.

He and Eileen established Kapell Real Estate in 1981. It specialises, says its website, in selling 'fine vintage homes', but also offers 'paintings and … furniture, folk art and pianos'. The couple's Subaru Outback is the latest model, but Dave tends to get around town in an old pick-up painted scarlet. Its gearbox is ornery and its steering floats, but he wrestles it with finesse. By 2003, Dave had mentioned on the Kapell Real Estate website that he was the son of pianist William.

The main purpose of my visit was to meet and talk with Anna Lou, who was in a nearby nursing home and in the last months of her life. Dave would accompany me, helping me to get the best out of what would be necessarily brief interviews. We agreed on two or three sessions of perhaps half an hour each.

These days a software architect at Oracle, Joshua is a rangy young man with thick brown hair his grandfather might have quiffed into a flourish. Like every member of the Kapell family, he is immensely proud of Willy. He remembers seeing Dave – his father – 'sitting alone in the den' and listening for the first time to the CD of the Chopin *mazurkas* (and the Geelong Chopin). 'He was visibly moved … and seeing that in turn really moved me. It's something that I'll never forget,' he says. Despite the pride the family has in Willy, Josh says there is also 'an inescapable sense of loss and sadness about his tragedy'.

In 1998, Josh was studying at Oberlin College in Ohio. He took a class on building websites, and to practise his skills he decided to construct williamkapell.com. It would be a 'small homage' to his grandfather, where 'people interested in his life and work could find information'. Josh hoped Kapell fans – indeed, all music-lovers – would gather there to exchange opinions and reminiscences. It would also be a repository for audio clips, articles and Alistair Cooke's precious movie. Email inquiries to the site went to both Kapell Real Estate and Josh's Oberlin College address.

★ ★ ★

Roy's house was sold in April 2002, providing ample funds for long-term care. His health was stable; Cambridge House – while not perfect – did its job, and he delighted in visits from old friends in TOSA and Maurice's constant surveillance and friendship. At one point, organist Thomas Heywood arranged to play a short private recital for Roy in the Melbourne Town Hall. A photograph shows Roy in a wheelchair admiring the organ's four manuals. His hands –

in black woollen mittens – are clasped in his lap, and he wears a grey cardigan. Heywood leans on the back of the organist's bench and is doubtlessly explaining something of immense interest to the old man.

Apart from visits to St Vincent's as an outpatient, Roy rarely left Cambridge House. There is a picture of him visiting brother Vic in the hospital. Roy has on a teal-coloured silk dressing-gown – Maurice thinks he must have been getting tests done. His eyebrows are white and bushy, his bare scalp a summit above an unruly horseshoe of white hair. (Vic is about to be discharged, and looks quite healthy. In fact, he died before Roy.) Roy has a faintly haughty air, the corners of his lips turned down, the *doppelganger* of Sviatoslav Richter towards the end of *his* life.

What happened next is unclear even to Maurice, who keeps pocket-sized – but scantly annotated – diaries in a travel pouch around his waist. Maurice hadn't heard of William Kapell until Roy mentioned the Geelong Chopin turning up on a commercial CD. And now and then in Roy's last years – over hundreds of hours of conversations – they would talk about the pianist and Roy's recording. They were intrigued by the uncanniness of the story. But they also realised the significance of something in which they had become unwittingly involved. What Maurice calls the 'incongruity' of Willy playing the *Funeral March* sonata then 'flying home to his death' had touched them. And then, a great improbability: his friend makes a recording of it that, somehow or other, gains worldwide release. Even more unlikely is that the cutting is of the greatest importance to the musician's place in the pianists' hierarchy.

Perhaps Roy *did* mention to Maurice that he had made other Kapell recordings, but Maurice is not at all certain of it. The idea of a collection of Kapell etchings perhaps churned in Maurice's subconscious over several years before something compelled him to act. Whatever force it was, in the end it was irresistible, and Maurice began hunting for Kapell acetates.

There was little order to Roy's etchings when Maurice began removing them to a back room of his modest suburban home. They were 'all over the place', he says. But it was fairly easy to sort them by their numbers into a chronological sequence. As it happened, Roy had cut no more than about thirty discs in 1953. Maurice began pulling them out one by one. He was alone, and he can't remember if at that particular moment he was 'deliberately looking [for Kapell] or just noticed them and put them aside for audition'. At the back of his mind was the idea that, if he found more Kapell recordings, Willy's relatives – if he had any – might be interested in copies of them. He had long ago been given ABC tapes of the great Soviet violinist Leonid Kogan, who had relatives in Toorak. Maurice rang them to see if they wanted copies. They already had them.

'WILLIAM KAPELL' was in red block capitals on the label of one of Roy's discs. Then in black type beneath, 'Prokofiev, sonata No. 7, July 25th, Melbourne T. H.' A Mozart sonata, said the label, was also on the acetate. He pulled out another. 'WILLIAM KAPELL', this time playing Debussy's *Suite Bergamasque* and a Chopin barcarolle, nocturne and scherzo. A third contained Willy performing Mussorgsky's *Pictures* and Bach, and a fourth, Rachmaninoff's third piano concerto.

We all listen to music in different ways, says Maurice, and for a man innocent of the Kapell genius he was not 'especially excited', he says. But there they were – pure gold for those who knew their value. Maurice rediscovered six acetates in all that day, some of them containing little Kapell playing. (Music of other genres – and at least one stand-up comedy routine – filled the other tracks.)

He believes that he would have told Roy immediately. But it was not something of great urgency because Roy would have known the recordings existed, even if he had never mentioned them. He never made a fuss over any of his etchings. Indeed, Maurice does not remember Roy's reaction to the discovery. 'Roy was not a demonstrative person,' says Maurice. 'He probably would have looked away, and you would have seen a little glint in his eye.'

More important was to see if this Kapell character had relatives. Because there were several acetates, Maurice reasoned, there was an even greater chance that a Kapell in America might want to hear the little collection. He Googled William Kapell and came up with the website Josh had built. On the morning of 25 October 2003, he emailed the only address he could find on it, Josh's at Oberlin College.

He began, 'Hello Joshua, for your interest and comment.' In the next four hundred words, Maurice explained about Roy's passion for recording, and that his discs were 'eclectic selections' of jazz, organs and 'symphonic work'. He mentioned the Geelong Chopin, and that it appeared to have found its way onto the Kapell nine-CD discography.

'Well, there is plenty more!' was his next sentence. Maurice would try to restore the tracks for computer files, but also keep a 'raw' file for more 'advanced restoration methods to take advantage of'. Then he listed what the discs contained.

The email bounced. Maurice tried again. It bounced again. Joshua had left Oberlin, and his college address had expired. Two days later, Maurice emailed Dave Kapell at his agency. He assumed Dave was related to William, he wrote. The address on the official website was returning his emails unopened, he complained. 'I have info re some rare broadcast [sic] from Melbourne Australia in 1953 that may be of interest'. Dave forwarded the email to Joshua, who responded immediately. Maurice wrote back to Joshua, who opened the message on 29 October 2003, fifty years to the day after his grandfather's death.

Within a week, Maurice had explained that one of his hobbies was 'restoring old 78 rpm records'. But he was having trouble getting the best out of the acetates. After having tried a 'wide variety of styli and cartridges' he still had reservations about the audio files in his computer. He offered to send Josh both processed and unprocessed files.

In the meantime, Joshua had emailed family members with the news, among them Rebecca, Willy's daughter, who lives in Washington DC. Rebecca Leigh, who is married to federal government lawyer Ned Leigh, gave up the law to bring up two boys, David and Eliot, who are these days in their twenties and asserting their pedigree. Eliot is a composer and producer of pop music, but also an engineer at a private recording studio in New York. In 2003, he was studying audio engineering at Indiana University. David followed his brother to Indiana, where he studies violin performance.

All of them were, of course, over the moon. In her first email to Maurice, Anna Lou could not contain her delight. 'How can we possibly describe the thrill we experience reading and re-reading your E-mails [sic] to Joshua?' she wrote. She had tried to get recordings of Willy's last concerts in vain. 'Ever since, I have dreamt of what might still surface as a result of music lovers like your friend having made their own recordings from those broadcasts.' She called the inventory of the discovered discs 'stunning'. The Prokofiev seventh and the Chopin barcarolle, in particular, were favourite performances.

★ ★ ★

When he heard about the discoveries from Anna Lou, Jon Samuels was at first sceptical. He believed they might simply be copies of the Australian Chopin, Rachmaninoff and Mussorgsky recordings that OPUS had released on LPs. But when he saw what was recorded he changed his opinion. He also suggested to Josh that he ask Maurice to date the performances – it would help to authenticate their newness. If the dates were plausible, then Maurice was very likely to be 'the real deal', he believed. And although discs had been made previously from tapes or pressings of Roy's work, what delighted Jon was that these were apparently first cuts, priceless originals.

Maurice enquired about the cost of shipping the acetates to America. The quote was '$282 AUS!' he told Eliot, the exclamation mark indicating that any imminent transfer was unlikely. He was, however, happy to lend the acetates to the family if a means could be found of getting them safely to the States. He copied Roy's work on to four CDs, one containing only data for Josh. By 20 November, they were on their way to Anna Lou, who gave them to Jon Samuels to make further copies and distribute them to the rest of the Kapells, as well as undergrounders Tim Page, Jerome Lowenthal and Allan Evans.

In Maurice's words, the family was 'blown away'. Like Roy, precise and cautious, Anna Lou was thrilled to hear Willy again.

In describing her feelings, she wrote on 1 December, 'Can you begin to imagine what this means to me? … Our gratitude to you is boundless'. Willy was in 'top form' on the acetates. The performances were 'fantastic', she told Daniel Wakin in the *New York Times* in 2004. They were 'breaking me to pieces'. Willy was alive and 'in front of me', she said. 'You can imagine what this does to me 50 years later.' Wakin reported Evans as saying that Willy's 'maturing was exponential in the last couple of years … He was shedding his past as an interpreter of Russian war-horse pieces … and deepening his study of Beethoven and Bach, Mozart and Schubert'. And he was at his 'absolute best' in concerts. The Australian recordings showed a 'very great artist in his prime, playing at his best.' Daniel Guss, director of the classical catalogue at BMG Music, said it was as if someone had found 'a dozen new paintings by Rembrandt or a lost film of Charlie Chaplin'.

For Jon Samuels, they were simply 'great', even if the sound needed work. They also confirmed his belief that a 'Roy' was out there somewhere. He and Evans and others had simply failed to find him. 'These are the discs I looked for five or six years ago.' He suggested to Anna Lou that they should approach BMG with a view to releasing them commercially. He was cautiously optimistic that the music giant would.

The big question, though, was 'how to transport the acetates you have so generously offered us', Anna Lou wrote. (Maurice says that at no stage did he say he would 'give' them outright to the family. In an email of 23 December, however, he told Anna Lou that he was 'even more convinced that you deserve the original acetates'.) She would probably make the journey to Australia and carry them back herself, she said. 'We are united in not wanting to lose them again.' She was deeply touched that Maurice was 'so willing' to share them. Could he, she asked, tell Roy Preston 'how grateful we are to have access to these Kapell performances?'

Maurice had kept Roy up to speed about the emails between him and the Kapell family. He can't remember Roy's reaction with any precision, but he would have looked away, he says, smiled faintly, and his old eyes would have sparkled. He no longer had the force, anyway, to be acclamatory. For a year he had suffered dizzy spells and minor strokes as a result of restricted circulation. He was also starting to lose the use of his hands.

Maurice had rigged up an old CD player and wireless headphones so that Roy could keep in touch with the music he loved most. The machine worked twenty-four hours a day. When they weren't being used, the headphones balanced on a triangle of stainless steel – a grip – above his bed. Once Roy put them on, the music played. When he replaced them, they switched off. But by the time arrangements were being made to ship his acetates to America, he was no longer able to grasp the headphones. Either a nurse – or Maurice – would have to do it for him.

By the last week of December – a month after his Kapell acetates had been rediscovered – Roy could barely speak. Maurice knew he was listening, but his responses to questions often amounted to only a barely comprehensible word or two. By now he was on morphine, and he managed to tell Maurice that he wanted to hear a recording he'd cut in 1952 of Stanfield Holliday playing Bach's *Jesu, Joy of Man's Desiring*. It was the last of his own recordings he heard. Two days later he was barely conscious, but he let Maurice know that the British dance bands he'd been listening to had been too light as music went. He needed to hear something more profound. He had a special request. Maurice bent low to try to understand what Roy was saying.

'Tur ... ang ... alila.'

'What, Roy?'

'Tur ... ang ...'

'Just a minute.'

Maurice dived into his travel pouch for his notebook and ballpoint.

'Say again, Roy.'

'Turanga ... lila', Roy whispered. 'Esa-Pekka Salonen.'

Maurice block-lettered Roy's words as phonetically as he could. He hadn't a clue what the old bloke was on about.

Not Kapell, nor jazz. Not even his favourite theatre organs. When Maurice explored Roy's CD collection that night he discovered that Roy wanted to hear Olivier Messiaen's *Turangalîla-Symphonie*. Drafted just after World War II, it's a sprawling ten-movement work whose title comes from Sanskrit words with many interpretations – perhaps it's a love song, or maybe a hymn of joy, a celebration of the rhythms of existence, or a meditation on death. Messiaen was devoutly Catholic. Maurice found the CD, a version directed by the Finnish composer and conductor Esa-Pekka Salonen, made a copy, and brought it in the next day.

Roy stared blankly into space, and a nurse said he hadn't long to live. Maurice couldn't make eye contact. It was pointless trying to talk to him, so he slid the *Turangalîla* into the player and placed the headphones on his friend. 'He closed his eyes. We knew he was listening, and that was it.' Maurice had errands to run, but within the hour his mobile phone rang. Roy was dead, fifty years and a month to the day after Willy.

A small plain memorial card was handed out to the few who attended his funeral a week later. Stating the dates of his birth and death and bearing a pencil sketch of Lance Sergeant Preston, it finished with the words, 'Music was his life, kindness his demeanour'. Roy's body joined the remains of his parents and brother Victor in an unmarked plot in the Methodist section of Coburg's 'Pine Ridge' Cemetery, a few streets from the big house in which he and his mum had lived when he was little. He never saw the point of spending money on headstones.

★ ★ ★

In return for finding the recordings, transferring them to CDs and sending them to America, Maurice asked for nothing. (Dave later sent him an ex gratia payment.) In February 2004, Anna Lou wrote that she was 'very moved by your offer to give us access to the acetates'. She and the family had talked 'at length' about what to do with them. They had decided that they should be transported by hand from Australia to New York, and Anna Lou herself would come to Melbourne to pick them up within three months. Maurice wrote back to say that he couldn't put her up in his 'very humble suburban cottage', but he would take her wherever she wanted to go and be her guide. He sent her several websites for bed-and-breakfasts.

In August, Anna Lou had great news. Old friends from Reed College days were visiting relatives in Melbourne and would pick up the recordings. 'It appears,' she continued, 'that BMG is quite interested in doing one CD and maybe more.'

Maurice packed the acetates in plastic bubble-wrap and a 'stiff cardboard box that previously held graphic arts sheet film'. Using black cloth bookbinding tape, he secured the box – which he had used in his printing days – on all sides, but it could be inspected if customs or quarantine officers insisted. He sent Anna Lou details of its weight – four kilos (8.8lb) – and size. On each side of the box he pasted a label: 'CONTENTS FRAGILE – HANDLE WITH EXTREME CARE – DO NOT SUBJECT TO EXTREME TEMPERATURE FLUCTUATION'. The notice also described the contents: 'Six historic broadcast recording discs on aluminium base'. (Acetate and the aluminium beneath it expand and contract at different rates. If temperature changes are sudden and extreme, there's a danger that the discs might crack. Recording surfaces can even break away from metal.) Maurice didn't want any return for his work: 'Being a vector of history is reward enough!'

Retired Portland lawyer Ernie Bonyhadi and his artist wife-to-be Shirley Gittelsohn shouted Maurice breakfast in their Melbourne hotel, the Windsor, on 27 September. An ornate Victorian pile, the hotel prides itself on its architecture, longevity and tradition. Maurice thought it was a privilege to have a meal with the couriers, though he found the place a 'bit posh' for someone of his lowly background. He remembers that Ernie wanted his hard-boiled eggs soft in the middle. He photographed the couple, hands on the package. Through the window behind them, you can make out the 19th century steps of the Victorian Parliament. Ernie grasps a distressed leather handle that Maurice has strapped to the package. It had been in the Austin family as long as Maurice could remember. Its pointed ends and their two brass studs scared him as a child; he thought they looked like the face of a hungry rat. A bright-orange 'FRAGILE' sticker is on each side.

Telling Anna Lou about the official handover, he wrote that the return of the discs was 'not a high priority'. If the 'children' thought they were important enough then perhaps they should remain with the family. The musical content was paramount, 'but the intrinsic value [of the acetates] is a judgment best made from your end'. Anna Lou was 'so happy' to learn that Roy's cuts were in good hands, she told Maurice. 'You have been [their] guardian angel and will receive all the attendant honours.'

Ernie and Shirley carried the cargo for the rest of their three weeks in Australia. They had no problems with quizzical officials, especially after explaining what was inside. When they were airborne, says Shirley, 'I held on to that case and sat it on the floor next to me.' For take-offs and landings only, it went in a locker above their seats. They weren't able to take the discs on a light plane to Heron Island on the Great Barrier Reef, and for a few days they were in the care of an onshore hotel. Shirley was 'scared to death that something might happen when they were out of our custody'. To be the couriers of such precious material was 'one of the most wonderful things we could have done for anyone anytime'.

They returned to Portland in the third week of October and took the recordings to New York three weeks later, again as hand luggage. They went direct from LaGuardia Airport to Anna Lou's Upper East Side apartment, using a door-to-door chauffeur service they trusted. Anna Lou was waiting on the pavement with Josh and Eliot. They moved to the lobby and the discs were taken up to the apartment. 'She was thrilled … She was just thrilled,' says Shirley. 'Even the doorman was excited.'

She and Ernie took Anna Lou and the boys to Brasserie 8½ on 57th Street for dinner. Josh remembers 'wine and a celebratory air'. To have 'the discs in hand' was incredibly exciting, he says. 'The fact these recordings even existed was miraculous and had seemed a bit surreal to me.' Josh held them, felt their weight (heavy) and convinced himself that what was happening was real. 'My grandmother was elated and visibly so.'

Anna Lou later told Maurice, 'It is impossible for me to articulate the great depth of my gratitude to you.' Dave Kapell corroborated Anna Lou's feelings. 'You have no idea how important your gesture [sharing the acetates] is, not only to our efforts to preserve and advance my father's legacy, but more importantly to the healing effect that it has had on my mother and our whole family,' he told Maurice. Their profound loss, he added, was mitigated by the only thing that survived Willy's 'tragically brief life: his music'. As painful as the recordings were to listen to, they were also the source of enormous pride and joy. 'I thank you from the bottom of my heart,' he finished.

And Maurice had a codicil to the story. He'd managed to contact Cliff Hocking and talk to him for three hours on the telephone. Cliff said he'd been trying to 'locate' Roy for years. They had discussed mutual friends, including Eric Wicks. Eric and Cliff had gone to school together.

★ ★ ★

Sony BMG – a fifty-fifty venture of BMG and the Sony Corporation of America – was created in March 2004. Jon Samuels worked for it in a freelance capacity. He talked to Daniel Guss, who was still on staff and a Kapell devotee. Daniel was immediately interested and got company support for remastering Roy's acetates and releasing them commercially. After the success of the EDITION, BMG had always been on the lookout for 'another Kapell', as Jon puts it. (This could also have meant, of course, the release of previously unknown recordings of another great musician, he adds.) His preference was for a new three-CD set that included all the Australian recordings, including a Prokofiev concerto, the Geelong Chopin and the Schubert impromptu tape. None of them was, in the end, included. BMG thought two CDs was a better market choice.

But first Jon had to work on them. He can't remember the date, but it was very early in 2005 that, one afternoon, he went to Anna Lou's apartment. He can't remember what he used to unpick Maurice's package – he suspects a sharp kitchen knife or scissors. Predictably, Maurice had done an excellent job; Jon remembers lots and lots of brown paper. Anna Lou's hands were shaking, but not enough to prevent her from taking photographs. She was 'terrified' at the opening, she said recently. He went carefully, making sure that he didn't slip and chip an etched surface. And then they were out – before them, on the kitchen bench.

Jon removed a disc from its sleeve and held it between his palms. He probably smiled, though he doesn't especially remember. Anna Lou's shutter snapped. 'This had a lot of emotional meaning to her,' he says. 'She thought she'd never hear anything like this again … She was choked up.' She wasn't weeping, he reports, but she was 'very emotional … this was as close to bringing him back to her as one could do'. Her emotion – verging on 'ecstasy', he has called it – thrilled him. For him, unpacking was a 'very heady moment', but he wasn't 'jumping up and down … This is my job. But I was pretty happy about it.'

Anna Lou asked him to take the discs home for safe-keeping. He took a cab across Central Park with the 'valuable cargo' and stored them upstairs, where he keeps other priceless recordings.

Lawyers tend to intervene in all natural processes, so it was not unusual for two years to pass before representatives of Sony BMG and Anna Lou had thrashed out an agreement on fees. It was only then that Jon was commissioned to remaster the discs.

Using a careful selection from three shelves of solvents and cloths, he began by cleaning them. Acetate surfaces can deteriorate, and some of the solvents are designed to remove chemical patinas. Fortunately, Roy's discs had degraded little.

Then he centred each disc in turn – precisely – on a Technics turntable, coated the acetate with distilled water, and began the process of sluicing electrons through high banks of electronic equipment, old and new, that crowd his small basement studio. For the Kapell recordings, he used a pair of fifty-year-old McIntosh pre-amplifiers containing glass tube valves. They help to give a warmer sound, he says. Not quite so ancient was a Pachburn machine aimed at reducing noise, the next station in the process. A Bryston pre-amplifier also nurtured the signals before they were sent down a cable to be converted into digital mode. He stored the music on computer 'cards' to create what he calls a 'high quality work station'.

These became the raw files he manipulated to remove as much and as many of the acetates' imperfections, the crackles and clicks inevitable in a fifty-five-year-old archive cut by an amateur at home from a radio broadcast. He spent two months, seven days a week, producing two-and-a-half hours of publishable music. Some days he was at his desk for sixteen hours. 'At one point, I lost track and stopped counting.' Eliot – Willy's grandson – assisted him.

There were easier ways of getting the job done. A certain 'device', says Jon, will let you remove all the 'ticks' at once. He tried it, didn't like the result, and took out the imperfections one by one. It's always a trade-off, he says. You try to remove the noise or try to improve the sound. You can do both only up to a point, he says. 'I decided to focus on the sound.' A good audio engineer has to try to re-create 'a sense of the hall, a sense of the piano'. He or she has to put listeners back in the seats of, in this case, Melbourne Town Hall in the winter of 1953, a genius at the Steinway.

And then he packed up, job done. *WILLIAM KAPELL reDISCOVERED*, a natty triptych, its central booklet separating two CDs, was released in May 2008.

And Roy's six original acetates? Where are they? They've disappeared.

CHAPTER FIFTEEN

Proof of Genius

'Someone might ask what all the fuss is about. The answer is simple: great as Kapell has always been, in the last year of his tragically brief life, his playing matured and blossomed in extraordinary ways.'

Jon M. Samuels's liner notes

'The playing on these discs, at least, is immortal; Kapell had worked very hard to make it so.'

Tim Page in liner notes

Roy's cuttings of Willy's concerts were immediately acclaimed. Typical of the critiques was Jeremy Nicholas's in *Gramophone*, an authoritative British magazine, who wrote that 'this is playing of a sublimely gifted artist'. Kapell's 'ability to see the big picture, his blazing intensity and wonderful control are heard at their best'. Terry Teachout in the *Wall Street Journal* wrote that while the sound was only 'fair', the performances 'are pure Kapell, headlong, vital and crackling with a vibrant immediacy that makes you feel as though he were playing in your very own living room'. Anthony Tommasini in the *New York Times* relished the CDs but added an astute perspective. These late performances were 'more mature'. It might sound absurd to speak of a 'late period' for an artist who died so young, he wrote, but Kapell was 'consciously striving to deepen his insights and expand his repertory during the last years of his life'. Prokofiev's seventh was played with 'breathtaking vigor and incisive attack, high-spirited yet never brutal'. Chopin's barcarolle was 'beautifully direct, lyrically supple', and his scherzo in B minor 'spellbinding, restless'. Tommasini said the recordings showed the results of Willy's 'growing maturity'. The Mozart sonata was played with 'clarity, grace … [and] sure structural cohesion'. His Bach was 'scrupulously honest and sensitive, full of character and dancing energy'. The Rachmaninoff third concerto emerged as 'intricate, cagey and innovative', ranging from 'surging power to ruminative lyricism'.

In his producer's note, Samuels mused that someone might ask what the fuss was all about. It was simple: in the last year of his life, Kapell's playing had 'matured and blossomed in extraordinary ways'. On another occasion, Jon called the Kapell Rachmaninoff 'one of the finest performances of the piece' he had ever heard. Willy's interpretations were different from those of most other musicians at the ends of their careers. 'Valedictory' recordings were historically important but often musically uninteresting. Willy's last performances were not only important for where they were in history, but they were made when he was 'at the peak of his skills'. And as far as the background noise on the CDs went, Jon said he had tried only to improve the sound of the music. Some extraneous noises had had to remain, and he had been criticised for it.

One of his critics was Donald Manildi, who was 'disappointed' in the quality of the transfers. Writing in the *Journal of the Association of Recorded Sound Collections*, he was, however, positive about the playing. Its significance could not be overestimated, and of special note was the Rachmaninoff, which had 'fierce intensity and drama'. It surpassed 'in every dimension' a 1948 version with the Toronto Symphony. Kapell's Debussy had 'poetry and restraint', and his Prokofiev 'blazing excitement'. In *The Plain Dealer*, Donald Rosenberg asked readers to listen 'through the noise, and you'll hear a magisterial musician who likely would have become even more towering'. Kapell's 'phrasing, coloring and wizardly technique combine here in cherishable performances that blend stylistic truth with artistic daring'.

Roy's acetates proved beyond doubt that Willy deserved his place among the keyboard immortals. In those last fourteen weeks of his life, he battered down the doors of the musicians' Pantheon and entered in triumph. Never before had his genius been so consistently and emphatically expressed. In Maitland and Melbourne, Bendigo and Brisbane – and ever so poignantly in Geelong – he played possessed.

Just why he chose to do it in faraway Australia in front of perhaps less sophisticated audiences than Carnegie Hall's remains a conundrum. Was he dying of cancer? Was he paying credence to a foreboding that his days were numbered? Was he simply signing off on Australia – forever – and did it with all the musical integrity and honesty he could muster? Or had he fallen victim to a bizarre obsession that drove him into a transcendent performing zone? Had the private, brooding Willy seen something, heard something, done something or understood something – been overcome by forces not even he understood, in other words – that induced a kind of other-worldly character to his art. We shall never know. And conjecture is unlikely to cease.

All we have are the forensics, the facts of his genius in seven major works performed in the vast shoebox of the Melbourne Town Hall. They are better than any of his earlier music-making – as sublime as his last turn at a keyboard, the Geelong Chopin.

Perhaps it was the Frick Collection's Steinway that inspired his pedestrian execution of Mussorgsky's *Pictures at an Exhibition* not five months before he gave a stupendous account of it in the Melbourne Town Hall. Several notes in the middle register of the Frick's grand are clearly out of tune, and over much of its compass the piano's timbre is jangly and banjoesque.

The differences between the masterful Melbourne performance, recorded on 21 July at Willy's first recital in Australia in 1953, and the Frick one, recorded in March, are enormous. In the former, a very great artist integrates a much-loved virtuoso work of widely contrasting musical colours, rhythms and dynamics. The latter exhibits no more than a fine pianist doing a professional job. Once or twice, indeed, Kapell sounds as if he has stopped concentrating.

Concert pianists and their audiences love *Pictures* to death. Based on drawings and water colours by Mussorgsky's painter friend Viktor Hartmann, it showcases a full palate of tonal colours. A jaunty walking tune links the images, which are of an old castle, a dwarf with crooked legs, quarrelling children in the Tuileries gardens in Paris, brawling women at Limoges market and the majestic Bogatyr Gates in Kiev, among other things. Many of the artworks that inspired the music are lost. Mussorgsky's music repaints them for us, brighter and in sharper focus than they were on Hartmann's paper.

The Melbourne performance is eighty-two seconds slower than its New York counterpart. Slower playing can equate with – and does in this case – a more thoughtful interpretation, longer and more dramatic pauses and more considered tempi. And as *Pictures* is an intense half-hour of sixteen integrated sections, for how long you pause and which tempi you use are crucial interpretative decisions. They are also fundamental to the work's wholeness. To perform a piece slower is also to take an extra artistic risk. But Willy triumphs. The Melbourne version is perfectly realised. From first chord to last, its thread is taut. Every note sounds right – as do the pauses between them – and the way Kapell hangs each of the 'pictures' seems completely appropriate. The images are sublimely rendered.

In the Frick's 'Old Castle', a strumming left hand accompanies the right-hand melody. And while this is logical because Hartmann painted a troubadour in front of the castle, Willy's thrumming is overdone, the guitar quality of the accompaniment diverting and a little kitsch. In 'Bydlo', a snapshot of a Polish ox cart, he exaggerates the eccentric wheels hitting ruts in the road: they do more stomping than rolling and are cartoonish. The Limoges market scene is rushed and in the vital late sections, especially in the ferocious Baba-Yagá (a hut on fowl's legs) scherzo, Kapell seems to lose conviction for the piece (and perhaps the piano) and accelerates through it. By the time he gets to the great gate of Kiev he sounds exhausted, struggling to nail all the images – and nail them up.

In Melbourne, they move and convince. The gnome gets about not only awkwardly on his crooked legs. He is also interrogative: why me? he asks. The mandolin is absent from the castle, the accompaniment just lightly staccato, which produces a more restrained, poignant and complementary bass line. This is consummate, expansive playing, the kind of interpretation in which its creator disappears and sharpness of line and colour dominate. The children in the Tuileries are quarrelling, but Kapell's depiction of them is light and deft. After all, children can't squabble too seriously, he says. The ox cart still drives leadenly, but its wheels resound on the ruts rather than stomp. Kapell's hands are less heavy, the picture no longer a caricature but an example of his own masterful brand of music-journalism. The women in the Limoges market are less rushed, Kapell exhibiting other sides to their characters. The huge echoes in the Catacombs are laden with portent and slowly executed. And in Baba-Yagá, the chord-striking is simply stupendous.

Five years after Kapell performed *Pictures* in Melbourne, Sviatoslav Richter, the amazing Russian whom many believe was the greatest 20th century pianist, especially of his compatriots' works, executed his legendary interpretation in a cough-counterpointed winter hall in Sofia. Kapell's Melbourne version is as good.

Willy had opened the program with Bach's suite (BWV 818), a piece he had recorded in RCA Studio 2 six years before. Listening to the performances side-by-side highlights dissimilarities. As with Mussorgsky, the Australian Bach is longer – nine minutes compared with eight-and-a-half in 1947. Where – and to what effect – did Willy put the extra thirty seconds?

The 'Allemande' that begins the suite is actually from the 1947 studio recording. For reasons never discovered, Roy Preston did not record it. The studio version, at any rate, is well articulated, muscly and energetic. The pianist appears to be goading the dance into a kind of urgency, somewhat forcing the issue.

The 'Courante' runs seven seconds over a minute in 1947. In the Melbourne Town Hall the pianist adds another thirteen. Whereas in the earlier recording it is dashing and emphatic, staccato notes foiling exaggerated rubati before cadences, six years later it is slower and more assertive. Willy has backed off and observed the suite from a distance, choosing the 'Courante' as its core statement. In 1947 the virtuosity is remarkable; in Melbourne it is invisible.

Only five seconds are added in Melbourne to the two following slow 'Sarabandes', which are sublime. The dances' ornaments are ice-blue, melodies husbanded with care. Pauses are sublime, arias liquid, and at times Willy turns down the volume to *ppp*, playing as softly as he can. Fruity coughing that accompanied the 'Courante' stops, and concert-goers crane to listen.

The 'Gigue' that ends the suite is twelve seconds slower in Melbourne than in the studio account. In a morsel of a little over a minute it amounts to a twenty per cent extension. In 1947, Willy employed staccato notes and bravado – foreshadowing the way Gould was to play Bach a decade or so later. In 1953, the 'Gigue' is a revelation. It is much slower yet still extroverted, a huge and deliberate contrast to the ethereal sarabandes that preceded it.

Four nights later at his second Melbourne recital, Willy opened with Mozart's B flat sonata K.570. Not known for his playing of the sublime Wolfgang, the pianist presents one of the most satisfying Mozart performances on record. The best interpreters of the little master have a trick to succeeding: let Mozart's music play itself. It is architecturally and tonally perfect. Generally speaking, absent from it are the nuances, surprises, syncopations and quirks that, say, Haydn would write into his keyboard pieces. The performer needs to run them up the mast. Provided you stick to the tempi, the notes and the dynamic markings, Mozart's sonatas play themselves. Let the pianist disappear, let the music conquer. Géza Anda could do it. Watching the sublime Hungarian, you felt as if he could leave the keyboard and whip out to the Green Room for one of the smokes he so loved, and the music would continue. (A year older than Willy, Anda died of cancer of the oesophagus at fifty-four in 1976.) He rolled out Mozart as if on glass, every note and its colour, length and strength transparent. But added none of himself. Mitsuko Uchida does something similar these days.

Two earlier Kapell performances of the middle movement of K.570 exist, both recorded in New York Town Hall, the first in 1949 and the second four months before Willy began his 1953 tour. In Melbourne, his execution of this movement – marked *adagio* or slow – is similar to the New York recording made earlier in the year. But in 1949, Willy had erred towards emphasising staccato marks in the third bar of the main theme, producing a cute, mannered effect.

He is not yet trusting the music to sing all by itself, feeling it needs help. As a Mozart pianist, he has not yet realised what is needed. In Mozart's day, the lowly infant piano – a far from powerful instrument – needed all the help it could get to bring music to life. A lot of staccato markings and ornamentation in 18th century keyboard music may be seen as compensating for the meagre volume of sound instruments far less sonorous than contemporary grands could produce. Four years later in Melbourne, Kapell avoids staccati almost completely. In all three movements, his tone is delicate, his louds and softs judicious, his melodic shaping definitive, his artistry over the keys exemplary, his deference to the composer total. For sixteen or so minutes, William Kapell has left the building – possibly gone for a smoke – to become a Mozart pianist.

And then, for the second and last item before interval, there was Prokofiev's seventh. His is a superlative version of a work new to the Kapell discography. First, it shows – as most concerts do – that music is best performed for other people and not microphones in studios. The essence of a piece of music is brought to life once a player sits down to present it to listeners who are nearby. He or she is nursing a composer's baby and knows it. There is a responsibility to treat it well. If he or she cannot bring a work to life, a musician is liable for the death or injury of a fragile newborn – every performance is a birth. Tragedy threatens, stimulating glands, winding up tension. The musician must bear up and will herself to succeed. Such pressure is hard to copy in the inert ambience of a studio. The burden of performing impels artistic vision. A performance should yell, kick and scream; it should crave attention. It should live without a smack on the butt. Almost all studio renditions seem routine and pedestrian beside their concert counterparts.

Richter's interpretation of Prokofiev's seventh is the benchmark. In *Notebooks and Conversations*, the Russian said, '[The composer] had just written [it] and had decided to entrust it to me with its first performance. I received the manuscript score only shortly before the premiére and had only four days in which to memorize it.' Being Richter, he achieved the goal. But not without being 'almost responsible for the death of Neuhaus's [Heinrich Neuhaus, Richter's teacher] second wife, Sylvia Fyodorovna, who was ill with a temperature of 40 degrees and whose apartment was the only place I could find to rehearse'. The piano was in her bedroom, and the 'poor woman had to submit to the onslaughts of the final movement ('Precipitato') for three or more hours at an end, over a period of four whole days.'

Prokofiev was in town and Richter, not yet thirty, visited him at the National Hotel to preview his interpretation. The composer had a piano in his room, but one of its pedals was broken. Pianist and composer got under the instrument to fix it. As they tried to straighten a metal connecting rod – it is easy to imagine Richter's murderous fists pushing and pulling – they banged their heads, almost knocking each other out.

When Richter played the work days later at Moscow's Hall of the House of Trade Unions, the seventh was a mighty success. (Ironically, it won Prokofiev a 'Stalin' prize.) Prokofiev was called to the stage to raucous applause, and several musicians in the audience, including violinist David Oistrakh, wanted Richter to play the sonata all over again. The pianist wrote that concert-goers 'clearly grasped the spirit of the work, which reflected their innermost feelings and concerns'. He was probably too polite to add 'in the dictator's wartime Soviet Union'.

In his book, Richter hints at how the seventh should be played. It was a piece that 'brutally plunged into the anxiously threatening atmosphere of a world that has lost its balance'. Chaos and uncertainty reigned. 'We see murderous forces unleashed.' But he argued that this should not mean Russians had to abnegate how they had lived before. 'We continue to feel and to love.'

A stupendous Richter rendition of the seventh at a Moscow recital in June 1958 has been released at least nineteen times under many labels. Richter executes the first movement at speed and note perfect. It is also wholly unsettling, a brutal plunge into an image of totalitarianism, the gulags and world conflict. (Prokofiev gave no specific metronome instructions about how fast or slow to play it, just that the performer should take it at an allegro pace and trouble the listener.) Richter's is pointed and unnerving art – great art. The movement's middle 'andantino', which Prokofiev directed should be 'sorrowful' (*dolente*) foils the first's violent atonality. It ambles lovingly and is exquisitely melancholic. And at no time – not even for a fraction of a second – does Richter relieve the pace or intensity of the *Precipitato*.

In the Melbourne Town Hall, Kapell played the seventh somewhat differently. He might not even have heard of Richter, who was yet to make his debut in the West. Masterful throughout, the seventh in Willy's hands is nonetheless more lyrical and not so tense. Willy's opening movement is jaunty – while still a little unsettling – its 'andantino' section contemplative and lovely. You could argue that it is too romantic, bearing in mind the work's history. (The seventh became known as the second of Prokofiev's three 'war' sonatas.) Willy fails, at any rate, to plunge the Melbourne audience 'brutally' into recognition of Stalinesque evils. (Like

Willy, both Stalin and Prokofiev did not see out 1953.) Not that the music is hurt by it. The 'Andante' middle movement is exquisite. It moves along faster than Richter's. And it is typical of Willy to make the repeated crotchets A flat and G – separated by a doleful semitone – toll pointedly and very softly a few bars before the short recapitulation of the main theme towards the movement's end. We may read nothing personal into these sad bells, because it is early in the tour – Willy's premonitions of his imminent demise came later. His *Precipitato* is relentless, loud and frightening. Both he and Richter never slacken the pace over those final two cacophonous pages. Confronting 1103 notes that need to be struck at a rate of twenty-five a second, some of the greatest pianists have baulked.

At his third Melbourne recital, Willy performed Debussy's *Suite Bergamasque* and three Chopin pieces. No other recordings exist of the Debussy, Chopin's Barcarolle Opus 60 and Scherzo No. 1 Opus 20. They are priceless.

The 'Prélude' that begins *Bergamasque* is elegant and whimsical. But it is also assertive and taken at a fair clip, its volume ranging between forceful and whispering. Perhaps Lindsey Browne was right – perhaps there *was* an 'American' style of piano-playing. At any rate, Willy's mastery over Debussy's material suggests it was written for him. The Frenchman's renowned interpreter Gieseking turned the *Bergamasque* into sedate – perhaps sedated – high romance. Willy energises and dramatises it. But he also unites the movements, plugging each into a shared grid tingling with several thousand volts. There is also extreme delicacy. The rising *glissando* that ends the 'Menuet' is played as softly as Willy dares. The result is breathtaking.

Halfway through this second section, the listener will also begin to notice interference, probably from another radio station. A male voice – a commentator of some sort – in a baritone Australian accent sounds as if he might be broadcasting from a greyhound track. It is impossible to understand what he is saying, but tone and cadences suggest that the dishlickers are being loaded into their starting boxes. A new track, Sandown Park, south-east of Melbourne was opened in 1953, and perhaps the rogue broadcast is straight from Sandown's sand. It joins, anyway, great recordings in which extraneous sound effects add interest and rarity, whether they be anti-aircraft guns defending Paris as Wanda Landowska records Scarlatti, Glenn Gould's atonal humming as he plays just about anything, and Pablo Casals's groaning during Beethoven cello sonatas.

Willy plays on, his sublime 'Clair de Lune' speedier and livelier than the habitual simper, the ending 'Passepied' playful and sinewy.

All three of the Chopin pieces – the third is one of the Pole's most sublime late nocturnes (Opus 55 No. 2) – reach the stratospheric standards Willy sets in earlier works. They are also emblematic of his style, interpretations tempered by intense musicality, coherence from first note to last, sensitive use of a wide dynamic range and, of course, his most obvious skill, peerless virtuosity. Notable are the introspection and mystery he brings to the barcarolle while stressing that life occasionally lends us shining moments. In the nocturne, the rising melody in the treble and its fainter echo – also played by the right hand – are weighted so perfectly that their twinning swells the heart. Willy plays brief semi-quaver decorations marked staccato in a restrained semi-abrupt fashion. The result is a jazzy and playful overlay in an otherwise meditative piece. Few pianists have mined these musical lodes with as much thought and originality. The scherzo is taken at horrifying speed, yet there are moments when Kapell pulls out of the dive to study the music. The result is other-worldly. Again we wonder how eight fingers and two thumbs can manage what he achieves.

On Thursday 1 October, four weeks before his demise, Willy played his last concert in Melbourne, Rachmaninoff's third concerto with the Victorian Symphony under Bernard Heinze. At home in North Fitzroy, Roy Preston inserted a new stylus. The result is gold standard. In his letter to the American music writer Joe Salerno, Cliff Hocking, who was at several of Kapell's Melbourne performances, said the Rachmaninoff 'appeared to take fire'. Listen to the 'sonically atrocious recording' he delivered to Gregor Benko, he urged Salerno. ' … [One] should have been there to hear that entry into the third movt. [sic] and the final pages – I was, and shall never forget'. (Hocking's letter continued by 'rambling on' about Willy's greatness. As far as he knew, Kapell 'must have been an isolated being, one well aware that in all the important moments of life we are truly alone … It was of this that his music spoke – and sang, and danced, the passionate utterance which lies well beyond common notions about life yet may well make contact with everyman'.)

Willy recorded the Rachmaninoff third with the Toronto Symphony in 1948. Comparing this rendition with its Melbourne counterpart is relatively easy. Although the much-loved first movement 'Allegro' is almost the same length in both performances, in Melbourne the 'Intermezzo: Adagio' and its contiguous 'Finale' are forty-six and forty-two seconds longer. Willy puts the extra time to best use, etching melodies with greater clarity amid Rachmaninoff's rich scoring. He takes with utter seriousness his responsibility to make the music sing – or at least show its potential to be sung. He nurtures the arias, caressing especially the soulful tune that inspired the first movement's lovely main theme. Too many times with the Toronto Symphony, the songs get lost while Willy demonstrates how well he can play all the notes – and very fast. The final two helter-skelter movements – a warhorse draped with copious garlands – makes sense in Melbourne, an achievement in itself. This is gorgeous, romantic pianism, music to luxuriate in, a performance to gasp over. And the Victorian Symphony collaborates to the full. Its wind work is lush, and the questions and answers between soloist and ensemble are balanced and clear.

In a piece as expansive as this, Hocking's assertion that Willy led the music from the keyboard must be seen as a personal response. It couldn't be done; he and Heinze collaborated as closely as any two musicians have. And Willy's long cadenza in the first movement has the ability to stop a listener's vital organs. Taken in its entirety, the performance is almost certainly everything Rachmaninoff desired of his music.

Tim Page's liner notes to *KAPELL reDISCOVERED*, echoed the thoughts of other commentators. It might sound strange, he wrote, to talk of 'early', 'middle' and 'late' periods in a pianist's playing, especially as Willy's career lasted only twelve years. '[But] there was a marked growth in Kapell's artistry over time, which we hear reflected in these interpretations, the latest of "late Kapell".' Page goes on to call Willy's Chopin 'some of the greatest', and the performances overall 'magnificent playing by any standard and a colossal enhancement of our understanding of [the performer]'.

Raymond Lewenthal, who died in 1988, heard only the Australian Chopin and Rachmaninoff performances. But he had already detected that Willy was 'growing at an alarming rate'. His playing had 'increasing strength'. Lewenthal wrote ironically that very little of the improvement was captured. He had heard, however, of 'vague rumours … about the possibilities of private recordings'. He would have loved the *reDISCOVERED* discs.

★ ★ ★

Anna Lou held my hand a long time when we first met. Propped up with pillows in her nursing-home bed, she seemed well aware that her days were darkening. She could scarcely talk, and had trouble clearing her throat. Yet her ginger hair and make-up were done to a blush, her beauty vintage but pronounced. She'd had a fall and a stroke the year before and was virtually immobile. She was occasionally helped into a wheelchair for a short excursion before returning to bed.

Her answers to my questions came slowly. With great effort, she could manage only a few words at a time. Dave helped me to understand her responses and give them context. The Geelong Chopin 'blew my mind', she said, when she'd first heard it. She had spent all these years trying to find recordings of other Australian performances because among them were pieces she hadn't heard Willy play in concert.

When we met the next day, Dave rugged her up against a crisp afternoon and wheeled her out behind the nursing home to a small lawn bordered by thin leafless trees, perhaps poplars. The sun shone feebly. She wanted to give me notes she had jotted for her autobiography, she told me, as well as transcriptions of letters to her parents that were written when she and Willy were courting. I had her permission to use them in my book. I was immensely moved. Throughout her life, Anna Lou had been vigilant on Willy's behalf. She had wanted only the truth told about her man, without whom − and despite her other achievements − 'life was nothing', she said. I was curious to discover if she could give me more specific reasons for the absence of a biography, but she was in no condition to answer. I concluded that it was because she cared so much about what people thought of Willy and his recorded legacy. He was hers.

She declined to comment on Willy's emotional state during the last weeks of his life − he was often 'anxious', she said. And she was well aware of the rigours of the tour and the vindictiveness of the Sydney critics. Yet he made music like an angel. No one − not even she − could pinpoint why.

There was a long pause. A small cold gust blew in off Long Island Sound and the sun disappeared. When it shone again, Anna Lou offered this: 'He had to show me what he was doing, and he had to show himself.'

CHAPTER SIXTEEN

Coda

'Something that serves to round out, conclude, or summarize and usually has its own interest.'
Merriam-Webster *dictionary*

'It was Roy that started all this … We are all just bit players in an amazing world of coincidence, chance, happiness and sadness.'
Maurice Austin, in an email to the author

'[A] concluding section … that is based, as a general rule, on extensions or reelaborations of thematic material previously heard.'
Britannica's *definition of a musical coda*

AMERICAN HUMANITIES PROFESSOR Stanley Fish has analysed *The Fugitive*, a television drama of the 1960s that was peerless at the popular examination of moral dilemmas. Dr Richard Kimble, the show's protagonist, is an innocent man on the run from a murder conviction. For an hour a week, he becomes entangled in the problems of a wide variety of ordinary Americans in a host of towns, hamlets and cities. He picks up any casual employment he can get. Fish analyses the episodes and runs a commentary on the politics and philosophies of personalities, professions, police and Joe Public.

His examination of an episode entitled 'With Strings Attached' echoes Willy's life. Its protagonist is Geoffrey Martin, an 'obsessive' young concert violinist driven hard by his coach and guardian, Max. Kimble, who was trained as a specialist in children's medicine, is hired as a chauffeur, and he is soon suspicious about what gives between Geoffrey and Max. The violinist's pet canary dies, his Stradivarius gets broken, and Geoffrey reports that Max has injured his (Geoffrey's) hand. Kimble suspects Geoffrey himself is doing the deeds. He's right, of course, and it transpires that Geoffrey is aiming to murder Max because he feels trapped by his violin – snared by the discipline and dedication required to become and remain a great player, resentful of not living an 'other' life. Before a concert, Geoffrey confronts Max: 'You took something from me … I'm taking it back. My freedom.' Max replies that Geoffrey lost his freedom when he was given 'the great gift of genius'. No matter what Geoffrey does to try to flee from himself, Fish argues, his 'compulsion to perform' will survive and rule his existence. The story ends at gunpoint, but rather than shoot Max, Geoffrey shoots his violin. All he wanted was to be free, he wails, and a narrator reminds us that some people are in chains from birth: 'They are their own jailors, their own prisons.'

As much as he loved them, Willy often hated pianos. At times, he couldn't bring himself to look at one. And before a concert, the big black instrument waiting for him on the stage terrified him. So far as we know, he never shot one. But, in a sense, he could not avoid turning a gun on himself.

Many great artists do. Moreover, they sense the inevitability of what awaits them. Literary critic Harold Bloom in *The Western Canon* comments on the agony of genius. He says Nietzsche – whom Willy read – taught a 'poetics' of pain. That to create anything memorable was to submit oneself to torture. Keats agonised over his sonnets. Excellence in every art, the poet wrote, required 'intensity'. He believed that failure was a good grounding for success; he would 'sooner fail than not be among the greatest'. Such was his obsession.

Bloom says the Czech writer Franz Kafka was iconic of the great artist's paradox: he became indestructible only by self-destruction. In his aphorisms known as 'He' – because he led each off with the pronoun – Kafka wrote: 'He has the feeling that merely by being alive he is blocking his own way. From his obstruction, again, he derives the proof that he is alive'. Kafka lived, he noted, on 'frail ground … over a darkness from which the dark power emerges when it wills and, heedless of my stammering, destroys my life'. Yet life was worse when he wasn't writing – 'wholly unbearable and has to end in madness'. Writing was a 'sweet and wonderful reward' but a reward, nonetheless, for 'serving the devil'. Speaking only as a writer, he might have been nonetheless voicing the predicament of every great artist who is 'the scapegoat of mankind'. Writers allowed others to enjoy 'sin without guilt, almost without guilt', Kafka wrote. And there is an irony to the indestructibility Bloom invests in Kafka: artists attain it – if they're lucky – sometimes only decades and centuries after they have returned to dust. Willy is indestructible now, and nothing – except the extinction of man himself – can diminish what he achieved and the archive Roy made of it.

And as much as great artists feel compelled to submit themselves to agony, they have the choice of opting out. Each of us tries to construct a world in which he or she is most at ease, and for many of the greatest painters, writers and musicians intense pain is an acceptable part of the job. And despite the terror his art compelled him to endure, there is enough evidence in Willy's own letters to show what abundant rewards he believed he received from playing the piano. He had come to terms with the life he wanted to live, however agonising and complex it sometimes was.

Events in his life – especially in Australia – manifest what Freud called the 'uncanny'. The father of psychoanalysis was perhaps the most important of several great minds that have wrestled with coincidence – what the Swiss psychiatrist Carl Jung labelled 'synchronicity'. But in the end, Freud and Jung, at least, or at most, came up with very little in the way of an explanation for the causes of uncanniness. There is description, but scant understanding.

Jung sought a principle to explain an eerie chain of happenings that could not be explained by cause and effect. Over more than a hundred pages, he grappled with the way lost articles get back to their owners, for instance, as well as the notion of extra-sensory perception. He cited the palolo worm, whose sexual segments float to the sea's surface on the day before the last quarter of the moon in October and November ... always. He undertook a long analysis of certain horoscopes, even applying mathematical models to them. But the best he could conclude was that 'synchronicity' was a 'highly abstract and "irrepresentable" quantity'. It was at the opposite end of the scale from 'causality'. Coincidences could be thought of as accidents of pure chance, he admitted. 'But the more they multiply and the greater and more exact the correspondence is, the more their probability sinks and their unthinkability increases, until they can no longer be regarded as pure chance but, for lack of a causal explanation, have to be thought of as meaningful arrangements'. Jung cannot have been happy with this explanation, and it seems as if he placed little trust in probability theory.

Willy was involved in several of Jung's 'meaningful arrangements'. He, Noel Mewton-Wood and Richard Farrell – all fine pianists, all dead at thirty-one. His referral several times to the short 'Life' line in the palm of his hand and his assertions that he shouldn't be alive only days before he died. His stating that he would never return to Australia. His deciding not to stop over in Honolulu but continue his fatal journey. The black cat's visitation at his last concert, assuming, of course, that black cats bring bad luck. (In some cultures, they are thought to deliver good fortune.) The similarity in looks of Willy and Roy. Several events – Willy's death, Roy's death, and contact being made between Maurice and the Kapells the most prominent – occurring on the twenty-ninth day of a month. And, perhaps the most important, that Maurice Austin met Roy, followed up his interest in Willy, and found the acetates of his best performances almost by 'happenstance', as he calls it. These coincidences – arrangements – have differing qualities, but they could all be classified under Freud's 'uncanny' heading.

Freud thought there was nothing remarkable in leaving a garment at a cloakroom and being given a ticket with sixty-two on it then being allocated a 'cabin', say, bearing the same number. But things changed if these events were close. If, for instance, we encountered sixty-two several times in a day, one would need to be 'steeled against the lure of superstition' not to think the repeated happenings had some secret significance, he wrote. Observers experienced an 'uncanny effect' when they blurred the boundary between fantasy and reality, Freud concluded. Their fault was to emphasise 'psychical' reality over 'material' reality. He could not deny the bizarre, but how forceful it was depended on how we balanced a see-saw – the real world, and what our minds made of it.

We have every right to interpret a set of events as we please. We may believe that some supernatural force scripted the story of Willy and Roy and moved its players. We are entitled to think that Willy was destroyed by appallingly bad luck. We may equally believe that his genius was resurrected by a stroke of the reverse. Or we may simply fall back on big numbers: so many billions of human events occur each day that, occasionally, a sequence of them will frame an uncanny narrative – such as Willy and Roy's.

Willy was tragically unlucky. But Roy captured some of his last – and indisputably best – performances in all innocence in a humble cottage on amateur equipment. And Maurice valued Roy's etchings enough to find them and begin the process that assured Willy of immortality. How it came about seems immaterial, in the end. It happened.

NOTES

Chapter One

1 Cook captained *Endeavour* on his first voyage (from 1768), commanding *Resolution* on his second and third. (*Adventure* sailed with Cook on the second voyage and *Discovery* on the third.) *HMS Resolution* was Cook's 'ship of my choice', so enamoured of it was he. The former coal sloop was fitted out with the latest navigational aids, ice anchors and equipment to distil fresh water from the sea. It had three masts and twelve cannon. At almost 111 feet long and over 35 feet in the beam, she was just a little bigger and broader than a DC-6.

Chapter Two

1 She was briefly married to a Russian engineer but returned to the States to try to forge her future on the American concert platform. At the age of twenty-five in 1905, she hired all 2800 seats of Carnegie Hall, an orchestra and conductor Walter Damrosch and performed Tchaikovsky's first piano concerto. She'd lit the touchpaper to what Harold Schonberg in *The Great Pianists* calls a 'brilliant career', touring the United States and returning for concerts in Europe. She made many recordings. Two years younger, Leopold Stokowski made his Paris conducting debut with the Colonne Orchestra in 1909, Olga playing a Tchaikovsky concerto. They married two years later, and Olga lobbied hard so that her less well-known husband could take up the vacant conductor's post at the Philadelphia Orchestra. (Stokowski would go on to become the world's best-known maestro, a champion of new music as well as the man who wielded the baton for Walt Disney's *Fantasia* score, his hurricane-struck white hair flourishing, his cues precise and imperious.) In 1923, Olga and Leopold divorced, and two years later she fell in her New York apartment, injuring her shoulder. From then on, she turned almost exclusively to teaching and writing about music. Ernest Hutcheson, the Melbourne-born dean (and formidable pianist) of the newly formed Juilliard School, invited her on to the staff, and she taught there and at the Philadelphia Conservatory for the rest of her life. William Kapell was her most famous student, but she is reported to have said that her

best was the New Zealander Richard Farrell. (It was the kind of remark she might have made in front of Willy, to spur him to greater heights.) She also taught the masterly Bach pianist and scholar Rosalyn Tureck.

2   Schubert wrote three piano sonatas as typhoid – some say syphilis – strangled his thirty-second year, and they are of such scope and significance that Alfred Brendel, a great Schubertian pianist, has described them as 'disguised string quartets'. (Among Beethoven's last and greatest works were string quartets.)

3   Professor Susan Hallam of the University of London recently analysed many studies on the benefits for children of learning to play a musical instrument. She concluded that it improved their behaviour, memory and intelligence. Playing music enlarges the left side of the brain, which dominates logical processes, analysis and language. Over time, children who study a musical instrument score several points higher in intelligence tests than their instrument-free counterparts, she discovered. Harvard University research has confirmed that playing an instrument leads to higher verbal ability and greater skill in recognising patterns. Other American studies have shown that piano students more readily understand mathematical and scientific concepts. They win more academic honours and awards than students who don't study instruments. The compounding effect of learning to produce organised sound and an increase in intelligence – and therefore analytic and interpretative skills – can't be denied.

4   It's said that you must put in 10,000 hours of practice if you want to be a virtuoso. It doesn't mean that if you do the time you'll become a great artist; the practice simply gives an aspiring pianist the equipment to try to become one. Professor Gary McPherson is the University of Melbourne's director of music. His special interest is determining why anyone would want to put in those 10,000 hours, bearing in mind that practically no one can practise intensively, repetitively and intelligently for longer than about three to four. Those who can shoulder the burden of developing their talent meet three criteria, he says: they have constant support from parents and teachers, they like repetitive work and they enjoy the developmental process. These seem obvious requirements, but Professor McPherson adds that research fails to support the myth of prodigies' stereotypical parents who shackle their children to the keyboard.

Chapter Three

1   Moses had taken an unusual path to the ABC's top job. A graduate of the prestigious Sandhurst military college in Britain who served in World War

I, he emigrated to Australia in the 1920s to join his father and brothers
growing fruit in central Victoria. The venture failed, and he tried selling
real estate and cars. Entrepreneurial, he even set himself up as a kind of
personal trainer. None of these moves was successful, however, so he
auditioned to be an ABC sports commentator. (He had been a handy
middleweight boxer and soccer player, and had a special interest in
competitive wood-chopping.) He got the job and very quickly vaulted up
the commission's ranks. In 1934, he was appointed federal controller of
talks. Tall, handsome, straight-backed and straight-shooting, he formed
an advisory body to find ways to present radio documentaries more
imaginatively. But his thinking also had an impressive and uncommon
cultural breadth that appealed to the commission's chairman, William
Cleary. Cleary and Moses discussed the ABC's role in society at length.
Moses felt the broadcaster should support local playwrights, composers and
music-makers.

   After a year as head of talks, he was – at thirty-five – made general
manager of the entire behemoth. Razor-sharp competition axes leant against
his office wall. Perhaps untrue, stories tell of his shaving guests' forearms
with them. Heinze and he strove to implement their ideas, and in 1938
they toured Artur Schnabel, the world's foremost Beethoven exponent, and
maestro George Szell. At a Sydney concert, Schnabel and Szell played both
Brahms piano concertos to a three-quarter-full house. But that wasn't the
point, Moses later stressed. The same concert could have been put on to full
houses several nights a week later in his thirty-year reign, he once recalled.

   War interrupted, and Moses served with courage and distinction in
Malaya and Singapore. Returning to the ABC, he moved quickly, securing
from state governments and capital-city administrations a share of the
money needed to realise his dream. Setting up state orchestras wasn't
immediate. But it was inexorable. He poached British maestro Eugene
Goossens from the Cincinatti Symphony to be the Sydney Symphony's
permanent conductor. (Moses and Goossens germinated the idea of a great
opera house in Sydney.) And central to his vision remained annual tours
by the world's best virtuosi. The breadth of his smile as he read Ormandy's
letter can hardly be exaggerated.

2 When Perth was dropped from Kapell's schedule, the ABC's Western
   Australia manager, a Mr Charlton, wrote to James with what he called
   anger and regret. He pleaded with James to make a 'final effort' to rearrange
   bookings so that Willy could play in his state. He continued, 'I have not

conveyed the information to the Women's Orchestral Committee whom I know will be ropable. They were very hot under the collar over the elimination of Ormandy (the year before), and now this one crops up. Your suggestion that Richard Farrell succeeds him (Kapell) I do not think a good one [sic]. We can certainly play up the youth side of it but do you honestly think that he is the one to succeed an artist such as Kapell is, or that his publicity would make us believe he is?' A little later, Perth was reinstated on Willy's route.

3   The son of a bricklayer, Dobell enrolled in night-school to study painting. He is reported to have told Willy that his father had insisted he learn the piano only after he had studied architecture. The report says Dobell studied for three years at Sydney Conservatorium, an aside that goes unmentioned in the *Australian Dictionary of Biography*. In return, Willy told Bill he had 'very good piano hands'. If he didn't start painting until he was twenty-four, then there was time for him [Willy] to become an artist, he was reported to have said. 'I paint from instinct', the quote went. 'I have no knowledge of fundamentals.' Dobell allegedly agreed to give him tips. According to the *Australian Women's Weekly*, he'd also sketch him in concert from the stalls.

4   The 'babe' 'Athena' was Mollie Maginnis, a friend of McCallum, who later married legendary Melbourne journalist and writer John Hetherington.

5   By 1939, Cardus feared the war in Europe might curtail his British career, and he accepted an invitation from Sir Keith Murdoch, Rupert's father, to cover a tour of Australia by the idiosyncratic conductor Sir Thomas Beecham. His reports were for Murdoch's Melbourne *Herald*, which was published in the afternoon. He found it inconvenient to cover evening concerts, so he negotiated a job as music critic at the *Sydney Morning Herald*. He was fifty-seven, pedantic, waspish, and supposedly at the height of his analytic powers. He held the post until he returned to England in 1949.

Chapter Four

1   Lewenthal was an unlucky pianist, if not so unlucky as Willy. In the summer of 1953 he was mugged in Central Park by a gang of louts wielding clubs. They broke seven bones in his hands and arms, and he left America for a painful recovery abroad that lasted more than a decade. He took an interest in the idiosyncratic French composer Alkan – he of the rattling virtuoso piano works – eventually bringing him to the notice of American ears in the 1960s. And he also resumed his concert and recording career.

Chapter Five

1   As Kapell completed the first half of his tour, which had stations at Perth, Ballarat and Brisbane as well as Adelaide and Melbourne, gushes and raves reverberated after every note.

Dr Robertson: 'Not for a long time have Adelaide concert-goers been granted playing so convincing in musical quality and so masterful in technique.'

Linda Phillips: 'The relentless drive of the last movement [of Prokofiev's seventh sonata] was almost frightening in the pianist's employment of modern piston-like mechanics.'

Dr B. V. Pusenjak: 'His was a performance of great beauty, tender in its phrasing, full of dazzling virtuosities and constrained to the tiniest details at the same time.'

The *Age*: 'Since his previous [1943] visit to Melbourne ... Mr Kapell has gained maturity and authority.'

'Fidelio': 'William Kapell played the piano superbly.' And again, 'My goodness! How that poet has grown in the seven [sic] years since [he] played here last!'

Eunice Gardiner: 'Think of the few great pianists you have heard and put the name of William Kapell beside them – for that is where it belongs.'

Ernest Briggs: '[His Brahms first] revealed a marked artistic and intellectual advance since he last played here.'

Chapter Six

1   Sinclair's revelations were made during Stevens's commemorative broadcast by the ABC on the thirtieth anniversary of Willy's death. Its most alarming exposés amounted to corroboration of Willy's frequent bouts of depression and his tenuous grip on commonsense. Stevens himself speculated about a premonition Willy allegedly had of his 'early death'. Patricia Tuckwell revealed that she had heard Willy work 'creepily' and obsessively on the *Funeral March*. Ray Humphries reported to a friend that during a trip from Melbourne to Bendigo, Willy had looked deeply troubled. Humphries asked him if he could do anything. Willy replied that he was trying to understand the psalmists, who wrote, 'Blessed are the meek: for they shall inherit the earth'.

To draw on for the broadcast, Jerome Lowenthal sent Stevens a draft of an article that would appear in the February 1984 number of *Clavier*. In a covering letter, Lowenthal hoped that Stevens would not be offended by the 'dark colors in which I paint Kapell's Australian tour'. He wrote that Willy was 'desperately unhappy' during it, and in paraphrasing certain of Kapell's letters he hoped 'to render the quality of that unhappiness'. Willy had found himself 'harassed by a hostile, even derisive press, and given no encouragement by indifferent management and an unresponsive public'. His schedule was 'horrendous', the repertoire requirements 'enormous'. Lowenthal continued, 'For anyone this tour would have been exhausting, but for Kapell, whose private formula of work-ratio to concert performances was inexorably demanding, collapse seemed inevitable. He did not collapse, however; except for a few days [sic] layoff in Melbourne because of severe muscle strain, he continued to work feverishly and to play gloriously. Australia had become a prison to him, and he passionately longed to go home, not in order to rest, but to be able to perform for those who would receive the message of his art'. His 'three-month nightmare' behind him, he wanted to lay a groundplan for a 'life of artistic exploration and growth with audiences who would follow where he led'. Lowenthal described it as a 'golden dream which the reverse alchemy of circumstances was to transmute into an ironic obituary caption'.

2 Using a Speed Graphic camera, Gemmell took a photograph of Willy at the keyboard of the Ellerys' grand early in the tour. He has stopped playing and is turned from the music, his eyes downcast and half-closed, his hair tousled, smile absent. Pensive, he looks every bit the great musician. The photograph was used for at least one record cover in America.

Chapter Seven

1 *King Kut Comedy No. 1* is a sixty-eight-minute retelling of the 'legend' of King Kut, who 'dwelt' in the mountainless Port Melbourne 'Alps'. Indeed, he ruled its 'empire'. The film opens with King Kut in the bath wearing a crown that looks as if it has been hacked from sheet tin with an axe. 'KK' is stencilled on the side of the bath, and an aide enters to tell His Majesty he shouldn't be in headgear while he washes. Fairly quickly, the scene shifts to the king's lovely daughter Katty. She and a bevy of handmaidens in swimsuits 'doeth' (says the caption) their morning exercises – rather like battery-powered ancient Egyptians. The Duke of Footscray, Czar of Carlton and Prince Slippery Sloper have major roles in *King Kut*, and Katty and her attendants disguise themselves halfway through as soldiers. Gender-swapping occurs frequently, and false moustaches and funny hats

are common. The Czar declares war on King Kut, but all is resolved when Slippery Sloper and Katty marry. (Royce Films, it might be surmised, could not afford to stage battle scenes.) There was no *King Kut Comedy No. 2*, at any rate, and it's surprising to think that *No. 1* and its histrionic captions, smudgy focus, bad acting and sclerotic cinematography was shot in 1929, just ten years before the colour and magic of *The Wizard of Oz*.

Chapter Eight

1   A month after the crash, *The ABC Weekly* quoted several of the commission's senior executives. Bill James, who had seen off Willy at the airport, was 'stunned'. Kapell was one of the great pianists of his generation, he said. 'The passing of so brilliant and serious a musician is a severe loss to the world of music.' Later, in a program foreword, general manager Moses spoke from the heart. The Willy Kapell he saw in 1953 had 'mellowed' after eight years. His devotion to music was 'almost fanatical', his marriage and family had enriched him, and 'one felt he was obsessed by a feeling of humility towards the Masters he interpreted'. He walked 'eagerly' to the piano, keen to show the 'beauties of the works he would play'. Then he became lost in the music. 'His habit of talking to himself or ... to the composer, did not seem affectation. He set himself very high standards of performance and worked himself to the point of physical exhaustion to achieve them. Often he would rehearse into the small hours of the morning, even on the night before a concert, to satisfy himself that his performances would not fall short of his own standards.'

2   In memoriam in 1983, Leonard Bernstein said of Willy, 'You spent so much of your abrupt life mourning your own daily deaths, grieving over what you perceived to be your failures, even as you celebrate your own flaming genius'. Eugene Istomin dictated that 'there has never been a better model for our young pianists'. He went on, 'He left the highest standard ever achieved by an American born pianist. His intensity, his translucent sound, his humble yet steely discipline and piercing intelligence, above all his powerful personality combined with a sometimes feisty integrity, describe him best as an artist and force of nature.' He remained 'unconsolable' [sic] by 'the abortion of his career'. And Jerome Lowenthal said, 'There's an aesthetic completeness about that driven, knotty, violent personality punching music critics, insulting conductors, creating hordes of enemies, and meanwhile being the adored hero of the public, playing ever more beautifully, and finally colliding with a mountain. That's the material of legend.'

In his essay on Willy, Raymond Lewenthal said that he heard about Willy's death from a radio news broadcast. 'I probably aged ten years that day,' he wrote. Willy was different from the rest. 'He changed, he shifted, and how he continued to grow! Certainly, he was nowhere near his peak when he died, although the level to which he strived was stratospheric.' He was in a hurry to fulfil his destiny – it was 'almost as if he knew he didn't have much time'.

3   Two years older than Willy, Stern was born of Jewish parents in the Ukraine. The family moved to San Francisco when he was a baby, and his first studies were at the city's conservatory. In his autobiography *My First 79 Years*, he wrote that he played his first 'really professional concert' at the age of seventeen in his home town with Pierre Monteux conducting. His performance of the Brahms concerto 'went quite well, because there was a ripple effect'. It started his career. Two years later, the New York *Herald Tribune*'s critic believed he was 'among the most important violinists now to be heard'.

Stern is remembered for his musicality and consummate technique, but also his generous partnering – he had three wives – and equally bounteous mentoring that beat paths for much younger string players such as Yo-Yo Ma and Itzhak Perlman. He led a campaign to save Carnegie Hall, which he called the 'Holy Grail' of music, from demolition in 1960. He was constantly on the lookout for ways to make classical music more appealing to more people and to improve the lot of music's practitioners. A rare performer, he loved the politics of art as much as its execution.

He had heard Willy play often, he wrote in his autobiography. They had performed together privately. 'Short, with wild black hair, a pimpled face, and a wiry body, he seemed to walk electrically; it was as if he needed only to touch the piano and it opened up to him. He was a brilliant explosive virtuoso, a Promethean pianist.' In the two years before his death, Willy's 'perceptions had matured; his palette of colors and ideas, the inner substance of his music, had grown larger, and he was able to give greater scope to his performances and develop more and more music of various kinds'. According to the violinist, there was 'no limit' to Willy's talent. He was headed for a 'major career', not only because he was a great musician. He had 'the "X" factor', which allowed him to 'extend across the footlights and mesmerize the audience'. Willy 'had it … [And] now he was gone. A terrible loss!'

4   The imperious Sir Thomas Beecham thought in 1940 that the Melburnian was the 'best talent I've discovered in the British Empire for years'. (Beecham usually owned most things connected with music. He once

demanded to know if an orchestral player had fly-spots in front of his notes because he was playing flat. The 'flat' mark in music, which lowers the note by a semi-tone, is little more than a flyspot with an aerial.)

Like Willy, Mewton-Wood had learned from Schnabel – he spent the European summer of 1938 with him. He premiered Benjamin Britten's piano concerto, Britten himself conducting, as well giving first performances of a concerto and sonata by Arthur Bliss. An only child of a piano-teaching mother, his playing was noted for its passion and physicality, which erred occasionally, some say, towards a brand of uncultured violence. Unlike Willy, Mewton-Wood was taciturn, swam often, played tennis, read medical texts, bred German shepherds and, when he lived in the country, kept geese. According to one source, he composed and wrote the books for and staged his own marionette musicals.

Chapter Nine

1   Haydn loved the tune, having written it as a birthday anthem for Francis II. He used it in both the quartet and a small set of piano variations he wrote late in life. It became the German national anthem.
2   In an interview late in life, Roy described Verdon's sight-reading as a 'miracle … But he might have played it at home'. Williams went on to become a respected musician, composer and conductor.
3   A month before Willy began his last concert tour, McKie conducted a choir of four hundred and an orchestra of sixty in the music he had devised for the coronation of Queen Elizabeth. He was knighted the same year.
4   'Wurlitzer' is 'Hoover' for theatre organs, which were invented by Englishman Robert Hope-Jones to accompany silent movies. Hope-Jones specified that his pipe organs should be able to imitate an orchestra and have a playing console that could be distant from the pipes. He built more than two hundred of them from the late 19th century into the early 20th before merging his company with the American Wurlitzer firm. Soon after, he committed suicide for reasons sources decline to specify. Hope-Jones's innovations included replacing draw-knobs with tabs the player could press to introduce an amazing array of timbres and voices. He developed pipes that had built-in vibrato and tremolo (frequency and amplitude variations), the fluttering sound for which theatre organs are best-known. Later instruments added bells, whistles and even such effects as the sound of breaking waves.
5   Roy reported that cover notes to Baker's LP were 'both irritating and interesting'. Interesting because they dealt well with all the items played,

and irritating because they 'ramble on about the organ being a superb "imitator" of the orchestra'. Roy pointed out that 'surely the operative word is "substitute" … If the theatre organ really sounded just like an orchestra would it have the select following it has?'

Chapter Ten

1   From his small timber Californian bungalow in Robbins Street, Ivanhoe, a middle-class suburb of nice Melburnians, Eric Truswell taught piano and violin to a host of students for several decades after World War II. I was one. He regularly plucked a fresh shoot of bamboo from a patch in his front garden to welt the errant hands of would-be keyboard artists. He dressed in olive-green corduroy trousers and tan suede shoes that not only trumpeted his modernity but suited his silvering Beethovian hairdo and swarthy skin. His much younger partner John – sharp-featured, his black beard pointed – would eye students through a crack in the door to the kitchen with the scepticism of a Velazquez prince. For Truswell's more talented players, however, Truswell was a demigod. Like Kapell and many others, he had learned from Schnabel, and he had the rare gift of conveying what musicality meant, how to identify it and how to manifest it. Through clouds of cigarette smoke, the best of Truswell's students were taught the usual Schnabel axioms: try to take in the whole landscape of a piece of music, not the pretty flower in bar twenty-one; play runs like strings of pearls; play the pauses; perform the whole piece as if it is a whole piece, not a collage. He was a skilled go-between, too, arranging eternal and ardent love affairs between music and many of his more vulnerable pupils. He tried to make them musicians. Hocking had been in good hands.

2   Part of Timmins's aesthetic existence involved membership of a small group with artistic and philosophical inclinations led by poet Harold Stewart. They mostly discussed traditional systems of belief. Stewart, Timmins and another of their number, Adrian Snodgrass, went in 1963 to Japan to be trained in Shin Buddhism. Only Timmins elected to become an ordained Shin priest. Snodgrass became a philosopher and has since contributed to hermeneutics – the study of interpretations.

3   Their first joint venture was to bring out Carl Dolmetsch, the French-born recorder virtuoso who may be credited with resurrecting the instrument's popularity in the 20th century. (His father Arnold made recorders that became a benchmark for quality, his craft the foundation of the revival of early music.) Carl was booked to tour for four weeks and eventually stayed

eight. Barry Humphries's second one-man show *Excuse I* ran for seven months from late 1965. Sarod master Ali Akbar Khan was next, followed by two tours by Venezuelan classical guitarist Alirio Diaz. By 1970, Humphries had toured again with *Just a Show*, Diaz had returned twice, and Hocking and Vigo had presented him in the United Kingdom. The Robert Pikler Chamber Orchestra, Sinfonia of Sydney and guitarist Paco Peña also entrusted their musicianship with the pair. They had few failures, relying on gut instinct to tell them if a musician or entertainer in a specialised field was likely to attract audiences. They toured only quality, and until Cliff's death in 2006 brought to music-lovers in Australia, the United Kingdom and the United States some of the biggest names.

Cliff got British jazz singer Cleo Laine and her husband, the saxophonist John Dankworth, into Carnegie Hall. It was the beginning of their immense success beyond the jazz cellars of London. He toured them through small towns in Australia and America. One Midwest town was so snowbound that only about ten locals could get to the hall. Laine and Dankworth performed. In another, the local entrepreneur was slow to produce Cliff's share of the box office. Cliff confronted him. Custom was, Hocking reminded him, that the talent and his manager were paid at the end of a show, sometimes before the last notes had faded. The local impresario pulled open a drawer, took out a pistol and banged it on the desk.

Elsewhere, Cliff was once paid in coins – bags and bags of quarters. He toured Stéphane Grappelli many times in Australia and the United States. Blossom Dearie, Pam Ayres, Leo Kottke, Frida Boccara, Stan Getz, Keith Jarrett, Dave Brubeck, Oscar Peterson, Ravi Shankar, Arlo Guthrie, the Sydney Dance Company, The Fureys, John Williams, Teresa Berganza, Shura Cherkassky, Victoria de los Angeles, Rowan Atkinson and Stevie Ray Vaughan, the blues guitarist, were all once or several times managed and promoted by Hocking and Vigo. After the last show of a successful tour, Cliff handed Stevie Ray a bonus – possibly a few thousand dollars, says Vigo – in a brown envelope. Vaughan was flabbergasted. 'People just don't give me extra money because things go well,' he said. He and David took on artists with surplus fire, Cliff used to say. They were so hot they were not just cool, but freezing. 'Ice can burn, you know,' Vigo says Cliff used to say. Cliff was the first person to be artistic director of both the Adelaide and Melbourne arts festivals.

4   Tureck later toured Australia for Hocking and Vigo without playing a note in public. Vigo heard her practising in the concert hall in which she was to

play that night, but later found her lying down, too ill to perform. She'd just come from India, she said, and had caught something. Days later, she was still too sick to play in Sydney.

5   Maurice eventually played electronic and theatre organs for his 'own amazement', as he puts it. He learned no instrument as a child, even though the family always had a piano. His older brother Don played tuba at Melbourne High School, and younger brother Roger was a drummer in a rock band.

6   Late in 1987 Ann Kapell – Bob's wife – met Clifford Hocking at a Tower Records store at Lincoln Center, New York City. They literally bumped into each other. On 21 September, she wrote to Cliff to say that she and Bob had heard on the radio the day before Cliff's contribution to a commemorative broadcast – probably on WQXR – about Willy. What he had said about their brother-in-law and brother had 'touched us deeply'. Ann thanked Cliff for contributing to 'our understanding of Willy's trip in Australia, especially how you and many others felt about him'. Willy, she wrote later in the letter, 'was made from stellar sources'. Ann had given Anna Lou's contact details to Cliff, and he visited her. Anna Lou could remember little of their meeting, but perhaps Cliff might have explained his role in the emergence of the bootleg recordings.

Chapter Eleven

1   Described as a nightclub owner, Ruby shot dead Lee Harvey Oswald in full view of television cameras. Oswald, the Warren Commission eventually decided, acted alone in assassinating President John F. Kennedy.

2   Todd Zagorec has reviewed a biography of Willis Ritter for the *Utah Bar Journal*. He describes him as 'crotchety', a 'quirky, grouchy judge' whose life was a 'Greek tragedy set against the law, politics and personalities of Utah'. Everyone who had ever known Ritter told stories about the 'iron fist' with which he ruled. At one point, his courtroom was above a basement of postal workers sorting letters. They used an elevator, whose rattlings carried to Ritter's bench. Declaring that the court was beginning to sound like a bowling alley, the judge ordered the elevator stopped. It continued, and he decreed the arrest of the offending sorter who was in it. Postal workers spent the day failing to learn from their colleague's mistake, and by the end of the sitting twenty-four of them were in custody.

Reportedly, Ritter at one time or another assaulted the owner of a nightclub, pounded the table at a restaurant (possibly several), and lost a game of 'strip' spin-the-bottle at Club Manhattan, a late-night Salt Lake City bar. For all that, he was an influential jurist who made brave – some said controversial – decisions such as removing the Ten Commandments from a downtown Hall of Justice. A New Deal Democrat, he was liberal in an America not especially amorous of people who did things differently. Defining the epithet 'ornery', he had enemies and an unhappy marriage. As he aged, he became lonely, bitter and, in Zagorec's words, 'vindictive, erratic, dictatorial, and at times just plain mean and uncouth'. Only alcohol, alone in his chambers, helped.

From a broken family, he had been a brilliant student, graduating from the University of Utah, the University of Chicago and Harvard Law School (with a doctorate in legal science). Professionally, he was acclaimed for much of his career. For all that, *TIME* magazine described the short, round jurist – of the drilling gaze from behind rimless spectacles, the cleft chin below them – as 'freewheeling'. He was fifty when he was promoted to the bench in 1949, and by 1961, as a senior federal judge he also sat beyond his home state.

3 Chester Bryant was a gripman on a cable car in San Francisco – he worked the long lever in the middle of cars that held tight to a running cable beneath the street. As he was entering the intersection of O'Farrell and Powell Streets one day, the lever thumped back, hitting him in the torso so hard that he appeared to suffer 'permanent palsy', as Melvin Belli put it in his biography, *My Life on Trial*. No one could understand how the accident happened, so no one could decide fault. Belli discovered that cars were operated by two different companies at the intersection, and if a Powell car, say, failed to drop his grip as an O'Farrell car approached, the O'Farrell gripman could get hit by the rebounding lever. But how could he demonstrate it in court? Not overly eloquent, gripmen were not good witnesses, he surmised. So he spent $300 – a lot of money then, as he says in *My Life* – to make a scale model of the intersection, cable cars and all. Bigger than a king-sized bed, it was brought into the courtroom along with a full-sized gearbox. Defence lawyers objected, but the judge allowed Belli's innovation. When he saw jurors inspecting the model and the gearbox, he saw 'frowns turn into smiles of understanding'. He realised that he was on to something. Next, he brought in a blackboard – another first in such a trial – to help him and the jury work together to calculate Bryant's award. Jurors agreed to compensation of $31,883.25, a 'big award in those days'. And long before the gurus of adult training had their say, Belli discovered that human beings learn best by seeing rather than hearing.

As formative was the appalling punishment he had witnessed early in his career. It provoked a recurring nightmare he had for years: he dreamt he was on the gallows about to be hanged.

San Quentin inmates Alexander McKay and Joe Kristy assaulted Warden Holohan in his residence, taking him and two parole board members hostage. They commandeered a prison car and drove away, hundreds of Marin County police officers in pursuit. Cornered in an old farmhouse, they gave up without harming the officials. (Apart from Holohan, who had a fractured skull from the assault.) Co-opted by San Quentin's padre Father O'Meara, whom Belli knew, the novice counsel visited the jail next day with nothing in his briefcase, as he writes, 'but his lunch'. He interviewed McKay and Kristy at length, understanding their side of the story. But Father O'Meara reminded Belli that 'sure as the Pope's in Rome they'll hang'. It was Belli's job to defend them as best he could, O'Meara said. The trial was quick, Belli did what he could, impressing the judge, but the prisoners were guilty on several counts. Death was the penalty, and he didn't believe in capital punishment. There was 'already too much brutality in the world'.

An execution date was set, and it was expected that Belli watch the hanging. On the eve of the judicial murder, he and Father O'Meara visited the condemned men, who were held in 'separate, slatted cages' in an old factory at San Quentin. The factory had once made doors, and Belli describes the air as 'heavy' with sawdust. It was lit with blue bulbs, and the aura was 'cloudy, unreal'. The gallows was designed for two, and, in a corner, 'three new manila ropes tied with hangman's knots … were being stretched by weights …' Two simple timber coffins were in front of a stoop, the prisoners only a few feet away. Rain beat on the tin roof, and for the rest of his life Belli was to remember McKay and Kristy whenever he heard rain on a roof.

It was still falling next morning, a soft tympani to foil a scratchy recording of *Clair de Lune*, a last request. Inside the factory, 'there was a smell of death and sweat and uneaten last meals in the air'. A crowd watched as McKay and Kristy were rushed past Belli and Father O'Meara up the narrow stairs. Belli croaked, 'So long, Mac. So long Joe', and a guard bawled, 'Quiet! There'll be silence in here.' Sudden and to plan went the hangings, and a furious Father O'Meara gunned his car out of the prison, Belli in the passenger's seat. They drove to the parish house, opened a bottle of scotch and drained it without a word. Belli says he woke up sweating three days in a row. Soon after, he began having the hanging nightmare that continued throughout his life, stirring when the rope was placed around his neck. For the young lawyer, it amounted to a trope for 'my own personal fight with established society'.

Chapter Twelve

1   Wendy Wicks, the eldest child, remembers Roy fondly. He was affable and kindly and would have made a great father, she believes. On holiday in 1951, he carried her more than eight hundred steps up the Giant Stairway to the Three Sisters outcrop in the Blue Mountains west of Sydney. He was a great walker, she remembers. All who knew Roy, in fact, marvelled at his strong, quick gait. His work-a-day commute to Myer and back was about five miles. He also walked in the bush. He would take public transport out to the Dandenong Ranges east of the city. (They are of similar elevation to the Californian mountains where *Resolution* crashed.) Setting off into eucalyptus forests and fern groves, he would carry only a rudimentary snake-bite kit – a handkerchief and a length of rubber tubing to use as a tourniquet. In those days, anyone serious about first-aid kept a small cylindrical vial with a metal lancet at one end and Condy's Crystals (potassium permanganate) at the other. (Lancing a snakebite and applying the crystals is these days condemned. As is applying a tourniquet.)

Roy got Wendy her first job – as a salesgirl in Myer over the Christmas and New Year school holidays. She was not quite fourteen, the legal age for sales assistants. In 1969, Roy and she stalked Myer for her wedding present. Eric got Roy to record Wendy's wedding, and she looked forward to hearing the exchanges of vows and the minister's sober advice. The recording consisted of the organ pieces that were played between the words.

Chapter Thirteen

1   Because he was Jewish, Gaston was unacceptable to his first wife's father. In the first week of her new marriage, Anna Lou again had to cope with anti-semitism. Her new husband asked her to help him tell his sons – twelve and fourteen – that he was a Jew. She replied that they probably already knew. He should say that they ought to be 'very proud' of their father's lineage.

2   'In 1979,' she said in the television interview, 'no one thought there was hunger in the US.' As she was documenting the plights of homeless New Yorkers, successive city administrations did little to fix the problem. Instead of providing dwellings for the less well-off and acting to improve welfare,

they ran a 'huge and highly skilled' public-relations campaign suggesting that city policies were decreasing the numbers needing aid. Under Mayor Rudy Giuliani's administration (1994–2001), New York simply stopped publishing statistics on those without roofs. Eventually, a legal ruling that ordered the city to provide shelter to all was partly due to Anna Lou's case studies.

3   Halfway through the 1980s, Samuels chose to take on a peculiar project. In the first half of the 20th century, Emanuel Feuermann was said to rival Casals for the title of world's greatest cellist. Recordings of his playing verify his stature. He died, however, at thirty-nine in 1942 of an infection following minor surgery. Jon's aim was to find every recording Feuermann had made. He chose to do it because the task fascinated him and he imagined the recordings would be few. He began to discover many that had never been released as LPs. It 'shocked' him. The year he had given himself to complete the project soon became four – unpaid – and he travelled to the United Kingdom and contacted people in Japan and Germany in search of Feuermann tracks. He was a good digger, he likes to say. (For a short while as a child he wanted to be an archaeologist.)

Having collected the recordings, he began to transfer them at home via a Thorens turntable and an open-reel tape recorder for broadcast on WKCR. Soon, he realised that many of his transfers were better than professionals' efforts, and he began looking for freelance work. He learned by trial and error, but soon took a job as chief audio engineer at the Museum of Television & Radio in Manhattan. A leap up the professional ladder followed when he joined BMG, which was one of the world's biggest record companies. He was employed as an audio engineer, and his main aim was to 'learn the equipment' that only the biggest companies can afford to buy. In 1993 he became a producer in BMG's Reissues Department, and seven years later he was responsible for all the company's re-releases of classical music. His CV runs to eight pages and includes two dozen awards. He considers himself, he says, a 'musician by temperament'. He got into production because he needed an outlet for his creativity. 'It sounds trite,' he adds, 'but I wanted to do something worthwhile and this was worthwhile.'

SELECT BIBLIOGRAPHY

Belli, Melvin. *My Life on Trial*. William Morrow and Company, 1976.

Bloom, Harold. *The Western Canon*. Harcourt Brace & Company, 1994.

Freud, Sigmund. *The Uncanny*. Penguin Classics, 2003.

Gát, József. *The Technique of Piano Playing*. Collet's, 1974.

Gollin, James. *Pianist*. Xlibris, 2010.

Jung, C. G. *Synchronicity*. Princeton University Press, 2010.

McCallum, Bonnie. *Tales Untold*. The Hawthorn Press, 1978.

Murray, Nicholas. *Kafka*. Little, Brown, 2004.

National Centre of Biography. *Australian Dictionary of Biography*. Online.

Page, Tim. *William Kapell, A Documentary Life History*. International Piano Archives at the University of Maryland, 1992.

Schonberg, Harold C. *The Great Pianists*. Simon and Schuster, 1963.

Sherman, John K. *Music and Maestros*. University of Minnesota Press, 1999.

Stern, Isaac. *My First 79 Years*. Alfred A. Knopf, 1999.

ACKNOWLEDGEMENTS

Many people contributed their efforts, thoughts, suggestions and memories to *A Lasting Record*. All of them were important.

I was enormously touched and privileged to be taken in – almost as a family member – by the Kapells. Though frail and very ill, Anna Lou herself made a tremendous effort to respond to my questions. I was deeply moved and thankful. Willy's son, David Kapell, and his daughter, Rebecca Leigh, were equally generous with their help. And I was given a detailed perspective on Willy's early life by his brother, Bob, and Bob's wife, Ann. They have been magnificent. David's son, Joshua, filled in the story of the first contacts between Maurice Austin and the Kapell family.

In Melbourne, Roy's carer, Maurice, anticipated my needs, supplying photographs, documents, eulogies and recordings that made my task so much easier. A busy man, he was never without time for an interview, and he read and re-read the manuscript, corrected errors and made valuable suggestions.

Christopher O'Donnell took me to the crash site south of San Francisco and provided appropriate documents and insights into the BCPA disaster and its aftermath.

David Rayner of Adelaide was the first person to alert me to the extensive file concerning Kapell in the Australian National Archives. For the cost of photocopying, he provided me with it, saving me considerable work. Without the hundreds of letters, contracts, memos, programs, reviews and miscellaneous notes and scraps retained in the archives my text would have been much the poorer.

Clifford Hocking's former business partner David Vigo spent hours rummaging among Cliff's 'boxes' to try to come up with material that might help us all to understand how the Geelong performance of the Chopin sonata – Roy's last cutting of Willy's playing – got from Melbourne to New York. Gregor Benko answered my questions about the conundrum as best he could.

At IPAM outside Washington DC, curator Donald Manildi gave me access to the archive's complete Kapell collection, including Willy's diaries, which are usually closed. At the National Archives in Varick Street, Manhattan, I was able to read the complete record of the Kapell–Qantas litigation, and the State Library of Victoria in Melbourne also pulled up documents important to my research. The Performing Arts Museum in Melbourne provided access to a recording of Milton Stevens's ABC memorial broadcast, which included interviews with people such as John Sinclair and the former Patricia Tuckwell. I was also able to look through its Kapell file.

Jon Samuels in New York submitted himself to two long interviews and countless email enquiries in an effort to fill in the details of the story's last chapters. Also in New York, Jerome Lowenthal and Byron Bray sketched aspects of Willy's character that gave me a greater understanding of the man and his music. Tim Page generously agreed to my quoting from his 'Documentary Life History' of Willy.

Bruce Ardley and Julien Arnold, Roy's friends from TOSA, and Wendy Wicks provided first-hand accounts of Roy's character, and I am indebted to Peter Inglis, who explained the intricacies of the Royce recording machine.

Alan Gemmell not only heard Willy play in Melbourne but photographed him and was inquisitive enough to try to uncover the state of his mind towards the end of the 1953 tour. Although unwell and in care, he was most helpful.

Ernie Bonyhadi and Shirley Gittelsohn told me about being couriers of the acetates, and Daniel Guss tried hard to uncover the sales of *WILLIAM KAPELL reDISCOVERED*. Sony has decided to keep them secret.

To all of the above, I owe an enormous debt of gratitude. And if I have overlooked other important contributors, I apologise in advance.

I pitched the idea of *A Lasting Record* to Roz Hopkins of HarperCollins, who liked it immediately. I am indebted to her for arguing its case at publishing meetings and succeeding in getting the company to agree to bring it out. A fine publisher, Jeanne Ryckmans, took over the book from Roz and applied her efforts and intellect to bringing out the best volume she could.

It was the product of an old firm. While Jeanne oversaw publication, Nadine Davidoff, one of Australia's best editors, made important suggestions and saw to it that the storyline was uncluttered by the time it reached printers. It was something of a reunion – we had last worked together on *Blackie*.

I am indebted – as always – to my friend and agent, Margaret Gee, for believing in my modest talent. She made the initial approach to HarperCollins, and you hold the result.